D0071765

CITIZENS OF NOWHERE

FROM REFUGEE CAMP TO CANADIAN CAMPUS

CITIZENS OF NOWHERE

FROM REFUGEE CAMP TO CANADIAN CAMPUS

DEBI GOODWIN

ANCHOR CANADA

Library and Archives Canada Cataloguing in Publication

ISBN 978-0-385-66723-4

Photos on pages 29, 31, and 79 courtesy of Halima Abdille.
All other photos by Debi Goodwin.

Book design by Paul Dotey
Printed and bound in the USA

Published in Canada by Anchor Canada,
a division of Random House of Canada Limited

Visit Random House of Canada Limited's website: www.randomhouse.ca

10 9 8 7 6 5 4 3 2 1

To the students of Dadaab—those who
have made it out and those who remain.

CONTENTS

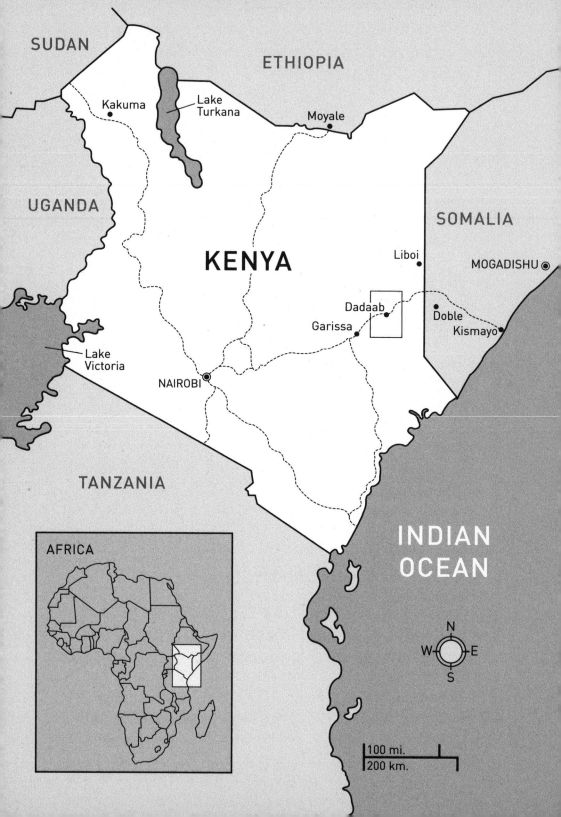

Map of Kenya and Somalia

SUDAN

ETHIOPIA

Kakuma

Lake Turkana

Moyale

UGANDA

SOMALIA

KENYA

Liboi

MOGADISHU

Dadaab

Doble

Garissa

Kismayo

Lake Victoria

NAIROBI

TANZANIA

INDIAN OCEAN

AFRICA

N

W E

S

100 mi.
200 km.

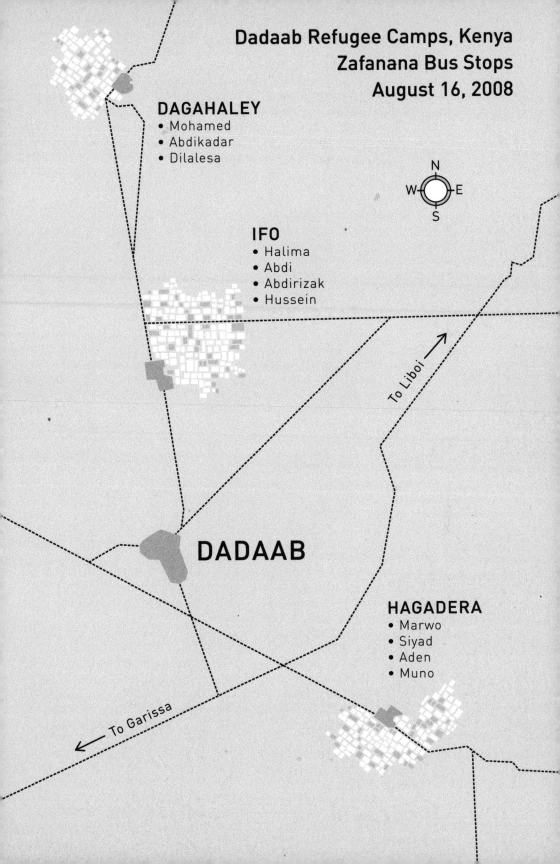

Becoming Universal

IN THE FALL OF 2009, as I was writing this book, my daughter left home and moved to a city across the country. She had finished university and was trying to figure out what she was going to do with her life. It was a good time for her to leave home—there was nothing unnatural about her departure. And yet for her and for me it was a traumatic event. The emotions of the departure, and of the days before and after it, made me feel more deeply for the parents and the young people you are about to meet in this story.

My daughter moved away from home to a city in her own country, and she understood that if things didn't work out for her there, she could always come back home. Even so, on her second day away from home, she called to say she didn't know where she belonged. The mothers and fathers of the young people in this story could hardly imagine the strange world their children were entering. Many of them feared that Western culture might change their children beyond recognition. And yet they let them go because it was the only choice that offered any hope for the future. Without the safety net of family, the students in this story left their homes in the refugee camps of Dadaab, Kenya. They had a one-way ticket to Canada and the knowledge that this was their best shot at a productive adulthood.

It may seem self-indulgent to compare the journey of an educated middle-class Canadian to students who grew up as refugees and came alone to a completely unknown Western country. But we have all had departures that tore at us, and I hope that those reading this story will draw on their own memories to understand the dislocation and the heartache and the challenges to their identities that these young people faced. It is too easy to think of "refugees" as a block, as something other, even as something to be feared. It is harder to take the time to realize that their individual stories have elements in common with our own. Refugees too often invite compassion fatigue instead of simply compassion.

Displacement is part of the human condition. Over the centuries, people have moved to avoid floods, wars and famine. In its annual report on global trends, the United Nations High Commission for Refugees, UNHCR, estimated there were 42 million "forcibly displaced people" worldwide at the end of 2008. Of those, 15.2 million were refugees in asylum countries, 10.5 million of them under the care of UNHCR. More than half of those under UNHCR care had been living in exile for more than five years with no solution in sight in what humanitarians call "protracted refugee situations."

Forty-two million. It's not a number easy to imagine. Forty-two million. It is not a number that suggests that solutions are around the corner. Forty-two million. It is a number hard to connect to individuals with sorrows, regrets, fears and despair, or with lives of marriages, births, songs and poetry.

Displacement is also a big part of the Canadian story. We are a nation of people who, for the most part, have come from somewhere else and, usually, because we had to. There were the Irish who faced "death or Canada" after the potato famine of the 1840s; the Doukhobors and the Jews who escaped pogroms in czarist Russia; the Ukrainians who settled in the prairies before the First World War; the Hungarians and Czechoslovakians who ran from Soviet oppression in the '50s and '60s; the "boat people" fleeing from Vietnam, Cambodia and Laos in the late '70s.

The blemishes in our record of accepting displaced people are part of our country's shame. There's the *Komagatu Maru* incident of 1914, when authorities in Vancouver would not allow steamboat passengers from India to disembark on Canadian soil, and the horror of the MS *St. Louis* in 1939, when Canada refused to accept nine hundred Jews escaping Nazi Germany. Those who did make it to Canadian shores often faced racism in extreme forms such as the "head tax" for Chinese immigrants, or the gnawing bigotry and discrimination faced by the Irish, by Italians and by the "DPs" of Eastern Europe after the Second World War to name a few. Yet despite the Canadian ambivalence to immigrants and refugees, they kept coming and we kept—and keep—accepting them. By 2006, one in five Canadians was born somewhere else.

About a quarter of a million newcomers came to Canada in 2008 alone. Among them were eleven students who had been isolated without freedoms in remote camps in the poorest region of Kenya, refugees living in one of the worst "protracted situations" in the world. Their adjustment to life here may seem like an extreme example of the disorientation all newcomers experience, but it is a chapter in that important Canadian story.

I first was drawn into the lives of the students of the Dadaab refugee camps in February 2007, when I met two remarkable young Somalis who had spent most of their lives in the Kenyan camps after fleeing civil war in their country of birth. I was in Dadaab as a producer for CBC Television, working on short pieces about the fresh wave of arrivals in the camps fleeing a new round of violence in Somalia. While I was in the camps, I started working on a documentary that would follow two students who were preparing to come to Canada months later. I met Nabiho Farah Abdi and Ibrahim Aden Mohamed in the main CARE compound for aid workers who provide services to the three surrounding camps. Nabiho and Ibrahim had come for a lesson on how to write essays for Canadian university courses. After the class they both spoke excitedly about having been selected for scholarships to Canadian universities. Nabiho said she wanted to become a "universal person" and to see what the real world was like. Ibrahim described Canada as the country of his dreams. The two were full of gratitude for the opportunity they'd been given. Although they knew little about Canada, they believed it was a country of tolerance. As the day drew near for their departure, their excitement became muted, tinged with anxiety and a growing realization that they were leaving everything they'd ever known behind. In Nairobi, before her departure, Nabiho told a CBC crew that she was "happy, but in another part not happy. It's so painful to leave your mother, your sisters and brothers." Ibrahim described his feeling as "a mixture of happiness and worry."

Six months after I met them in Dadaab, I arranged for CBC crews to follow Nabiho and Ibrahim during their first days in Canada for *The National* documentary "The Lucky Ones," which focused on the initial shock of displacement. When Nabiho arrived at the airport in Regina, she tried to go around the camera to hug me. I was the only face she knew in a strange new world. She cried as she waited for her luggage, thinking of the mother who had raised ten children alone in a refugee camp and encouraged them all to learn about the world beyond the camp, encouraged them to study—a mother who was now so far away. On her first morning in Canada she called home telling her mother she wanted to go back. After three days of realizing she'd gained new freedoms but had lost everything familiar, she said her chances of adapting were fifty–fifty. I bowed out of her life then, only occasionally checking in on her adjustment.

Since I had not seen Ibrahim arrive, I decided to invite him to our home for dinner later in the fall. Over the course of his first year, my family entertained him several times, and at each meeting I realized how long and hard the adjustment was. On one snowy night in December, as we wiped our car to drive him back to his residence, he looked up into the falling snow and said, "I can't believe anybody lives here."

For most journalists there are some stories they cannot forget. This is mine. And so I decided to go back to Dadaab in August 2008, alone, to meet eleven more students, ten of them Somalis, who would be making the same journey to Canada. And this time, instead of shooting a short glimpse of their lives, I would follow them for one year as they adjusted to Canadian universities, weather and food, to Western culture and to the loneliness of leaving families behind.

They were preparing for their departure when I arrived. My time in the camp had been cut short because the Kenyan government, not the aid agencies, now controlled who got into the camps, and my permission to enter had been held up. I waited in a hotel room in Nairobi as a group called Windle Trust Kenya pleaded my case. I despaired that I would not meet the students, who were waiting in the camps worrying that something might happen to prevent them from leaving. When I finally did get to Dadaab, I met most of them for the first time in a morning session arranged by their teachers. They had been filling out forms and answering questions in interviews for over a year to win the scholarships and the right to come to Canada—and it showed in the rote way they recited the biographical details of their lives. At that initial meeting I asked basic questions. They gave basic answers.

There was a shift, though, as we sat under neem trees on that hot morning drinking cold sodas. They were under the impression that I was going to pick one of them to write about. And the young men assumed I would choose one of the three young women, since journalists who'd come before had focused on girls' education. I had in truth thought of selecting just a few of them, males and females, but after meeting them I knew I couldn't choose. As they outlined their lives, they each said something that sparked my interest. When I told them I would like to see all of their homes in the camps and then visit each of them in Canada, they became more engaged and started planning a schedule for our meetings. Over the next days, they guided me around the different camps where they lived and welcomed me to their family compounds.

Once the students were on Canadian soil, our relationships shifted dramatically. I became part of their first year here. I was there for a first phone call home, a first bout of homesickness, a first Tim Hortons French vanilla cappuccino (which strangely enough brought back memories of home), a first subway ride and the evening after a first final exam. I watched their bewilderment at the confusing, and sometimes shocking, new world they encountered. I listened to their concerns about their studies, about finding new friends, about the desperate situation of those still in the camps. I witnessed them as newcomers and came to observe myself as the born Canadian sometimes challenged by their values and by the exchanges between us. I asked my questions, but I offered advice too. They answered my questions and shared deeper worries. Sometimes they shared more than they meant to, and as the year drew to a close they suddenly realized they had disclosed information too personal for any book.

As a journalist, I struggled with this. I talked to them about their concerns to figure out ways around them, and in the end I did not include some details that could open up old wounds or harm reputations that are so critical in the Muslim Somali community of Dadaab. All of the young women talked to me about the Somali practice of female genital mutilation. One of them changed in her thinking on the matter after her time in Canada and wanted me to include the issue in the book without revealing her personal experiences. One young man requested I not discuss his clan; clan warfare had destroyed the lives of the students' families and sent the country of Somalia into a chaos from which it has never recovered. Those who grew up in the Dadaab camps, removed from the violence of their homeland, had forged lives together as refugees. They wanted to move past the tribalism that had killed so many of their friends and relatives. They saw that as the only way to save Somalia. Most students talked to me openly about their clans. They did so to fill in their histories, not because they wanted to make clan an issue. Even though I have worked hard to respect the students' wishes, there will still be some things I know they won't like reading. The students I spent a year with are all private people who came from a strict world. One young woman agreed to the "sacrifice" of telling her story because she hoped it would help others in Dadaab by bringing attention to their plight.

This is a snapshot of a refugee's first year in Canada, in particular a snapshot of refugees lucky and clever enough to win university scholarships and permanent resident status before arriving. It is a snapshot of the challenges to their identities, of the changes in their attitudes toward their own culture and their new country. Like any snapshot, the action continued after the image froze. Many of the opinions the students held at the end of the first year and the careers they'd chosen at that point will have changed, perhaps many times, by the time this book is read. Certainly, the situation in the Dadaab camps, where the students came from, and in Somalia, where most of the students were born, will have gone through many alterations possibly for the worse or, one can only hope, for the better.

I couldn't predict the future of the students I followed for a year, but in my curiosity to see how their lives might unfold, I sought out others who had come to Canada as refugee students in the years and decades before them. Each of the stories of struggle and adjustment I heard from past students could fill a book of its own. In the context of the Dadaab eleven, their stories provided me with clues to how new identities and new attachments are forged. One former student in particular, Ambaye Kidane, confirmed my growing understanding of the significance of that first year in Canada. Ambaye had been a student in Ethiopia in the '70s and was imprisoned and tortured during the years of the Red Terror. In 1983, he came to Halifax's Dalhousie University on a scholarship. Even now, as a senior civil servant in the Ontario Ministry of Finance, the landscape, the food and the people he first encountered in Canada remain as vivid in his mind as if it were yesterday. In 2008, at an event in Toronto, he sought out my husband, whom he quickly identified as the fourth person he had met in Canada. Twenty-five years had done nothing to dim those memories.

During the Dadaab students' first year in Canada, emotions about their new world were still raw, memories that would eventually take shape still blurry first impressions. The world they'd left behind, however, was sharply focused in their memories, clear in every detail. Over the course of the year they all provided me with immense amounts of information about their cultures and their daily lives in both Africa and Canada. Their need to talk about their two worlds was so intense that they were able to transport me into their lives. And through the year they welcomed someone who would listen to and possibly understand their feelings of dislocation. But in the end, I was a witness. Someday, I know, some of them will write their own stories with their own sensibilities. I hope they do. One year in Canada, is, after all, just a beginning.

PART ONE

Leaving Home Behind

CHAPTER ONE

Out of the Sealed, Dark Room

DESPITE THE SHOVING and the wailing at the bus stop in Hagadera refugee camp in northeast Kenya, the conductor for the Zafanana bus company tried to do his job that day. He herded, sometimes pushed, those with tickets onto the colourfully striped bus. It was almost nine in the morning and the bus was already an hour behind schedule. If the driver didn't leave soon, he wouldn't make it to Nairobi before dark. Expected and unexpected stops by Kenyan police to check travel documents could further delay the bus, adding to the urgency to begin the long drive west on the packed sand road.

Outside the bus, parents, friends and siblings blocked the entrance and surrounded those trying to get on board. Through an open window, a young man held onto his father's hand. Inside, one young woman, not yet twenty, sobbed uncontrollably while another watched the most important woman in her life walk away. Eleven young students were among the passengers leaving on the Zafanana bus that day. They were leaving, perhaps forever, their families and others they loved, and the only world they had ever really known. It was August 16, 2008, a day they would remember for the rest of their lives.

———

Less than a week before the students zipped up their suitcases and boarded the bus, UNHCR did a head count in the three sprawling camps of Hagadera, Ifo and Dagahaley. Collectively, the camps in Kenya's remote North Eastern Province are known as the Dadaab refugee camps. UNHCR officials knew that numbers were on the rise in the camps, knew that each month about 4,000 people were sneaking across the closed but poorly guarded Somali border less than one hundred kilometres away from the town of Dadaab, sneaking into Kenya to seek asylum from the violence in their homeland. On August 10, 2008, UNHCR found 206,639 refugees in Dadaab, up 20 per cent from the first day of the year. Dadaab was fast becoming one of the largest refugee camps in the world. Because of its location, the vast majority of both the new arrivals and the older residents in the camps were Somalis. Only about 3 per cent of the population in Dadaab came from places like Uganda, the Democratic Republic of the Congo, Sudan, Ethiopia or Eritrea.

When UNHCR drew up the plans for the Dadaab camps in 1991, it foresaw a maximum of 90,000 people taking refuge there. Tractors cleared land previously used as rangeland for livestock, and over the next two years workers laid out plots for three camps encircling Dadaab, a small town near the equator where temperatures can reach 45 degrees Celsius in March. Drills bore through the semi-arid land to reach the precious water supply. That was the year Siad Barre's dictatorship of Somalia ended in a bloody civil war. Hundreds of thousands of Somalis fled enemy militias and the destruction of their homes, fled on foot with whatever they could carry into Kenya, overwhelming the country's ability to absorb refugees. Over the next few years the Kenyan government pushed as many refugees as it could find to the farthest, poorest corners of the country, into the camps of Dadaab in the northeast and Kakuma in the northwest, far away from the vibrant capital of Nairobi. The population of the Dadaab camps swelled as high as 400,000, more than four times the projection, before dropping well below 150,000 and then rising again.

Seventeen years after the Dadaab camps first opened, they had taken on a dispiriting feel of permanence, with tin-sheet schools, ill-equipped hospitals and even markets selling clothes and fresh food. CARE International provided elementary and secondary schooling and other programs designed to make life easier. It also sanctioned the markets, after entrepreneurial refugees wanting to fill idle time and their pockets asked for the space, often using money sent from relatives abroad to start their businesses. With no sign of peace in Somalia and few opportunities for resettlement, there was an unrelenting sameness to the days of those stuck in the camps. For most of the refugees, August 16, 2008, was just another day divided into equal parts darkness and light. Another day of stretching rations with whatever sugar or canned goods or vegetables they could afford to buy from the markets. Another day of lining up at communal taps to fill yellow jerry cans with water from deep inside the earth. Just another day marked not by nine-to-five jobs or by three daily meals, but by five prayers of Islamic submission. It is no wonder that Somalis have a word for the longing to be elsewhere, to earn resettlement to a third country. *Buufis,* they call it—a longing so strong it can make people lie about their identity, or drive them crazy, they say.

But before the chill of night left the air on that August day, before any hint of light tinged the sky, the family and friends of the eleven students leaving Kenya prepared for a very different day. Behind the *kamoor*—the high fences woven out of sticks that separate the compounds from each other—Somali families rose earlier than usual. Sisters and mothers lit kerosene lamps and poured the batter of flour, water and salt that had fermented overnight onto flat iron pans over freshly lit fires for thin pancakes known as *anjera.* They squatted or bent to toss unmeasured but exact amounts of loose black tea and crushed spices into aluminum pots of boiling water for the sweet, milky drink that added flavour and a burst of energy to every morning. In the Somali compounds, ten young people with few memories but these daily routines witnessed them for the last time. It is hard, they say, to make Somali men cry. Many did that day.

A typical kitchen in Dadaab. Even those who can afford solid mud houses for sleeping and living usually build their kitchens from twigs.

And in one compound in a corner of one camp where minority Eritreans and Oromos lived, the eleventh student, a single young man, looked around at his fellow Oromo teachers and began to weep, knowing he was the only one among them who would leave.

With more and more refugees flowing into the camps each day, the eleven students from Dadaab were going against the stream. They had given up their refugee papers, become subtractions from the count. They had all beaten the odds. Now they were off to Canada, a country they knew next to nothing about, to become permanent residents and university students, to be resettled in another country because they could not go back to their own and there was no future for them in Kenya beyond the sameness of life in the camps. What they knew about their third country, Canada, could fit on a single page. It was a cold place, they had heard, but all they knew of cold came from touching ice, and surely air couldn't feel like that. And snow—what was it exactly? Something white that falls mysteriously from the sky. Looking at a foreigner's picture of a patio table covered with a dome of January snow ten times thicker than the tabletop, one of the students asked, "Is that inside a house?"

They knew that Canada was a democratic country, and they had heard—and they prayed—that it was a tolerant place where they could practise their faiths with freedom. In school they had studied the politics of Kenya, Great Britain and even the United States. Canada, to no surprise, was nowhere to be found in the curriculum. Some thought there was a queen; others were sure there were elections. A couple of them knew there was a prime minister. None of that really mattered. *Canada was not here.* Canada would give them papers and let them move freely, study at universities and get jobs that could help their families.

Packed in suitcases ready to go were sweaters never worn, jeans, running shoes whiter than a fresh Canadian snowfall, photographs, hand creams and deodorants that surely couldn't be purchased in Canada, sticks for cleaning teeth, hijabs and flowing scarves, Qu'rans and prayer mats. Some of the Somalis, those who could find them, had bought prayer mats with plastic compasses glued to them, compasses that would always point them in the right direction for prayer, toward the holy city of Mecca.

Dagahaley Refugee Camp

The Zafanana bus company had a garage in Dagahaley camp, where it began its journey to the capital just after dawn. A commercial company, it carried passengers with Kenyan identity papers and UNHCR travel documents to the city of Garissa, one hundred kilometres southwest of Dadaab, or on to Nairobi, five hundred long kilometres away. Those travelling all the way to the capital could reserve a seat for 1,000 Kenyan shillings, about $15 Canadian. The International Organization for Migration (IOM), overseers of the resettlement of refugees, had given each of the eleven students precisely 1,000 shillings to buy their tickets ahead of time from conductors who lived in each of the camps.

Before sunrise, the bus driver, the main conductor and the mechanic making the journey that day ate in a small lodge in Dagahaley where they had spent the night. Dagahaley is the most remote of the three Dadaab camps, seventeen kilometres north of the town of Dadaab and eleven kilometres from the nearest other camp, Ifo. Almost all of the population of Dagahaley is Somali and more than half had been nomads in their former lives. Walking long distances is something they are used to. Three students would board there: two Somalis, Mohamed Abdi Salat and Abdikadar Mohamud Gure, and a refugee from Ethiopia, an Oromo teacher known to the others as Dereje Guta Dilalesa.

There was barely enough light in the sky to make out the edge of the camp when twenty-three-year-old Mohamed started walking that morning. He lived with his mother, his twenty-one-year-old brother and young half-siblings in a compound in one of the remotest blocks of the remotest camp. At one end of the fenced compound, Mohamed and his brother shared a mud house. The house had two sleeping mats and a hole near ground level for ventilation. There, Mohamed,

Mohamed with his mother in their compound in Dagahaley, days before leaving home, perhaps forever.

a fan of the BBC, often listened to a borrowed transistor for news about Somalia and about his favourite soccer team, Manchester United. A new radio would have cost almost $20, so he had settled for buying four D batteries for $1.50 every fifteen days. The cost and value of merchandise were concepts he understood well.

At the other end of the compound, his mother and the girls lived in a separate house. In between stood the family's kitchen and sitting room, domed structures made of twigs and covered with bits of cloth, structures somewhat like the houses of the nomads they belonged to—houses built to be taken apart quickly. But there had been no need for that here. Mohamed and his family had lived in Dagahaley for almost seventeen years.

That morning Mohamed hired a neighbour with a wheelbarrow to carry his luggage for the twenty-minute walk to the bus stop. There was a light breeze as Mohamed's mother and brother walked with him through a wide, open strip of sand along the edge of the blocks of housing. They passed the acacia tree that sheltered the homeless new arrivals to the camp. UNHCR had announced that month that Dagahaley had reached its capacity. There were no more plots of land left in the camp, so new arrivals spent day and night under the tree waiting to be registered to get food rations, waiting for somewhere better to go. As Mohamed passed the tree, the new Somali arrivals looked at him, in his clean khaki pants and fresh button-down shirt, as a stranger with a life worthy of envy.

To Mohamed the walk toward the centre of the camp that morning was like a dream. He tried not to think about what he was leaving behind. He forced himself to think ahead to the journey, to the room waiting for him at the Scarborough campus of the University of Toronto. Most of the information packages from Canadian students who would greet the eleven upon arrival had not found their way to the students or had been held for them in Nairobi. But Mohamed had received his, complete with a welcoming letter addressed to "Mr. Salat," a brochure with pictures of the university president and the campus, and snapshots of the young people he would soon meet. While excited at the opportunity to study at such a beautiful university, Mohamed feared the changes he might undergo in Canada. He had learned from his friend Ibrahim, who had left the camp a year earlier, that many of the Somalis living in Toronto acted more like Canadians than Somalis. Just as the new arrivals from Somalia eyed him as someone different, he considered those Somalis who had changed in Canada to be different from him. Would the new country change who he was? He realized he might have to make small, insignificant changes in how he dressed and how he spoke, but he was determined not to stray from his religion or the basic rules of his culture.

Mohamed's mother walked quietly beside her tall son with the kind smile. She was a woman accustomed to loss. Two of her husbands had already died. Mohamed's father died three years before the war when Mohamed was a young boy. Her second husband died in the camp. A third husband, still living but suffering from hypertension, lived in another camp with his other family and was often too sick to visit her. She did not cry the morning Mohamed left, but after, whenever she walked the same route, she would think of the son who had gone so far away.

Her two sons were her breadwinners. They both taught in schools run by the aid agency CARE. Although the government would not allow refugees to take paid jobs, all the agencies gave "incentives" to those who worked as teachers, translators or assistants in the many projects in the camp. Together the brothers brought home a little more than $100 Canadian a month and helped raise the family above the poorest of refugees. Now all that responsibility would fall on the shoulders of Mohamed's younger brother. Mohamed vowed to himself to send money home as soon as he could. He knew how much it would be needed. He could rattle off the costs of groceries at the market and list without hesitation the exact amounts of rations the World Food Programme distributed every fifteen days.

For the seven people in his compound, the rations were twenty-one kilograms of wheat flour, twenty-one kilograms of maize, seven cups of oil, seven bowls of dried beans or peas, seven bowls of dried soybean porridge and seven spoonfuls of salt. Sometimes there was more; sometimes there was less. There was never enough. And with new arrivals came new demands on the market goods from Somalia and eastern Kenya. A kilogram of meat could cost double the price of a year earlier, and sugar, a necessity for Somali tea, was on the rise too.

Mohamed was the first of the three students leaving that day to arrive at the Dagahaley bus stop. Abdikadar, another Somali student, twenty-two years of age, arrived soon after with his father and his brother. Abdikadar had fled Somalia with his family when he was five, after their farm was attacked by members of another clan and all the animals were stolen and some of his relatives killed. His mother was beaten so badly that she died during the long trek to the border. Both Mohamed and Abdikadar were popular teachers in the camp. The crowd around the bus stop grew as both teachers' students came to bid them farewell.

It was the arrival of Dereje, as the other students knew him—or Dilalesa, as his Oromo friends called him—that caused the greatest stir. At twenty-five, Dilalesa was a handsome man with thick black eyelashes any Maybelline-wearing Western woman would kill for and muscles any sports club in North America would call well defined. He had come to the camp as a grown man just four years earlier. In Ethiopia he had studied some philosophy in university and had become a teacher. That was before the government accused the Oromo teachers of organizing student protests and he, along with nine other teachers fearing for their lives, had walked across the border from Moyale, Ethiopia, to the safety of Moyale, Kenya. There the teachers turned themselves in to the police.

In his four years in the camp, Dilalesa had set about creating a life as full and as healthy as possible. He'd used his knowledge of four languages to get a job as an interpreter for UNHCR, and with his incentive income he bought vegetables—potatoes, tomatoes and wedges of wilted cabbage. He was a vegetarian, but he found no other way to flavour his soups than the packets of Spicy OYO (an imitation of OXO) Beef Mix sold in the market.

When a German aid agency had handed out small, fast-growing neem trees to families to improve the environment and beautify their homes, most took one or two trees and planted them in corners of their compounds, opting to keep the dirt areas between the houses open so they could lay out mats to rest on or sit on to drink tea outdoors. But Dilalesa wanted a garden and took all the trees he could. On the day he left for Canada, the trees, with their fresh green leaves, stood taller than him, a small forest beside his house.

Inside the house, he'd painted the supporting centre pole an intricate orange and green pattern. On one wall he'd hung a computer-generated sign that read "Never Write Off Manchester United!!" Beneath it, on a wooden table, he'd laid out objects that sustained him: a red jersey—"Number 7 Dilalesa"—boxes of Colgate toothpaste, a car battery to run his radio/CD/cassette player, books, an issue of *The Economist* and rows of water and juice bottles.

The water and juice supported his sports habit. Dilalesa exercised religiously and had designed a rigorous rotation of activities for himself that included playing soccer for the minority team in the camp's league and jogging in the bush, despite the heat and the oppressive air. He owned what had to be the most inventive pieces of sports equipment used in the camps. Managers of a CARE construction project had allowed him to take some concrete, with which he'd fashioned two barbells. To form each fifteen-pound barbell, he'd poured concrete into two large tins and joined the tins by inserting an iron bar. He'd also

Dilalesa holding one of his homemade barbells.

hoped to perfect his skills in the martial arts, but that would have to wait until he got to Canada.

Respect for the environment and respect for his own body were matters of faith for Dilalesa. Many of the Oromos of Ethiopia had converted to Islam or Christianity, but Dilalesa had stayed true to his traditional animist roots. To the camp's uneducated, as he called them, he was a *gaal*, a pagan—or just another Ethiopian, a man from the country now fighting in Somalia. Some in the camp spat at him. Others avoided him in the food distribution lines or wiped the nozzles clean at the water stations after he used them. But none of the other students leaving for Canada treated him with such disrespect. With them, he could share his thoughts on the unfair treatment of the Oromos in Ethiopia. Some of them came from a clan of Somalis who lived in Ethiopia and had fought for freedom in the past.

Dilalesa was the chairman of the Oromos in all three camps. In return for his services, on the eve of his departure, his friends honoured him with a party and then, in the morning, followed him to the bus, openly crying over their loss. Dilalesa could not stop crying either. He hated the idea of leaving his friends behind in this hostile environment of harsh weather and devastating floods, a place "that spoils your life," a place that forces you to "sleep on an empty stomach." To leave his friends in such misery when he was getting a new life overwhelmed him with sadness. He would study philosophy again, this time at the University of Saskatchewan in Canada, a country he felt certain would be democratic, peaceful and tolerant. And he had someone to go to the city of Saskatoon with: Abdikadar, the Somali student from the same camp, a young man who had become his friend.

A week earlier, Dilalesa and Abdikadar had walked hand in hand, as is customary for male friends in Africa, when they guided me around Dagahaley and took me to their homes. Dilalesa proudly showed off the Oromo Christian church near his house that he had helped build even though he wasn't a Christian, a church made in the ubiquitous mud-and-dung style, with wooden rafters supporting the roof. On one cracked, yellow wall a wooden cross hung above a small pulpit. The church leader, a man who could have been a well-preserved sixty-year-old or a worn-out man in his forties, led us to white plastic lawn chairs outside and explained that Christian Oromos in Nairobi had donated the money for the church so the ten Christians in his congregation could worship together. The church leader was stuck here but hoped interviews for resettlement to Canada would turn into reality. Around the corner from the church stood a timber-and-twig mosque with a green tin door for the Oromos who were Islamic. "We all live in harmony here," Dilalesa said.

He took us to a friend's compound, where an Oromo woman was bathing her baby daughter in a plastic tub. The compound belonged to a young man who had been rejected for a scholarship to Canada for single students after it was discovered he was married and hadn't disclosed the fact. "He couldn't go to Canada," Dilalesa said, "so he made the baby."

The two young men led me outside Dilalesa's compound and along narrow paths between the fenced compounds toward Abdikadar's home. People strolled past us yelling or talking softly into their cellphones. With an unreliable mail service and only limited—and expensive—Internet in the markets, refugees in the camps had embraced the cellphone as a means of keeping track of each other and staying in touch with those in the outside world. The cheapest cellphone cost about $35 and represented a major outlay, but the charges to use one were low and easily controlled. The chip to connect to the service provider cost $1. Cards providing five to twenty minutes of calling time sold for 50 cents to $2. All incoming calls were free, and some people in the camps purchased phones with no intention of using them except to receive calls.

At his compound, however, Abdikadar sent someone to find his father in the market where he earned extra money for the family by carrying goods for businesses using the cart he owned. The man who soon appeared was a shorter, heavier version of Abdikadar, with the same high forehead, the same facial hair outlining his chin, although his was more of a beard than his son's pencil-thin line. Through his son's translation, Abdikadar's father said he was happy that a visitor from Canada had come to see how the students lived and that he was grateful to Canada for accepting his son. All the family sat on a mat in their sitting room as they talked to me, making a point of asking Dilalesa to join them. Dilalesa, who played soccer with a team manned by minorities in the camp, nodded across the small room at a rival in his league, Abdikadar's brother, who played on a team of Somalis.

Abdikadar walks through the narrow laneways of Dagahaley.

A while later the two students guided me through another maze of passageways to the heart of the camp. We came out in the market near a "hotel," a building much like the other wood-and-tin buildings in the market. There are no rooms in the hotels of Dadaab; Western visitors are not allowed to stay overnight in the camps. Instead, the hotels are the cafés and restaurants where people with a few extra shillings come. All the Dadaab market shops have a major advantage over the camps' residents: electricity. With electricity they can offer Internet services, cellphone-charging and, in the case of the hotels, cold drinks from refrigerated cases. Without the odd treat of a cold drink from the hotel, the refugees had to make do with water they chilled in jerry cans wrapped in dampened cloths and stored in the shade.

There were few customers in the small hotel we entered. It was the middle of the afternoon and the market was quiet. Empty chairs at the long tables all faced a blank television mounted on one wall. On a table under the front window were jugs filled with a mixture of milk powder and juice, a drink known as *attunza*. A glass of *attunza* costs pennies, a bottle of Sprite or Fanta from the cooler more than double that but still less than a dollar.

We sat at a table with our soft drinks, surrounded by a few boys, listening to the hotel's jazzy music, a change from the Somali music that pounded through most doorways. The young boys looked briefly at me, the Western woman who had come in the hotel's front door, before turning back to each other. Abdikadar pointed to a second room at the back. "Women," Abdikadar said, "come in the back door and go in there." He said it without contempt or apology. It was just the way it was.

We talked about Saskatchewan. They had heard it was a prairie. Dilalesa said he feared the cold. One time he had travelled to Nairobi in the winter. "It was so cold," he said, "I slept for a week." Gently, I told him that the 10 degrees Celsius of a winter's night in Nairobi was considered a nice spring day in Saskatoon.

Now at the bus station, as Dilalesa wept, someone, probably the conductor, grabbed his arm and led him to his seat so the bus could pull away from Dagahaley.

Ifo Refugee Camp

The sun had already risen as the bus driver, trying to make up for lost time, turned the Zafanana bus south and drove fast over the sand road to his next stop, Ifo camp, where the dust blows freely over a long, flat plain. Early in the morning the road was not as bumpy as it would be later in the day after the constant passage of aid vehicles turned it into corduroy ridges. Eleven kilometres later, as the camp came into sight, a high sign on rusty metal poles could be seen through the bus window. Beneath a blue metal sign identifying the site as Refugee Operations Ifo, six white metal plaques ran between the poles. The top plaque read: Government of Kenya. Then, in descending order: UNHCR, World Food Programme, CARE International in Kenya, MMZ/UNHCR/GTZ Partnership Operations and The National Council of Churches of Kenya. These were the same plaques mounted outside all the camps—constant reminders that life was possible here only through the generosity of others.

At Ifo there was even greater chaos and further delays. The bus picked up four more students: Abdi Hassan Ali, Abdirizak Mohamed Farah, Mohamed Hussein Ismail and the first young woman in the group, Halima Ahmed Abdille.

The night before, twenty-year-old Halima didn't sleep. All day she'd walked through the narrow lanes of the camp between the walls of dried branches, stopping to saying goodbye to people she knew, listening to warnings that her culture and her religion would come under threat in the West, wondering if she would see any of these people again.

She had hoped to stop at the salon in the market during the day to have henna designs applied to her hands and her thin arms, but the line had been too long and she'd been too anxious to wait. Back at her compound she found it impossible to eat or even sit still, and she spent the evening hours visiting in the next block. Guests had come for a wedding celebration, and for four hours Halima answered all their questions about her imminent departure. It was midnight before she arrived home and she had her decorations yet to do. She finished her henna pattern of leaves at around two in the morning but still couldn't fall asleep.

Halima was a statistical anomaly in the camp, a daughter with two living parents, both of whom had encouraged her to stay in school. A report written one year earlier by staff from Bates College of

Lewiston, Maine, found that for every three boys in the primary schools run by CARE there were two girls. By secondary school, however, boys outnumbered girls four to one, and the remaining girls had trouble attaining marks as high as the boys'. It was Halima's father, in particular, who had helped her beat those statistics. He had recognized her intelligence and ruled that in his compound none of his daughters would do kitchen duty in their last year of secondary school so they could concentrate on studying for their final examinations.

And Halima had grabbed at the opportunity to learn. On weekends and after class, students often gathered to study together in empty classrooms or in family compounds throughout the Dadaab camps. They knew that getting high grades in the exams for the Kenya Certificate of Secondary Education was the only ticket to higher education, the only chance at the few scholarships available to them. Halima had never wanted to be in a study group with girls. She loved sciences and mathematics and wanted to study with the more serious boys. She'd become the only girl in a study group with twenty male students from Ifo Secondary School. The group often gathered at her compound, sometimes studying all through the night before exams. When neighbours complained to her father that it was wrong for a girl to be with so many young men who were not her relatives, Halima spoke up for herself and her father listened. She had always accepted the place of women in the Somali world of Dadaab. She wore the sombre-coloured hijabs, accepted that men had the right to marry four wives and that young girls needed to remain chaste, accepted the certainty that women could never be leaders. But she believed in the right of girls to be educated, and she convinced her father that the study group was necessary if she was to succeed. In the end, she graduated secondary school with a B– average, high enough to apply for and win a scholarship at Mount Saint Vincent University in Halifax, Canada.

Six days before her departure, Halima invited me to a celebration in her honour. Friends and family filled the compound. The house

Halima shared with her sister had been cleared out, a mattress shoved to one end, the walls draped with orange floral sheets. Thin sheet linoleum covered the dirt floor. With three adult children working for agencies, the family was well off—in refugee terms. Halima's older brother rushed from group to group of guests taking pictures with an old camera before pulling out a video camera with fake wood panelling on its side, which he aimed at one person after another to get single shots, waving at people to stand still.

In the twig kitchen, Halima's older sister laboured over a pot of boiling oil. From green plastic tubs filled with water, she scooped batches of potatoes cut like french fries and dropped them in to cook. Outside, women bent over the fire to heat water in kettles and aluminum pots. Plates and stainless-steel cups for serving drained on a small wooden cart.

Before the food was served I was summoned to another house to meet Halima's father. He was eighty-five or thereabouts. Records of his birth date are long gone. An old man with a bright red hennaed beard was lying on one of two small beds that took up most of the space in the close house. "He suffers from diabetes," Halima said.

Halima with her 85-year-old father who encouraged her in her studies.

Her father pulled himself up, and I was invited to sit across from him on the other bed. His thin legs were skirted in a traditional *ma'awis* and he wore a Somali patterned cap, but his green T-shirt sported a drawing of a running shoe and the word *NIKE* in pink letters. He told me he was happy his daughter was going to Canada. China, he said, is not a good place for Somalis. Neither is Italy. But in Canada there are human rights. He told me he was happy to pass his daughter on to me. I wondered if something had been lost in the translation and hoped he had meant to say that he was passing his daughter on to *Canada*.

When the feast was ready, women brought a large tin platter into the party room. The men sat around the platter on the linoleum floor and with bowed heads ate handfuls of rice, sliced tomatoes, boiled goat and chips, some the natural potato colour and some tinted red, stopping occasionally to pour spicy tomato sauce on their rice. When a platter that could feed six was set down in front of me, I protested, and the young female students were sent in to share it with me.

Throughout the party, Halima vacillated between a look of giddy hysteria and one of utter sadness, as though she would break into tears at any moment. There was a mercurial quality to her, but it was hard to tell if I was seeing something of her personality or just the enervating effects of a party day and the life-altering journey ahead of her. Before leaving, I touched her arm beneath the black hijab to say goodbye and tried not to show my surprise at how fragile I found her arm to be.

At four-thirty on the morning of her departure, it was time for Halima to get ready. She didn't want to eat, didn't want to bother with the photographer her brother had asked to take pictures. Instead, she took out the disposable camera she would carry to Canada and posed with her family against the sky that was still deeply blue in the early hours. Her last moments with her mother were captured on camera as they hugged and her mother's strong hand pressed down on Halima's head. Her mother had decided not to go to the bus stop with Halima, had decided it would be too emotional for both of them.

Halima's father, younger sister, brother and cousin would take her in a van borrowed for the occasion; otherwise, it would be a thirty-minute walk to the bus stop—a difficult walk for her father. Today, for the pictures, he stood proudly, his right hand resting heavily on a cane. It was the hand with a missing finger, lost in an assault when the family was escaping Somalia. He wore a patterned *ma'awis*, a checked shirt, a shawl thrown around his shoulders to guard against the chill, and a multicoloured cap. He stared directly into his daughter's camera with a smile that seemed to want to reassure the young woman who would examine the picture so far from home.

The other students from Ifo were at the bus stop before her. Among them was Abdirizak from Halima's study group. He was twenty-four years old but had the bearing of someone far older. Neither of Abdirizak's parents was with him that day. His mother had died in the camp from gunshot wounds she sustained in the fighting in Somalia, and his father

Halima's last moments with her mother on the day of her departure from Ifo.

had disappeared in the chaos of war. Abdirizak and his sister had lived in their uncle's compound for eleven years, enduring the indignities of refugee life. Now Abdirizak was off to University College at the University of Toronto, where he planned to study economics, a field he'd chosen because he wanted to understand "why some people in the world are so poor when others have so much."

Walking with Abdirizak days earlier on the wide lane through Ifo camp, commonly called "Ifo Highway," I had decided he was an earnest man, more reserved than the other students. I could understand why the others saw him as serious enough, responsible enough, to be their leader. We talked about how different highways were in Canada and he asked if I would take him for a drive in Toronto. Along the way, trees known as "early grow" leaned over the sandy path providing shade in spots as we walked.

The early grow trees had been introduced to the camp by a German aid agency because they grew so quickly, but they had spread wherever they wanted, becoming a nuisance. Their thorns, Abdirizak told me, could cause illness and even kill livestock. Families passed us, pulling carts filled with plastic bags of rice or grains. Children rolled jerry cans of water back to their homes. Abdirizak walked down the road with graceful intent, like a king with no need to hurry, head held high, unsmiling. He told me he walked eight kilometres a day in the heat and the rain back and forth between his home and the school where he taught. When he was a student, he had used a bicycle because the teachers would close the doors when classes started, keeping tardy students out. When he was a teacher, he didn't have the same worries of being late, and he'd grown tired of his years of riding the bicycle back and forth, so he walked to the school. As I walked slowly beside him, I thought there must have been times when he'd been especially late or had wanted to get out of the rain, but, adjusting to his calm, lion-like steps, I couldn't imagine him breaking into a undignified run.

A group of old men, their heads wrapped against the sun, stopped Abdirizak and talked at him loudly, waving their hands at me, the white woman walking with him. I could hear only the guttural sounds of the Somali language and understood nothing. Abdirizak said a few words to the old men and walked away. Curious, I followed him and asked, "What did they say?" He answered quickly and somewhat slyly: "They asked who the woman was and why I didn't introduce them. I told them you were a relative." He said it with such a straight face that it took a moment for me to catch the sharp sense of humour behind his words.

Twenty-one-year-old Hussein, who was heading to Grant MacEwan College in Edmonton, wanted to study economics like Abdirizak. His father had died the year before and he hoped a degree in economics would guarantee him a good job so he could bring the rest of his family to Canada. That day his mother and brother came with him to the Ifo bus stop. Later, he would go over and over the moment he'd had to say goodbye, finally using his lessons from English composition to capture his unruly emotions on a sheet of lined paper:

The moment came where my heart skipped and my blood rised to its highest pressure. The last moment, the time I had to say goodbye to my mother, the factory of all my success, the only one in my life, the guide in my eyes. I gathered all my courage and had to face the challenge of saying goodbye to my mother. When I stood in front of her, tears trickled down my face, large hot drops of tears. My hands became limp. I could not move my body and the worse came when mother shed tears of love, tears of sadness and worry of seeing me for the last time. My older brother joined me and only added on to my worries when he clinged onto me.

On the sidelines in the Ifo market, near the bicycle rental shop where the Zafanana bus stopped, twenty-one-year-old Abdi squatted, in blue jeans and the thin black leather jacket he'd purchased in Nairobi for the cold Canadian climate. He chewed his nails and watched the scene around him with a worried expression. He had done all he could for his relatives and friends. He'd given away his houses and his cellphone and had organized a lottery to give away his bicycle, a luxury in the camp, but none of that did much to erase the guilt he felt at leaving everyone behind. Abdi hoped to study political science and economics, although there was something of the philosopher in him. "To be a refugee," he mused, "is like living in a sealed, dark room." Life had to be better out there than it was here in hot, dusty Ifo, where there was "no freedom of movement, no good jobs if you have an education, no work permitted even if you have the education. And sometimes you go without food."

"I lived alone in the camps," he said, "struggled without a mother and a father, without having family. I think I will find it easier in Canada." Still, he could not erase the film of sadness that covered the day. To ease his guilt he told himself, "Some should escape outside and see what's going on in the outside world."

He would begin seeing that world at Huron University College in London, Ontario, although he still would not allow himself to believe he'd actually get there. He had waited until the last days to officially resign the position he held with CARE because nothing in life could be taken for granted. It was like a saying he'd heard: *Man proposes. God disposes.* And it was hard to forget what had happened to relatives still living in the camp, relatives who had made it as far as Nairobi in the resettlement process before their flight had been cancelled on September 11, 2001. There was a good reason the expression *Enshallah,* "God willing," was repeated so frequently in the camps.

Abdi had become an orphan during the civil war when militia gunmen from a rival clan burst into the family's home in Kismayo, Somalia, shooting wildly in the living room and killing both his parents and his three brothers. Only he and his sister escaped, but in the madness of the moment they became separated. In another time, on another continent, Abdi could have been the inspiration for a Charles Dickens novel. He'd shown the same pluck as Dickens' orphans by fleeing through the back of the house and following neighbours on the exodus to Kenya, where people connected him with an uncle— his mother's younger brother—in the camp. His sister made her way years later as a married woman to another camp, where she lived with her in-laws.

As a child, Abdi ate his meals with his uncle's family, but when he was about twelve he started living in his own compound, sleeping in a brick house he helped build. The solitary life suited him. He was a very private person who wanted to keep his painful history to himself. When he felt lonely after a tiring day at work, he stopped by his uncle's compound to listen to stories about his mother. He would miss his uncle's stories.

After the flood of 2006 had washed away his first house, he'd built two more in his compound, a sitting room and a sleeping room out of mud and twigs, houses supported with the strongest timbers money

Abdi beside the sleeping house he built in 2006.

could buy. Abdi could afford the houses and the bicycle, could afford to return his uncle's kindness, because he received one of the highest incentives given to refugees: 5,700 Kenyan shillings, about $87.50 a month at the time. After secondary school he'd taken an incentive job with CARE, ending up in a group dealing with sexual and gender-based violence, where he gave talks about the hazards of female genital mutilation and mediated in domestic disputes. It was work he believed in, but it was work that often drew jeers from other men, who wondered why this young, skinny guy was interfering in traditional matters. "Feminist," they called him. As if it were a bad word.

I met Abdi in the main CARE compound on my first day in Dadaab, one day before the other students came to meet me. We sat in an area between the agency buildings and the mess hall at a round picnic table covered with a round umbrella. Perhaps because he wore a beige baseball cap with the word CARE on it and told me people had nicknamed him "American" because he was lighter-skinned than some, or perhaps because he knew how to communicate so well, I went past the simple biographical questions I had planned for our first visit. There was a thoughtfulness to him, a certain gravity but also a willingness to engage and an eagerness to find humour in situations. Perhaps because of all that, I asked too much. He told me of his parents' deaths. He told me what clan his family belonged to and what clan had killed them. I didn't probe further, but I had already probed too much.

Two days later, I received an email from Ibrahim, his friend in Canada. Ibrahim advised me strongly not to ask questions about clan in the camps, where young people were trying to move past tribalism and where such questions might make them wonder who I really was. Ibrahim didn't mention Abdi's name. He didn't have to: Abdi had been the only one I'd spoken to about clans.

When, days later, I went to visit Abdi in his home, he greeted me graciously and laughed with good humour when I pointed out how much taller his nephew was than him. As we walked in the camp, I told him I would not ask any more questions about clan while I was there. He seemed relieved. It was a lesson for me, not just in sensitivity, but in awareness of how quickly news spreads among Somalis, wherever they are.

The morning of his departure, Abdi started walking to the bus stop before sunrise to greet his friends there and to make sure he was on time. Now he squatted, nervously waiting. The bus was late. When it finally came at seven-thirty, he got on board, the first step of a journey where so much could still go wrong. The conductor tried to keep order, to find the passengers among the forty or so people crowded around the bus. When Mohamed from Dagahaley descended to stretch, he had to convince the Ifo conductor he was a passenger because he had left his ticket on the bus. Fortunately for him, the main conductor on the bus recognized him. Finally, with most of his passengers on the bus, the conductor, in frustration, yelled at a tearful Halima to leave her family and pushed her toward the door.

——

The Town of Dadaab

Before the Zafanana bus could travel to the last refugee camp, Hagadera, it had to stop in the town of Dadaab, where it would go through the first of half a dozen checkpoints on the drive to Nairobi. The students dreaded the checkpoints and feared the Kenyan police who ran them. It was not uncommon for the police to reject travel documents that were perfectly legitimate or to take a person's papers, hide them and claim the passenger had nothing. "They are hard and they can do what they want," Mohamed said.

Abdi anticipated problems. One time he had been travelling with Halima when she was hassled because her picture was fuzzy. And another time he had been held even though he had documents that allowed him to go to Nairobi for the TOEFL, the exam that demonstrated the proficiency in English required for his scholarship. The police had finally let him take a later bus, but he could never relax near checkpoints after that.

The Dadaab checkpoint didn't scare any of them nearly as much as the one they'd cross later at the Tana Bridge, a checkpoint that divided the region inhabited by Kenyans who were ethnic Somalis from what was known as the "real" Kenya. Abdi recalled a sign at the bridge in Swahili that translated into English as "Have a Safe Journey," but he didn't believe the police meant it. At various times students had been pulled from buses at the checkpoint and taken to the police post next door, for no apparent reason, before being suddenly released.

If the police didn't hold them back, they might try to bribe them. Abdi and the others knew all too well the code words the police used to make things go more smoothly, words like "chai," or "soda," which were really a request for cash. Or, in Swahili, the police might ask for *kitu kudogo,* meaning "a small thing." The bus drove six kilometres east to the town of Dadaab, travelling past scrubby bushes with leaves grey with dust and the tall, noble acacia trees off in the distance, past the large red termite mounds that looked like unfinished sculptures. Outside of the town, the bus passed fields of garbage where torn bits of plastic hung from the ends of thorny bushes, and goats and marabou storks competed for slim pickings. The ungainly storks, known by aid workers as "rats of the sky," are scavengers, survivors, and they are everywhere. Atop acacia trees their enormity mocks all sense of proportion. On the sides of the road, they dwarf young girls wrapped in red or yellow cotton. In the middle of the road, they stop traffic before raising oversized wings and awkwardly flying off.

For the last time, the students passed Dadaab Primary School with its sign that read "Kick AIDS out of Dadaab" and its other sign from the Danish Refugee Council, listing all the good it had done for the school in providing desks, toilets, girls' uniforms and sanitary belts. Electricity and water flowed in the primary school, courtesy of CARE. Over the years, the agencies had given more and more help to the local community, which had become more and more vocal about the refugees in their midst using their resources and getting better education and cleaner water.

The bus slowed on the main strip in Dadaab to avoid the dips in the road and the shoppers who walked by the tin shops and the Al Rhama and Blue Nile hotels.

There is little to recommend the town of Dadaab to visitors. Announcements for positions with the major employers in the region, the aid agencies, insist that applicants "have prior knowledge of living conditions in Dadaab" and warn that "during the rainy season, mosquitoes, snakes, scorpions, bugs and insects are in abundance." Even for types who like their travel rough, it's hard to find Dadaab in any guidebooks. A search online through the Lonely Planet site might ask if you meant Madaba, in Jordan, and offer nothing on Dadaab. The town sits less than one degree north of the equator, too far away for a marker that tourists could pose by with smiling faces and thumbs up, and the barren landscape, often frequented by *shiftas*, or bandits, invites neither picture taking nor hikes. As small and as remote as Dadaab looks to the outsider, it is less small and less remote than it was before the camps came. A population of a few thousand in the early 1990s has more than tripled because of the employment opportunities created. Thanks to the camps, roads in the area are better maintained and communication with the rest of the country and the world has improved. In 2004, Kenya's mobile phone company, Safaricom, extended coverage to the area.

On the left, the bus drove past the steel gate and the razor-wire fencing of the main aid compound, and on the right, it passed the Islamic Centre and Dadaab Secondary School, with its library and laboratory funded by UNHCR. It came to a stop at the checkpoint at the edge of town, where police in camouflage uniforms checked the identity papers of the Kenyan nationals and the students' travel documents. That day there was no problem, and Abdi believed it was because there was safety in numbers. Seven students were already on board and they all yelled that they were going to Canada to study. The guard lifted the spiked yellow metal roadblock and allowed the bus to pass into the open road ahead.

Hagadera Refugee Camp

Ten kilometres southeast of Dadaab, the bus stopped at Hagadera camp, known for the red sand that makes walking difficult and riding a bike impossible. Here it picked up the final four Somali students: Aden Sigat Nunow, Muno Mohamed Osman, Siyad Adow Maalim and Marwo Aden Dubow.

It was a good thing the bus was late that morning, because Muno was having trouble leaving her compound. "There was no moving," she said. She stood between the tin door and the goat's twig shelter of her home in Block B5 thinking up excuses each time her father called from the bus stop to hurry her along. Muno could count on one hand the number of times she had slept away from this compound, away from her sister and mother. Just shy of twenty, with a pouty, plump, beautiful face, she was the youngest student leaving that day, perhaps too young for such an unimaginable departure. She assumed life would be better in Canada than it was here, but everything she had learned about life had happened here, in this compound, in this camp. She had read her first books here, anything she could get her hands on—Swahili books, English books, joke books, it didn't matter. She had read collections that had intrigued her, like the stories of Sherlock Holmes, to her a real detective. She

had read great books, such as *The Headsman* and *The Kite Runner,* the latter a gift from a Kenyan teacher who had recognized her hunger for reading. In this compound Muno had decided she wanted to be a writer who would tell the stories of refugees and of her religion. She knew she had to leave to do that. She knew there were more books out there—a whole library of books at the Mississauga campus of the University of Toronto—knew she had huge holes in her knowledge she could never fill here. And yet the price she had to pay for the opportunity to

Muno in her family compound in Hagadera, the only home she'd known in her life.

get that knowledge seemed so high. She had never suffered the obsession of *buufis*. It was not longing for resettlement that finally made her move from that doorway, not even her personal longing for endless shelves of books, but the knowledge that this opportunity, the chance to study at a university in Canada, would give her the means to help her family.

In Block C1, near the Hagadera market, Marwo, the third female student leaving that day, had already said her goodbyes to her aunt, the woman who had sheltered her after her parents died in the conflict and her grandmother died later in the camp. It was her aunt who had stepped in to care for her and who called her "daughter." There was nothing sentimental about the woman. "Hard," Marwo

Marwo in Hagadera with her aunt.

called her aunt, meaning it as a compliment. Marwo's aunt was divorced, a midwife and a woman who believed in getting on with life. She had not brought Marwo into the world, but she was determined to send her out into it, even if it meant losing her best companion in a lonely place.

A week earlier, I had sat across from Marwo's aunt in the centre of her compound. The acrid smell of burning garbage wafted over the walls. We sat—me on the only stool in sight, her on a jerry can—smiling at each other and making small talk through Marwo's translations. I expressed admiration of her work as a midwife. The aunt expressed joy over her niece's move to Canada. We smiled again at each other. A few drops of rain fell from the sky and Marwo's aunt rushed me into her house along with Marwo, Muno and a young Kenyan teacher, Catherine Kagendo, who had accompanied us around Hagadera camp. Marwo offered tea. I requested mine without milk because of the stories of Westerners sickened by unpasteurized African milk.

41

The rain stopped within minutes, but we stayed in the darkened room drinking the clear, sweet tea, sitting on mattresses that were wrapped in patterned sheets. There was a quiet intimacy to the moment, the noise of the camp muffled inside the house, the absence of men freeing the women to talk openly. Muno and Marwo spoke about how girls in the camp kept away from men during their periods, how girls stopped playing sports with boys when they reached puberty. CARE, they said, had delivered sports outfits for girls that totally covered their bodies, but people had scorned the girls who wore them. They said that CARE had been more successful when organizers had found an enclosed area where girls could play together, because girls and women like their privacy from men. Privacy is everything. Marwo and Muno explained that there are some women who cover their faces for extra privacy in the camps, although others do it to avoid the dust—that there is nothing in the religion that demands the face be hidden. Muno, in particular, worried that privacy would be harder to find in Canada.

The young women wanted to know if there were dogs in Canadian homes. When I said there were, Marwo asked, "Will they hurt us?" I said that they would not if they were treated well and that most dogs were treated like companions in Canadian homes. I told them about dogs trained to guard property but said they wouldn't have to come in contact with them. Muno—the daughter of a man who is both an imam, the prayer leader at his mosque, and a sheikh knowledgeable in Islamic teaching—explained to me that any contact with a dog is considered a heavy impurity. If a dog touched her, she said, she would have to wash her hands seven times before praying. She went on to list the mid-level impurities of blood, pus and the urine of an adult or a baby girl. The least offensive impurity, she said, is the urine of a baby boy.

Throughout the visit, Muno constantly busied herself, fingering the Swahili novel she carried with her as though she wanted to get back to it, checking her cellphone and reading a newspaper that Marwo had found and kept for her. Marwo liked to read too but not as much as her friend Muno did. Muno searched the paper for words she didn't know. When she came across the word *lingerie* in a joke, she asked me if it was just the underwear part or the top as well.

That morning, she had kept us all waiting, phoning several times to say she was on her way, admitting, after arriving an hour late, that she had been reading her novel while she was cooking breakfast and had lost track of time. She did, however, get through most of the novel.

We came out of the house to the bright midday light and the chirping of chickens caged by Marwo's aunt for their healthy eggs. Children were running everywhere, some from the families of new arrivals now enlarging the population of the compound, and I suddenly understood the desire to retreat into those houses. On the way out of the compound, Marwo ran up to me with a message from her aunt. I should take milk in my tea. It was the health advice of a midwife to another woman.

Marwo and Muno guided me toward Hagadera market, where they had to do some final shopping for their trip. On the way, we passed a donkey cart piled high with wood. Marwo told me the load, a three-month supply, cost 1,000 shillings, a price they had to pay. The ration of wood allotted to them as refugees was insufficient for all the

A load of firewood in Hagadera.

cooking needs of the compound and her aunt wouldn't allow Marwo to gather wood in the bush because women who foraged there were often raped. As we walked, Catherine, the Kenyan teacher, and I wore scarves wrapped loosely around our heads. Catherine told me children would throw stones at uncovered women. Even with the scarves, she admitted, they sometimes still did. Marwo and Muno both wore the hijab, the ubiquitous outfit for women and school-aged girls: a circle of cloth with an opening for the face, it flowed loosely to the knees and was worn over a long skirt. When I stumbled in a rut of the sandy laneway, I heard a chorus of "sorry," from Muno and Marwo. By then I had heard the word used by most of the students in the camps. Whenever I brushed away a mosquito or my shirt caught on a loose fence twig or I told them about something that had gone wrong in my day, they said "sorry," very softly, with a depth of empathy I found moving. I wanted to tell them they would fit in with Canadians, who were reputed to use the word "sorry" even when they were not at fault, but I couldn't figure out how to explain the joke.

The market in Hagadera where Marwo and Muno buy last-minute provisions for Canada.

In Hagadera market, we passed a shop with bolts of material and a sewing machine outside. Marwo said that a hijab, like the one she wore in a washed-out lavender colour, cost 250 shillings—200 for the material and 50 for the sewing. At another shop she pointed out the bottles of powdered henna they could mix with water to decorate themselves for Muslim holidays. The bottles varied in price from 10 to 50 shillings for one of the highest quality. But today they both needed new prayer mats. In Marwo's case there was some urgency to find one with a compass, since she would have to pray as soon as she got to her room in Victoria and wasn't sure anyone at the university would know the direction to Mecca. Muno was looking for a plain mat; a student from Dadaab was already at her campus in Mississauga and could help her face Mecca. As we walked past stalls filled with stacks of flip-flops and rolls of linoleum, Muno said that memories of the market would haunt her. She would miss its liveliness and the pleasure of spending time there with her friends. The two young women pointed out the shop where they usually bought their henna. The saleswoman, her face covered, saw our interest and pushed the

shampoos and creams. She had the gift of a born salesperson, teasing the young women and joking with me that Marwo and I looked alike, challenging again my idea of who had a sense of humour and who did not.

Most of the stalls were sold out of the mats with compasses. At one, Muno picked up a rather gaudy-looking mat in bright orange and greens from a pile of mats without compasses and asked our opinion. Both Marwo and I shook our heads, and Muno decided on another one in various shades of blues, arguing with the salesman until he lowered

Muno with the prayer mat she will take to Canada.

45

the price from 300 shillings to 270. Catherine said the bargaining was tougher in Nairobi. Muno responded, defending her home, saying that there were not as many choices here in the camp market. Finally, at another stall, Marwo found a mat with a white plastic compass. The saleswoman demanded 550 shillings and wouldn't take less than 500, a price Marwo considered too high. Her friend Siyad had paid much less for his. In the end she decided to buy a plain mat and asked me if I could email the young woman who would be meeting her in Victoria to find out which direction she should face for her prayers.

In her years living with her aunt, Marwo had learned how to be sensible. She had chosen to study international relations at the University of Victoria because it seemed to be a "marketable" field, but she was keeping her options open. Maybe once she was at the university she'd find another field that would give her what she wanted: an education, a good job and money. When she had all three, she knew, her life would change.

The compound Marwo and her aunt shared was a busy one with little space between the buildings that housed other relatives, including the new arrivals from Somalia with nowhere else to live. Marwo's aunt was not a woman to turn people away. That morning, Marwo's aunt had risen early from the house she shared with her niece to prepare a solid breakfast. That taken care of, she set off for work at the hospital, leaving it to other relatives to wait with Marwo at the bus stop.

In his home in B5, twenty-three-year-old Siyad had also said his most important goodbye. His father, the constant in his life, had a religious class to attend and couldn't go with him to the bus. Siyad's stepmother, sister and friends walked with him to the bus stop. Seeing all the crying faces around him, Siyad started to cry too until a friend asked him, "Why should you cry? This is not the end. Your parents will still be here." And he realized he could come back. If he became

Siyad with his father, the man who has been the one constant in his life.

a doctor, as he hoped, he could return and care for the sick in Dadaab or in Somalia. He imagined the photo from the University of British Columbia's website, and this buoyed his spirits. It showed a young man and a young woman sitting in opposite directions quietly reading. It was sunny outside. This, he was sure, was what Canada would be like.

Aden was also thinking of becoming a doctor. It was a profession that topped his list of choices, at least, right below pilot. At twenty-one, Aden had no experience with planes—had never flown in one—but he had seen airplanes in movies, and he had watched them fly high over the camp's air space. And that was enough to fuel his ambition. To some, his method of choosing a career might seem odd, but for Aden it made sense. His face shone with curiosity and ambition. Highly intelligent, he had graduated in 2006 with an A– average as the top student in Hagadera and tied for best in the region.

Aden described one of his hobbies as travelling, which, at first glance, seemed another quixotic notion for someone who had grown up in a refugee camp. But Aden was a guy who knew how to work around restrictions. He'd repeatedly visited an uncle in the Nairobi suburb of Eastleigh, using a student card from a high school there to travel back and forth. In Eastleigh he could receive tutoring in chemistry and Swahili and ensure that his grades in the final examinations were the best they could be. One time, he had gone to Nairobi for a mathematics competition and had travelled to nearby Lake Naivasha, where he'd seen vast flocks of flamingos. He assumed he would be able to expand his hobby of travelling once he got to the West.

He was a man who thought big, who couldn't wait to get out of the sealed room permanently and play. Even his cellphone expressed his desire for more. It rang with the title of Jamaican rapper Sean Paul: "(When You Gonna) Give It Up to Me." Aden had bought one of the most expensive cellphones he could find, a Sony Ericsson K750i for which he'd paid $200, because he liked "fancy phones."

Aden chats on his expensive cellphone, a luxury in Hagadera camp.

Aden wanted it all and he wanted it fast: cars and cameras, life in a big city like Toronto. He felt sure he would find people to help him in Canada, maybe someone who would buy him an airplane ticket so he could visit his mother the following summer. Ironically, the big, confident guy with the biggest ideas was headed to a university in the smallest city: Brandon, Manitoba.

In Hagadera, Aden was the man of his household. His father, who had lived separately from the family before the war, had disappeared in the fighting. His older sister's husband lived in New Zealand and sent money back to support his wife and their children in the camp. Both women pampered Aden: his sister had taken him to Nairobi to buy his clothes and two big suitcases for

Aden with his mother (far right) and sister (centre).

Canada; his mother had baked cookies for his journey. That morning the two women cried as they walked with Aden to the bus stop near the Hagadera police station. Although he felt sad too, Aden wouldn't let himself cry. "I was trying to be hard," he said later, "but I was crying inside."

When the bus arrived, crowds surrounded it, once again blocking the door and frustrating the conductor, who was still trying to make up some of the time they'd lost. The four students had to force their way inside. The bus was so late leaving that Marwo's aunt had time to return from her morning work and Siyad's father from his religious class before the driver pulled away. Siyad, already seated near the back, reached through a window and took his father's hand one last time. Not far from him, Muno cried inconsolably. Like a chain reaction, the sound of her sobs set off Halima and Dilalesa. As the bus drove off and Marwo watched her aunt turn away and walk home, all her bright hopes for change were doused by the singular thought that she should have stayed.

———

The Zafanana bus that carried the Dadaab eleven out of their sealed box that day was brown with a zigzag design of red, orange and yellow stripes on its side. Later, none of the students could recall exactly what that bus looked like. It could have been pale blue. It could have had green stripes or maybe green and red stripes. They had paid little attention. Their eyes had been focused first on the faces of families and friends and later on the land they might never see again.

CHAPTER TWO

A List of Heartbreaking Events

THE GLASS WALL THAT FRONTS the Jomo Kenyatta International Airport in Nairobi divides the world into two distinct groups: those who have valid airline tickets and those who do not; those who are leaving the city, the country, perhaps even the African continent and those who are not. For the eleven students from Dadaab, the glass wall cut their past from their future, separated them with gut-wrenching finality from all they had loved and loathed so far in their lives.

During the early evening hours of August 19, 2008, the students sat on the hard, red-tiled floor inside the terminal in the international departures area. In the days spent in Nairobi before their departure to Canada, they had caught up with relatives and friends in the city. Out in the city at night Hussein had run-ins with Kenyan police officers who demanded to see his identity card. When he couldn't produce any identification one time, they handcuffed him. He called his brother, a student in Nairobi, who came and bribed the police to let him go. Now Hussein's brother and a few of the students' friends and family members who had followed them to the airport stood on the other side of the glass waving, before finally wandering off for good.

Each of the Dadaab students had been briefed that day at an International Organization for Migration centre in Nairobi, given a final medical and handed an American twenty-dollar bill for their personal needs in transit. In the late afternoon the students, along with other refugees, piled into buses for the half-hour drive to the airport in a suburb southeast of the city. They arrived hours before their midnight flight to London, too early to check in and head up the escalator to the departure area, a hallway congested in the evening hours with people both arriving and departing, and lined with shops selling dusty carved giraffes and zebras, coffee beans in vacuum bags and duty-free items.

There wasn't enough room on the benches against two walls in the departure zone for all of the students. Sudanese students from Kakuma camp who were also headed to Canada and a few of the students from Dadaab took up most of those seats. Others sat on the floor, getting up to take turns standing in the nearby long line to sign for their travel loans from the Canadian government and receive the documentation they would carry with them in white plastic bags imprinted in blue with the letters IOM and the organization's symbol. They waited, exhausted and impatient to leave, to experience whatever their new lives would bring.

Abdi couldn't let go of his anxiety. There could still be delays, changes of plans or an accident that could prevent them from departing. Most of the students had slept little in Nairobi after trying to pack a lifetime of visits into three short days. They were all tired and they were hungry, but there was nothing to buy in the check-in area. Aden shared his mother's "cookies," cooked balls of dough that looked like Tim Hortons Timbits but tasted less sweet. Abdikadar was the only one who still had a cellphone. He lent it to all the students from both Kakuma and Dadaab so they could call their families one last time. To tourists returning home from game parks or businessmen flying back to Europe, they must have looked an odd sight: young people huddled on the floor, with backpacks and carry-on luggage, sitting next to a cart piled with suitcases wrapped in white tape, passing around a single cellphone. Some clutched the white IOM bags, proof that they were students in transit, refugees in limbo.

Ten of the eleven students from Dadaab leaving that night were Somalis who had known little but limbo all their lives. They were three years old or four or six when their world and their country collapsed in 1991. The youngest of the students, Muno, says she remembers nothing of living in Somalia or leaving it, only the red ration card in Liboi, a temporary camp just inside Kenya where her family spent its first few years in the country. She would go with her mother to get their rations. "There was rice and meat. The rations were good."

For the rest of the ten, some scattered memories of Somalia before the war remain: a two-storey house, a ride in a father's truck, a visit to the cinema, a whole family eating dinner together. They were born in a country held together by a tyrant, but they were born in peace. And although they hadn't lived in Somalia for years, they still proudly called themselves Somalis, studied the country's tortuous history and followed each twist of its violent present. It is the way of Somalis. No matter how lands were divided in colonial days, Somalis everywhere know they are a people who share the same ethnicity, speak the same language and, for the most part, practise the same Sunni branch of Islam. The flag of Somalia reminds them of this; the five points of its white star represent the areas where Somalis live: Somalia itself, Somaliland, Djibouti, the Ogaden region of Ethiopia and northeastern Kenya. The flag was created decades before refugees resettled in the Middle East, Europe and North America. The ten students would become part of the growing diaspora, but they would always be Somalis.

Well before their families left their homeland in 1991, the country had been scarred by clan rivalries and more than a hundred years of interference from global powers. Somalia's long coastlines on the Indian Ocean and the Gulf of Aden have always appealed to foreign powers for their easy access to major shipping routes. During the colonial era, Britain and Italy controlled most of the country, feeding the animosity among clans to keep control. On July 1, 1960, the British and Italian sections of Somalia joined together to form an independent democracy. It lasted just shy of a decade until an army commander named Mohamed Siad Barre led a coup against the government just one day after the funeral of assassinated president Abdirashid Ali Shermarke.

Siad Barre promised that his regime would turn the country into a socialist state where Somali would be the official spoken and written language, where there would be no room for tribalism, where banks and businesses would be nationalized. But he fuelled the eventual eruption of clan warfare by favouring members of his own Marehan tribe, a sub-clan of one of the largest clans in Somalia, the Darod, and by his brutal repression of any challenge to his authority.

During the Cold War, Barre's machinations turned his country into a pawn in the politics of the Soviet Union and the United States. At first the socialist state found a sympathetic alignment with the Soviet Union. In the 1970s, when Barre took his country into war against Ethiopia over the Ogaden region where ethnic Somalis lived, the Soviets backed him. Then Ethiopia pronounced itself a Marxist state and the Soviet Union began backing that country, too—a country it saw as more important in the region. That left Barre one other potentially rich ally: the United States. He promised to switch his allegiance to the Americans. They responded by pouring millions of dollars of military and economic aid into Somalia, creating a prosperity that could not last. Like the gun that appears in the first act of a play and has to be used by the final scene, the small arms that flowed into Somalia during that Cold War period would become a means for later anarchy.

By the late 1980s, Barre was having trouble holding the country together. Clan militias both in the north and around Mogadishu rebelled against his tyranny. Barre's army responded with bombings and shellings that killed thousands. The American government could no longer ignore reports of human rights abuse. With the end of the

Cold War, the region became less important, and in 1989 the United States cut off aid to Somalia. By 1991, rival clans forced Siad Barre out of power, sending him fleeing for his life. Prior to his departure, in a foreshadowing of the murderous chaos that would follow, *Time* magazine reported on January 14, 1991, that "the rebel factions had no political program: the only principle that unites them is their hatred of Siad Barre and their determination to oust him. Their organizations are completely clan-based and divided by hundreds of years of intramural fighting. With no restraining influences from abroad and the superpowers attending to other concerns, Somalia's future is likely to be sadly similar to its bloody past." The ensuing bloody period of clan against clan and sub-clan against sub-clan changed the lives of the ten Somali students from Dadaab forever.

Aden wasn't even school-age when the war reached his home in the town of Jilib in Somalia's Juba Valley. Yet he still has memories of his family's beautiful home: a brick house covered with white stucco and topped with a tin roof; a garden with tall trees; and the river nearby, where he swam, always mindful of the crocodiles. In the house, they had a sitting area as well as a dining area where his mother served meals. There was a cinema behind the house, owned by his maternal uncle, where he could see movies for free. He still remembers his mother taking him to Qu'ran school before he was old enough to go to the regular school. His parents were part of the Darod clan. His mother worked in a bakery in the market. His father was a police officer.

When the civil war broke out, people threatened to attack government authorities. Aden's father fled, and the family lost track of his whereabouts. Aden lived with his mother and siblings until the war came to town. He can't recall the exact date his life changed or who exactly changed it. He knew only that there was a war going on and that militias from other clans or sub-clans could kill them. Aden does remember the sound of gunfire, knows that it came from a rival clan that his mother feared. After they saw houses around them demolished and heard reports of neighbours killed, they ran. But the militia stopped them before they could get out of town and let them pass only after a tenant of Aden's mother, a man who belonged to the rival clan now controlling the city, intervened. "She's my landlady," Aden remembers the man saying. "She doesn't belong to those guys."

The tenant's intervention is not the only thing that Aden is grateful for. During the attacks and the long walk to the Kenyan border, he never saw a dead body, something he knows would have haunted him to this day.

Hussein was not so lucky. His memories of the time have the vivid detail of a lingering nightmare. Hussein's family came from the same clan as Siad Barre and became targets for reprisals from clans such as the Hawiye who had brought Barre's government down, even though Hussein's father was not affiliated with the government. He was a truck driver in the southern port city of Kismayo, working for a company that exported oranges and bananas from the surrounding orchards to Libya. Hussein remembers the ripe, yellow bananas his father would bring home and the rides in the truck on his father's day off. He remembers, too, how on Fridays his father would take them to the ocean and, to tease him, dip him in and out of the azure water of the Indian Ocean. "Life was good," he recalls with a nod and a smile.

Good until militia gunmen broke through the gate of the family compound. Hussein's father was out of the house at the time. If he'd been there, Hussein is certain, his father would not have survived the attack. The gunmen were targeting older boys and men of other clans; nonetheless, they opened fire in the house, and his grandmother and an aunt died in the random shooting. He has little memory of their deaths, but he does have three strong memories from the escape to Kenya. He calls them his "list of heartbreaking events." First on his list is the helplessness he felt as a boy who watched a street gang strip and beat his mother with a gun as the family tried to get away from the city. "I'm just a kid, a small kid, so I can't do anything," he says, describing the event in the present tense as if he is still on a street in Kismayo, unable to defend his mother. Second on his list: the dead bodies he saw as he, with his mother and siblings, moved to a safe zone of the city, where they reunited with his father. What made that memory more horrifying to him was thinking he'd seen a method of torture used elsewhere in Somalia, called "nailing," where an attacker pounded a nail into the head of a victim. Later, in the camp, Hussein wasn't sure if he had actually seen nails or if he'd mixed his own memories of bloodied heads with stories he heard from other survivors. He can't remember how many days the walk to the temporary camp in Liboi, inside Kenya, took. He remembers only that his family borrowed a neighbour's donkey cart to carry his injured mother, who was having trouble walking. The strongest memory of that walk, the final item on his list, is the leaves they ate for moisture when the family couldn't find any water.

Halima's only early memory comes from her family's escape to Kenya. A toddler at the time, she knows from what she's been told that her parents came from different clans and lived on a subsistence farm in the south of the country before the war. But her first clear memory, the one she can picture as her own, is from the end of their walk to Kenya, as her family neared the border and safety. She can still see the armed bandit, a strong-looking man entirely covered except for his eyes, who jumped out in front of them and ordered them to follow him deep into the bush and sit facing away from him. They could hear him searching through their belongings. The man took a book from Halima's father and flipped through its pages before tossing it away. "Why are you doing that?" her father had asked. The gunman pointed the gun at him, and at that moment her brother ran off. The man fired in the air, in warning, and, to the relief of Halima's mother, her brother came back. Then the gunman ordered Halima's mother and elder sister to remove their clothes so he could search for gold or other valuables they might have hidden.

Throughout the search, Halima's father feared the man would rape his wife or his daughter. "My dad," Halima says, staring off as if she can still see his face from that day. "That was actually difficult. He had escaped all that was happening in Somalia. And this was the end.

And my dad was like, *I can't let this happen.* And he cried. I could see my dad crying, because we were all facing in the same direction. I was young, but I can remember that." The gunman quickly ran off, taking what little money he could find, Halima believes, leaving her mother and sister untouched. Before collecting the family's scattered belongings, before getting up from the ground to walk the last kilometres to safety, her father prayed.

Sometimes it was looting and the threat of violence to come that drove families away from their homes. Both Siyad and Mohamed came from pastoral families who had little but the livestock they grazed in the bush. Mohamed's family belonged to the Marehan Darod, the sub-clan of Siad Barre, although they lived far from his seat of power. As a boy Mohamed learned to take care of the family goats. He gave each of the goats its own name and singled out one for his special attention. One night the family received news of an approaching rival militia. "They were coming," he recalls, "and what they are looking for was 'Are you from this clan?' It's not like, 'Do you have a gun?' or anything. But if you are from this clan, all of your animals are taken away. Women would be raped. Men would be killed. We had to run away." Siyad remembers the small house his whole family shared, a circular house made of twigs—remembers that their animals were looted in the night. He doesn't know who stole them, but since his family was from a small clan aligned with the Hawiye, he assumes the thieves were Darod.

Mohamed and Siyad, sitting together in the Nairobi airport, were two young men who shared similar stories but were from clans who had been enemies in the war. If they had stayed in Somalia, perhaps they would have grown to hate each other or would have picked up guns themselves. But in Dadaab they had both been refugees, boys growing up with a common belief that their generation of Somalis had to end the clan distinctions that had torn their country apart. In Dadaab, people avoided questions about clan, "especially among the young," Mohamed said. "They don't care about clans and those things. They have the same religion, the same appearance, no difference."

The other Somalis sitting with them in the airport shared his view. "It says in the Qur'an, we give you tribes and clans so you will know each other," Muno said. It was wrong, she believed, to discriminate or fight on the basis of clan. Aden said he didn't need to know which clan anyone else in the camp came from: "Provided we are good friends, we can all live together." Abdirizak said there was too much concern with tribalism in his culture: "That is one thing I want to dedicate my life to, to be above it."

Those leaving with the greatest pain from the war were those whose parents had died as a result of the fighting. Abdi lost his father and his mother, as well as his brothers, in a matter of moments. And he also lost track, perhaps forever, of his stepbrothers and stepsisters, his father's children from another marriage—children who could still be alive in Somalia or elsewhere. He wants to find out what happened to his half-siblings, but he believes no good could come from dwelling on his parents' death. That is in the past, and he has to move on.

Marwo has no photograph of her parents, but she will never forget their faces. Sometimes, in the camp, she found it hard to reconcile that her neighbours might well be from the clan that killed her father on the streets of Kismayo. "He was just a businessman," she says, "who played no part in the fighting." She remembers the big, beautiful house her mother and siblings had to leave behind, and the long, tiring journey to Kenya. She was six, and in her memory she is exhausted and crying, listening to her mother urging her on: "Just walk. You can walk." She remembers the relief whenever a truck came along and they could ride for a while, remembers that those few rides were not enough to get her sick mother medical attention in time. Marwo's mother died in the Somali town of Doble, less than twenty kilometres from the Somali border.

Abdikadar's mother is buried near that same border, somewhere in the Somali bush, somewhere her son could never find again. Like Hussein, Abdikadar had stood crying as he watched men severely beat his mother in Kismayo because they wanted money from her. He saw many of his relatives die—cousins and nephews, the older males—and he saw more bodies on the street with blood and guts spilling from wounds to the stomach and the head. "You cannot forget that," he says. "It is terrible." His father reconnected with the family during the twenty-day walk to Kenya. They kept to the bush and took turns carrying Abdikadar's mother which slowed the family's pace. After his mother died and they buried her, there was nothing to do but join the flood of people crossing the border into Kenya.

They entered a country that took them in but did not welcome them. Before the arrival of more than 400,000 Somali refugees in 1991 and 1992, Kenya had allowed refugees from African countries such as Sudan, Uganda and Ethiopia to move freely within the country and to find employment that made them self-sufficient. That was when Kenya could measure its refugee population in the thousands, not in the hundreds of thousands. Claiming to be overwhelmed by the numbers and the increased security threats from arms flowing in from Somalia, the Kenyan government moved quickly to close the door on its open asylum policy and to hand the care of the refugees over to UNHCR.

James Milner is an assistant professor of political science at Carleton University in Ottawa, a researcher and adviser on refugee issues. He has written extensively on refugees in Kenya and on how the history of that country's relationship with Somalia led the government to a policy that denied refugees basic rights guaranteed to them by the United Nations in 1951. He points to the government's long history of tension with the North Eastern Province, which represents one of those five points of the Somali flag, an area almost exclusively populated by ethnic Somalis left in another state during the great colonial division of Africa. In 1963, two weeks after Kenya became an independent country, guerrillas in the province seeking union with the Somali Republic began an unsuccessful, four-year campaign, a campaign known pejoratively in Kenya as the *shifta,* or bandit, war. Two years after that war ended, when Siad Barre took power in Somalia, he called for the reunification of a Greater Somalia, reviving fears in the minds of Kenyan leaders that they could lose the remote North

Eastern Province. Barre's 1977 invasion of the Ogaden region of Ethiopia, a second point on the star's flag, reinforced those fears and led to the continued oppression of ethnic Somalis in Kenya into the 1980s. In that historical context, the Kenyan government saw the arrival of hundreds of thousands of Somali refugees in the 1990s as an invasion, another reason to adopt a policy of control and containment, another reason to ignore their rights. "The history of mistrust and suspicion goes back to the beginning of the Kenyan state," Milner says. "And it's through that prism that all issues to do with Somali refugees are viewed. There's very little distinction between Somali refugees, elements coming in from Somalia and ethnic Somali Kenyans. They're all viewed as a collective problem."

The 1951 Convention and Protocol Relating to the Status of Refugees was designed to protect the rights of refugees after the Second World War, but it remains the gold standard for their rights today. The convention states that refugees are governed by the law of their host country, that they have the right to take on wage-earning employment and to move freely and obtain travel documents. At the time, refugee camps were envisioned as temporary asylums until one of the three recognized "durable" solutions could be found: repatriation, integration or resettlement. On World Refugee Day in 2008, two months before the students left Dadaab, UNHCR reported that 11.4 million refugees were in its care. The majority of those refugees had been stuck in camps for more than five years, in "protracted" situations with no durable solutions available to them— conflicts still continued in their countries, making repatriation impossible; host governments in some of the poorest countries in the world, plagued with concerns about their own security and economic problems, refused to allow refugees to integrate; resettlement opportunities remained few and far between. It all adds up to stagnation. Human rights advocates, like the US Committee for Refugees and Immigrants, claim governments like Kenya's are "warehousing" refugees as an "all-too-durable solution." And the rest of the world is complicit, ignoring refugees stuck in protracted situations. Donors, it seems, have forgotten the people in these camps and are more likely to send their money to aid current crises that they see pop up on their television screens.

Like many who study refugee issues and look for solutions, James Milner has the passion of someone who has witnessed the stalled lives of refugees with no way out. A dusty photograph in his office at Carleton University shows him as a young man in Malawi in 1992. He was there to further his knowledge of conflict issues, but he couldn't forget the refugees he met from Mozambique. "The more I learned about refugee situations, the more I came to see refugees as the most innocent victims of conflict who are held hostage by a lack of political solutions," he recalls. He went on to graduate studies at Oxford and to work with the UN in the developing world, and did a stint with UNHCR as a resettlement officer processing claims, finding solutions for individuals. He describes that job as "the most rewarding and fulfilling work" he's ever done. It confirmed his conviction that the question of refugees can't be excluded from academic work on conflict and peace building.

In protracted refugee situations, where there is no way out, resentment can fester and refugees may choose to support wars in their homeland. That protracted refugee situations can be detrimental to peace is not surprising news. After the Second World War, tens of thousands of displaced people were stranded in camps across Europe. In 1955, the High Commissioner for Refugees, Gerrit Jan van Heuven Goedhart, called the camps "black spots on the map of Europe." He said that they "should burn holes in the conscience of those who are privileged to live in better conditions" and warned that "there can be no real peace in the world as long as hundreds of thousands of men, women and children, through no fault of their own still remain in camps and live in misery and in the greatest uncertainty of their future." He added that if the world did nothing, if we waited too long, the uprooted would "become easy prey for political adventurers."

It took some twenty years to settle the issue of displaced people in

Europe. The issue of Palestinian refugees from the same period remains unsolved. The Palestinians do not fall under the UNHCR mandate, but as of 2008 there were about thirty other protracted refugee situations around the world that did. In his academic research, Milner has been part of teams that have visited some of the worst refugee camps, but he found few worse than Dadaab. "I think what is striking about the Somali refugees in Kenya," he told me, "is how isolated they have been, how minimal the assistance that they have received, how desperate their living conditions have been. It is impossible to believe that people have been living in these conditions for more than a decade, and it was reflecting on the harshness of those conditions, the limitations of rights, the lack of a prospect of a solution that led us to think: is this a problem that is systemic or is there something unique about Dadaab? And what we found is that there are dozens of Dadaab-like situations around the world. But of all the situations that I have visited, the conditions in the Dadaab camps, the vulnerability of that population are among the most stark."

The Dadaab camps were starkest in the early years when the students crossed the border into Kenya. While there was greater security in the camps than in Somalia, the incidences of rape, theft, murder and clan revenge were high. In fact, crime was a daily occurrence that few could hide from. Mohammed Qazilbash, former senior program manager for CARE, said he knew of "one horrible day in 1995 when there were one hundred reported rapes."

As children, the students lay awake at night in their first home of twigs and plastic on plots of land given to their families by UNHCR, listening in the total darkness to the silence and the occasional scream of hyenas, listening for the movements of looters.

Halima says that when she did fall asleep at night, she never knew if she would wake up safe the next day. Mornings, she would hear talk that "so and so is missing" or learn of someone murdered. She feared for her father, who was a prominent community leader. He feared for the four females in his household. Halima recalls that girls would often hide in the latrines overnight to avoid being raped. And sometimes those who were raped would not tell anyone, in order to save their families from dishonour.

Aden remembers seeing his first gun, his first "gangster," in broad daylight when he was playing as a child in the bush near Hagadera camp. Later, when he was thirteen, a gunman came to his neighbour's house one night: "They had already captured the family and they were looting them and beating the girls. And then, all of a sudden, my mom wanted to visit the family. She was wondering why the family was quiet all the night and when she went there she was told to sit down and keep quiet. My older sister went and was captured too. I saw one man standing at the neighbour's gate guarding the other guy [the one inside the compound]. I saw him and then I ran away to the other side and I made some noise. That's when they ran away."

Although many refugees just wanted to get on with their lives, there were times when clan-related violence did surface in the camps. Siyad remembers mornings when his family would wake up to find bodies between the blocks of housing in Hagadera. He said the killings were related to old wounds from the fighting in Somalia: "Maybe your brother was killed by someone who now lives in the refugee camp. Then you come and look for them. Sometimes it used to happen between the camps. There used to be a war among the tribes within the refugee camps."

The *kamoor* fencing most families built around their compounds did little to keep intruders out. If *shiftas* or old enemies came to the gate at night with flashlights and weapons, families had no choice but to let them in. To deter them, a second type of fencing, called *dhamaajo,* made from thorny branches, was constructed around blocks of compounds, but it was only when new policies were introduced that the security situation greatly improved.

Milner credits three initiatives that UNHCR and the local community undertook in 1998 with a tenfold decrease in crime between 1998 and 2003. First, the Firewood Project supplied refugees with

30 per cent of their firewood, since most violence against women occurred when they went into the bush foraging for wood. Second, a "security package" was instituted: more police officers—better-trained officers—were hired and posted in dormitories in the three camps and in the town of Dadaab. Third, UNHCR, with the Kenyan legal system, introduced a mobile court, which arrived in the camps on a bus three or four days every month to try the cases of bandits and rapists. Before that, court officials had had to make costly and logistically difficult arrangements to take the accused to Garissa, a city one hundred kilometres away. Under that system few cases actually made it to trial, but the new system saw a greater number of offenders held accountable for their crimes.

Five years after the Dadaab camps first opened, Abdirizak joined the others students in exile. Abdirizak was born in the Somali capital, Mogadishu, but his family had moved to Kismayo shortly before the war broke out. His parents were Darod of the Ogaden sub-clan. When clan fighting broke out in Kismayo, Abdirizak's father fled separately and his mother was shot in the left shoulder. Despite his mother's wound, she began the long trek toward the border with her children.

The area near the border was chaotic when they reached it. There were no soldiers, no police. It had become a free zone for bandits. "They stop you on the way just like traffic police will do," Abdirizak said, "and they will point their guns at you and they will ask you for money, something like that, and you will have to give them whatever you have, you know—sometimes jewellery, nice items, just like that."

The family retreated from the Kenyan border, farther into the interior of Somalia to a small farming town called Bu'aale, where they found safety with members of their clan. The border region was frightening, but they were also hesitant to leave the country without word of Abdirizak's father. "We were expecting to find or maybe to hear from the rest of the family, Father and so on," he recalled. "That didn't succeed and we stayed there for a number of years."

They stayed "holed up" in the small town until 1997 when the war caught up to them. "Life became a little bit unmanageable in Somalia," Abdirizak said. "The war actually spread like wildfire everywhere so the little peace that we enjoyed in this town was now destroyed. So we had to move out of the country this time, and many people as we heard had moved to Kenya and lived in relative peace and life could go on. We didn't like the idea of moving to a refugee camp or any other country at all, but with the situation we didn't have another choice."

Abdirizak's mother had never received proper medical attention for her bullet wound. She made it to Dadaab with her children but died there one year later.

The year Abdirizak left Somalia, Amnesty International reported "scores of deliberate killings as well as hostage-taking and rape" carried out on unarmed civilians "by militias of clan-based factions." By then the West had lost any appetite for stepping in to help. In 1992, after a drought and years of factional fighting that had disrupted agricultural activities and the flow of food within the country, horrifying pictures of starving Somalis had begun appearing in the Western media. Late that year, a United Nations mission called Operation Restore Hope descended on Mogadishu to ensure that relief food arriving on ships and airplanes got to those who needed it, not into the hands of clan militias that were using it to finance their attempts to take control in the power vacuum created by Siad Barre's departure.

The mission brought some order to the distribution of food but was plagued by conflicts with the most powerful warlord in Mogadishu: Mohamed Farrah Aideed, head of the Habr Gidr sub-clan of the Hawiye, leader of the revolt against Siad Barre. When the United States decided to create a separate mission to capture Aideed, they underestimated both the support he had and the anger Somalis felt at American interference. In the Battle for Mogadishu on October 3 and 4, 1993, eighteen Americans and thousands of Somalis died. Aideed remained free. The television images of two downed American helicopters and a dead American soldier being dragged through the streets of Mogadishu shifted American public opinion dramatically away from helping in Somalia to getting out of the country as quickly as possible.

The humiliation of "Black Hawk Down," as the battle was popularly named, ended the American involvement in Somalia and killed American zeal for humanitarian intervention for years. Tragically, it was also a major contributing factor to the United States' failure to listen to Lieutenant General Roméo Dallaire, head of the peacekeeping mission in Rwanda, when he pleaded for more men and material to prevent the genocide that would occur six months later.

Canada faced its own humiliation during the UN peacekeeping mission in Somalia. The elite Canadian Airborne Regiment deployed in Operation Deliverance spurred a military scandal when two members of the regiment took trophy pictures of the torture they had performed that led to the death of Somali teenager Shidane Arone at the Canadian base near Belet Huen. The "Somalia Affair" and the public inquiry that followed led to the disbanding of the discredited regiment. Somalia became, in Canada, a synonym for our own shame. For fifteen years, until news stories of Somali pirates captured Western attention, Canadians didn't want to be reminded of that country at all. Yet despite the appalling acts of Operation Deliverance, Somalis, especially those in the camps of Dadaab, continued to think of Canada as a place of refuge, a destination of hope.

By 1995, the last of the UN troops had pulled out of Somalia, taking away all support for those civilians who were trying to work outside of the clan system, civilians trying to find ways to bring peace and order to their country.

While there seemed to be no end to the war in Somalia and no possibility of integrating into Kenyan society, many of the refugees of Dadaab placed their hopes on resettlement. Although all the students understood the concept of *buufis,* that longing to be elsewhere—to migrate to the West in particular—most did not know the origin of the word. Some said it was slang. Author Cindy Horst, who did fieldwork in Dadaab for her study of how Somalis coped in the refugee camps, discovered that *buufis* is derived from a Somali word meaning to "blow air into or inflate." The word probably refers to the inflated desires blown into someone's mind. Someone who has their head filled with *buufis* often becomes obsessed with finding ways of getting out. "Somalis like resettlement more than I can say," Siyad told me. "They feel they are not in a safe place. So they will say anything to get resettlement."

All of the students know the stories of people who pretended to belong to minority tribes like the Bantu who were resettled earlier than others because of the abuse they received at the hands of other clans in the camp. Siyad recalls a time when a tribe no one in the camp had ever heard of received a group resettlement: "There was this program of the Somali Sudanese. That can't happen: Somali Sudanese. So they just make up a thing and they form a group and make a name. There are minorities there and they are treated badly but others used names to get resettlement." Another student tells of cases where families who were to be resettled would sell the "space" of a dead family member to an individual desperate to escape. The individual would pass himself off as the lost child or parent.

While some refugees certainly used deception, some humanitarian workers in positions of authority took advantage of the refugees' desire to get out of the camps. Stories of clerks who demanded bribes to push through resettlement claims led to an investigation in 2001 by the UN Office of Internal Oversight Services. It issued a report in January 2002 stating it had evidence that seventy people in the Nairobi office of UNHCR were involved in a scheme to extort bribes of $3,000 to $5,000 U.S. to guarantee resettlement. Marwo reports that there was sexual exploitation by aid workers in the camps too. Girls who didn't have the opportunity to go to school as she did were sometimes sexually exploited when they sought resettlement. The girls would say they wanted to resettle in Canada, the United States and Australia, and workers would demand sexual favours in return. Marwo became aware of the practice when she worked with the organization FilmAid International, which uses film and video to educate refugees on health and social issues. She remembers a film the organization prepared to remind people that aid workers offered services for free and to warn girls against exploitation.

There were those who refused to cheat the system and there were those who didn't want to leave at all, hoping that they or their children would be able to return to Somalia someday, fearing that they would lose their culture if they moved to a foreign country. Community leaders in the camps knew that if people were going to be in the camps for a long time, they would have to find a new kind of normal, a way of bringing hope to the lives of their children. "Hope" is one of those words that can be easily dismissed as hokey, but in a refugee camp it is the only real motivator.

The UN's World Food Programme supplied refugees with rations. CARE International created infrastructures for their other needs, such as clean water and latrines. But elders believed that the greatest hope for their children and their grandchildren lay in education. So they pushed hard for schools, which UNHCR, CARE and other donors built for them. Eventually, the schools began teaching the Kenyan curriculum in upper primary and the four secondary forms. Students learned English, a language that could help them if they resettled in North America or Australia, and received a Kenya Certificate of Secondary Education if they passed the national examinations at the end of Form 4. The certificate could lead to a higher education whenever they got out of the camps and wherever they went.

Windle Trust Kenya is a non-profit organization that promotes education for refugees from its airy headquarters of small, white buildings with red-tile roofs in a leafy neighbourhood of Nairobi. The trust's executive director is Marangu Njogu. Before he became the head of Windle Trust, Njogu worked in Dadaab for CARE, first in the development of schools and later as the manager of all CARE's programs. He confirmed that parents in Dadaab see education as a way for their children to escape from poverty: "It is the only thing they will take from the camps. They will not take property from their parents. At fifty, parents see that their functional life is over. They see young people with education as the future for their country or for lives elsewhere."

Hanging on a wall in Njogu's office is a photo of "Father Hugh," Hugh Pilkington, the founder of Windle Trust—a tall, skinny, white Kenyan who studied at Cambridge University, a man who lived a privileged life and taught religious studies at the University of Nairobi back in the 1970s, when refugees were permitted to move freely in the city. When Pilkington hired two Ethiopian refugees to teach him the language of the Ethiopian Orthodox Church, he was shocked to discover how underprivileged their lives were. They had been university students in Ethiopia, and had been forced to give up their studies and resettle in the slums of Nairobi rather than stay in their country and suffer further consequences of the repressive regime. Pilkington, appalled at what he saw as a waste of humanity and brains, devoted the rest of his life, and much of his wealth, to finding education opportunities for refugees. After Pilkington's death in 1986, his work continued with Windle Trust International. The Kenyan branch received an annual grant, but the money was never enough for all the work it hoped to do, so it began to advertise and to fund-raise, which the publicity-shy Pilkington would never have condoned.

Pilkington would, however, have approved of the organization's goal of finding university scholarships for Dadaab students. After secondary school, education comes to a full stop in the camps. There are no colleges, no rooms filled with computers where students can take long-distance courses. There is only the hope that one of the hundreds of incentive jobs will open up. Too many students graduate with nothing ahead of them but time on their hands. During my first visit to Dadaab in 2007, as part of a CBC Television crew, I met a young man named Dini who lived in Ifo. Dini spoke four languages and understood computers but could not find a job in the camp. He said he didn't know what to do with his time: "You just lay on your mat and think over and over you don't have nothing to do. You are a refugee." It's easy to spot the young men without jobs hanging aimlessly around the markets. Some of the young turn to qat, or *miraa,* as it is called in Kenya—a plant chewed as a stimulant. A few youths simply disappear, either illegally walking away from the camp in an unofficial attempt at resettlement or slipping over the border to Somalia. Either route is dangerous and detrimental to the reputation of those left behind, reinforcing in the minds of the police that the refugee population is not to be trusted. Those who struggle to stay sane in the camps gather for tea and conversation. There is a meeting spot in Hagadera camp known as Stress Corner, where young men talk about sports, resettlement and scholarships.

Apart from resettlement, a scholarship is the one sure, safe passage out of the camps. Most young people in Dadaab know the pauper-to-prince story of Abass Hassan Mohamed, who was plucked from Dadaab in 2005 and taken to Princeton after a visiting professor who learned of his high grades arranged for him to take the SAT, the standardized application test required for admission to American universities. While some harbour dreams that such an unlikely event could happen to them, others aim for a far more realistic objective: one of the annual scholarships offered in the camps. Windle Trust, relying on American, British and German donors, offers scholarships to students in both Dadaab and Kakuma for study at universities and colleges in Kenya. It also manages scholarships to British universities for Windle Trust International and serves as a partner to World University Service of Canada (WUSC), which offers a select few scholarships to Canadian universities. In 2008, Windle Trust helped prepare forty students from Kakuma and Dadaab for universities in Canada.

The few dozen hard-won scholarships have never been enough to go around. The students who win them are "a needle in the sea," as one student put it. For the past few years, over two hundred qualified students have graduated each year from secondary schools in Dadaab but have not won scholarships. They sat for the difficult Kenyan national examinations in a minimum of seven subjects based on the material from all four years of their secondary school. They passed those examinations with high enough grades for acceptance at universities. They have nowhere to go.

Other students fall by the wayside long before the end of secondary school. According to Njogu, 2,200 students finished primary school in Dadaab in 2007, but there was only space for fewer than a quarter of the graduates in secondary schools. That's because there were five primary schools in each camp but only one secondary school. In total, the three secondary schools of Dadaab could take only 480 students. Once again, the community elders pressured for more; CARE and UNHCR came up with space for an additional 120 students. That still left 1,600 students locked out of secondary education. In March 2008, the refugee community of Dadaab decided that that just wasn't good enough and took matters into its own hands. It asked CARE and UNHCR for classroom spaces in primary schools in the different camps, and raised enough money to hire secondary school graduates as teachers for almost 500 more students. Book Aid International provided some books. Students who had already gone to Canada on scholarships helped out too. By the end of 2008, they had raised $2,000 for books and stationery for the community-school classrooms.

It makes sense that Njogu, a former teacher and education advocate, would applaud any move toward universal education. But there's a practical side as well to his desire to see every child get a chance. As a Kenyan, Njogu knows how suspicious his countrymen are of the Somali refugees, knows that Dadaab is often seen as a passageway for small arms from Somalia to the streets of Kenyan cities. When al-Qaeda carried out two successful attacks in Kenya, the attacks fuelled the belief that the group had links to Islamist factions in Somalia and was carrying out training there. In 1998, Nairobi shook with the bombing of the U.S. embassy in an attack planned by al-Qaeda; most of the 213 people who died in that attack were Kenyan citizens. Then, in 2002, al-Qaeda blew up an Israeli-owned hotel in the coastal city of Mombasa, killing 13, and fired two surface-to-air missiles on an Israeli charter jet but missed. As the nearby lawlessness of Somalia deepened, so did Kenyan fears that terrorists could make their way into the Dadaab camps to hide out or recruit young men to return to Somalia and join groups with intent to harm Kenya. Some of the students told me they had heard of young people going back to Somalia, perhaps to find jobs or family, because they had nothing to do in the camps. It is possible, one student admitted, that "when you are idle and you have all this stress, it makes you do a lot of things."

Education is a real way of protecting his country, Njogu believes: "Not educating those young people who are completing secondary school in the camps is a big security threat. These are young people who are energetic. These are young people who want to have education. Now, if they continue staying in the camp, particularly in Dadaab, which is near Somalia, then these young people can be enticed by these other groups to go for training in the camps in Somalia, and therefore they will become not only a threat to our country, but also a threat to the international community. The world should take this seriously. Take these young people, take them to the universities out there not only in Kenya, but to universities outside, so that young people can be transformed and get education that will help them start thinking positively."

By 2006, the Kenyan government had begun to take the issue of refugees in hand again. It passed a refugee act designed to regulate and manage all refugee affairs. By the time the students left in the summer of 2008, the act hadn't translated into much other than an office in the town of Dadaab near the police station where one government employee, Omar Dhadho, was stationed as refugee camp officer. Kenya's Department of Refugee Affairs seemed content to let UNHCR handle the protection of the refugees once they were in the camp. The government just wanted to figure out a way to control who got into the camp. "The only area we need to address immediately is the area of registration: the registration and reception of refugees," Dhadho said from behind the wooden desk that took up most of his office. "That's very important because the government is supposed to be the one to receive anyone cross-ing the international border and coming into Kenya to seek asylum," he insisted. "So UNHCR is doing the reception at the moment, which is not the right centre. It's not their assignment, so we will have to take over refugee status determination. There's a lot of sus-picion that most of the people who are seeking asylum may be just people who have other interests, so it is crucial for us to cross-check from the beginning."

At the UNHCR compound in the town of Dadaab, sub-office head Anne Campbell said the agency was trying to adjust that summer to working with the government presence. She knew that with UNHCR's large budget and the number of refugees under its care, the organization was not leaving any time soon: "UNHCR is still not in a place where we are ready to exit. There's not an exit strategy. So what we are doing for the time being is working as partners, and as the years go on UNHCR will begin to hand over different functions to the government and then our agency will phase out, but it will be done gradually and it also will depend on the number of refugees here because our agency has such a huge protection role that we have to play vis-à-vis refugees. And at the moment the situation isn't look-ing like anywhere near exit."

Amid the crisis of the growing population in the camps and the dealings with the Kenyan government, Campbell tried to keep her vision for the camps alive. By the summer of 2008, she had worked with UNHCR for fifteen years and had been in Dadaab for less than one. She had come hoping to replicate a model from her experience with Cambodian refugees who were given training that helped them rebuild their country: "I would like this to be a place where we have a huge injection of talented people that are going to be able to return to their home countries, or even overseas, better able to manage. I would like to see that we would invest a good amount of money in primary education with a lot of girls on board, secondary education as much as we can. I'd like to see that we can do a lot of informal education so that those people could do distance learning programs.

I would like to look out for our camps as much as we can so the people have a decent standard of living, something dignified and decent for the period of time they stay here, so that children growing up in this environment have a sort of positive memory of what it was like, even though it is a refugee camp."

Campbell spoke rapidly as she described her vision. She sat on the edge of the sofa in her office staring not at those listening to her, but past heads, as if she could visualize different camps from the ones that surrounded her. Dressed in a sparkling white T-shirt and pressed blue shirt over white jeans secured with a gold-coloured leather belt, she seemed ready to defy the dust that was bound to settle on her clothing once she stepped outside. She knew that the priority of finding more homes for new arrivals took precedence over her vision, and she was under no illusion that peace was imminent in Somalia. She also knew the biggest threat to her plans for the camp was the indifference of the world to a situation that had gone on so long: "There's a huge donor fatigue. That's why I allow a lot of missions here. I want the people to see that there are human beings here, loads of children and youth. When we had the assistant secretary of state here, these young women were fighting each other because they wanted to tell him how they needed education."

The schools the students attended in the Dadaab camps were long, tin buildings with iron sheet roofing. Each building is divided into classrooms lined with rows of wooden desks and benches. On particularly hot days, when the temperature stretches past 40 degrees Celsius, the heat inside the classrooms becomes unbearable. "Almost every season is hot," Abdirizak says, "but in March, the hottest, you feel like your head is boiling." Muno recalls that on the worst days her teacher would take the class to the laboratory, in a separate, larger brick building where it was cooler. There was a blackboard there that he used to finish his lessons.

Beyond those visits, the teacher took Muno's class to the laboratory three times a year to use its equipment for science experiments that never quite turned out the way they did in the textbooks. Muno says the equipment in the lab was a hodgepodge of spoons, test tubes, bits of mercury and jars of crystals. Since there was a Bunsen burner but no fuel for it, the teacher used hot water from the tap to heat substances—with less than satisfactory results. "We would put whatever crystals we had in the test tubes," Muno recalls. And since they used tap water instead of distilled water, "sometimes you would see green in the test tubes when you were supposed to see yellow." Abdirizak says the laboratory in his school in Ifo was well equipped with fuel and other supplies, but it was still a laboratory in a refugee camp and couldn't compare to laboratories in the West. Although his laboratory had equipment, the seats were much higher than the desks, "so it was like you were bending or you'd be forced to stand the whole day."

The majority of the teachers in the schools had no formal training. There were a few Kenyan professional teachers and some of the "incentive" teachers had received extra courses, but for the most part teachers came directly from the graduating classes of the secondary school and stayed in the job until they got resettlement, which often never came. Some graduates had been teaching in the school for more than a dozen years.

School was not a nine-to-three affair for students determined to graduate. Each day, they walked twice back and forth between their homes and their school. Sometimes, in the dark, they would cross the camps to borrow textbooks from other students so they could finish their assignments. To achieve top marks in finals, they studied long into the night, in study groups or alone in their houses. Since darkness arrived consistently at six-thirty in the evening, they studied by kerosene lamps, which emitted hydrocarbons, damaging their eyes and irritating their lungs. Each morning they rose early enough to put on the clean uniforms required by the schools: the boys wore clean white or blue shirts, depending on their level; the girls wore hijabs in pink or blue, depending on the camp.

While parents pushed their sons to get educated, they were

reluctant to see their daughters go to school. Some parents saw education as a waste for girls, who would likely marry, possibly when they were as young as fifteen. Most saw girls as essential to running their households. In Somali culture, boys do little domestic work while girls are expected to do the bulk of it. And the chores were endless: before school there was the family breakfast to prepare, and after school, supper, cleaning and laundry. Halima, one of the luckier girls, whose parents encouraged her, described the life of most schoolgirls this way: "You've been doing all this stuff at home. Then you come to school. You're tired. And you do all the same things as the guys are doing. I wish our parents would understand this and could know that a boy and a girl can be just equal."

In an effort to persuade parents to send their daughters to school, CARE distributes free uniforms to girls enrolled in primary schools. Halima said support like that from the agencies has made a difference. More important, she said, is the understanding seeping into the camp that young women who have gone to the West have done well

A shy Halima (far right) turns her head away from a photographer in her first year at Ifo Secondary School.

at universities and have often been more diligent at sending money to their families back in the camp than the young men.

When Halima was in Class 4 of primary school in 1998, there were twelve girls in her class of fifty-four pupils, but by Form 4, the last year of secondary school, there were only three girls in a class of sixty-four. "You can imagine three girls studying with all those boys," she said. In the privately run Qu'ran schools in the camp, girls studied separately from boys, but in the secular schools run by CARE, they shared classrooms. Sometimes parents worried about the morality of the arrangement; sometimes they worried that education might transform their daughters from obedient Muslim girls to more Westernized ones whom they might not be able to control. Brothers, some young women from Dadaab told me, could be worse than parents in making sure a girl didn't misbehave or become too ambitious. "Brothers can be bossy and domineering," one woman said. "They tend to get annoyed if they see their sisters doing anything they wouldn't like."

Halima maintains that it's up to each girl to convince her parents of the benefits of an education: "This has something to do with who you are, your personality, because you can really change your parents. You can persuade them to let you go to school, and for a really good parent, very understanding, I don't think any logical parent will do anything to stop [a girl who works hard]."

When Halima left the camps, she planned to study biochemistry at Mount Saint Vincent, but before leaving she already possessed a keen sense of Darwinian principles. She instinctively knew the importance of standing up to those who didn't want to see her finish her schooling. "It is what you call survival of the fittest. For you to survive, you have to have some kind of weapons"—weapons like strong language to spar with boys who tried to demean her. "If you have the feeling to challenge men, to challenge guys and to tell them to get out of your face, it really makes a difference." And it could earn their respect: "If they see you are very competitive, you are really hard working, not all boys are the same and not all boys have the same kind of mentality towards girls. Some will feel really very proud."

While Halima had her father's support, Marwo had her aunt to push her through school. None of Marwo's siblings or cousins did well in their classes, so Marwo's aunt treated her special niece differently, discouraging her from marrying young as most girls did. "You are a very important lady," Marwo remembers her aunt telling her. "This is the only girl who does well in school, and I will support her and sometimes shout at her," her aunt would say.

In an issue of *The Dawn*, an English-language newsletter for youth in the camps funded by CARE Canada, Marwo wrote an editorial supporting girls' education:

> *We have brains that are just as capable as those of boys in learning and succeeding. Let us take a stern decision about early marriage, for it is hampering our way to education and a bright future for girls.*
>
> *Finally, I urge all girls to work hard to improve their academic abilities and adopt the motto: girls, just like boys, deserve education.*

It is not only communal beliefs about how girls should behave that hold them back; it can also be their health. Most of the girls in Dadaab have been circumcised in one of two ways in accordance with Somali culture. One method, called *sunna* circumcision, involves cutting off the hood of the clitoris but leaving the rest of the genitals intact. Another method, the more common and more invasive method, causes a variety of health problems for the girls as they mature into women: in pharaonic circumcision, women—relatives, often—remove the clitoris and some or all of the labia, suturing the vaginal area so that there is a small opening for urine and menstrual blood to leave the body. In this infibulation practice in the camps, thorns are often used for suturing and are removed only once the wound has sealed shut. A caring parent might buy clean razors for each of his or her daughters being circumcised, as well as antibiotics to save the girls from infection. Girls are often preschool age or slightly older when the circumcisions are performed.

Even before they reach adulthood and experience the problems associated with intercourse and childbirth, adolescent girls often suffer such painful menstrual periods that they have to miss school for three or four days every month. Sometimes when they go to class anyway, they faint from the pain.

For those opposed to the practice, female circumcision is known as female genital mutilation, or FGM. The World Health Organization has condemned the practice and reported that in Africa three million girls every year are at risk of mutilation. In Dadaab, CARE developed a program to eradicate FGM in the camp. But it was up against long-standing beliefs that girls must be circumcised to keep them pure and make them fit for marriage. It's unlikely that many still believe the old tales that say the clitoris grows to a woman's knees if left uncut, but the association of a clitoris with an immoral, animalistic female remains strong.

When he was a teenager, Abdi became a crusader in the fight against FGM. He'd attended a lecture by visitors who came to the camp to discuss the practice. Abdi, who had lived by himself for years, was used to making his own decisions and coming to his own conclusions, and he quickly decided that FGM caused suffering to the women around him and should be stopped. In secondary school he took part in a debate arguing against FGM. His job after graduation resonated with his beliefs. He became a program assistant with CARE's Sexual and Gender-Based Violence sector. His job sent him out into the community to talk and to listen. Frequently, he heard from adults that girls needed pharaonic circumcision to stop their sexual sensitivity and to control their sexual urges. Why is it, then, he wondered, that some prostitutes in the camp had been circumcised? Logic and compassion told him the justification was flawed. What disturbed Abdi most were the harmful effects women experienced throughout their lives. One time a woman came to him who suffered constant urinary incontinence after childbirth, a common problem among circumcised women in the camp. "She was a young woman of the age of twenty and it was her first childbirth," he said. "I was very scared when I saw her. I was feeling very sympathetic to her, and I told my workmates to go out and look for such women in the camp. We found ten of them, five of them with serious cases." CARE sent the women to Nairobi or Garissa for treatment.

Most women suffered the pain and indignities associated with FGM without medical help. The young women of Dadaab tell stories of friends whose husbands used knives to prepare them for intercourse on the wedding night, or friends who almost died in childbirth, saved only by a last-minute Caesarean delivery. Still, many of the young women in the camp accepted that FGM was necessary to keep them respectable. "That way they behave," one young woman explained.

But even those who were opposed to FGM did not want to talk openly against it. One young woman told me that although she thought the practice was wrong, there was too much attention paid to it by aid workers and journalists who ignored more pressing issues in the camps. "There are so many problems," she said. "People are sick; some people have no food." She defended the Somali culture, saying that other cultures have problems too yet people don't abandon them. The way she saw it, eventually, when people became enlightened, the custom would change.

Abdi grew most frustrated when he encountered people who said that female circumcision was required by the Islamic religion. He argued, usually in vain, with women and men far older than he was that FGM is a cultural practice, not a religious requirement. He argued that Africans of different faiths practise it and that not all Muslims do. He never claimed to be a Muslim scholar, but he attended the debates of religious scholars at a conference in Garissa. None of the scholars defended pharaonic circumcision, although some did argue that the less severe *sunna* circumcision was among the teachings of Islam.

The campaign against FGM has made slow progress in the camp. Despite the health risks, many parents believe no man would marry their daughter if she were uncircumcised. Abdi said that in his camp,

Ifo, there were about two hundred girls who were not circumcised—less than 2 per cent of the female population—and even those girls were still at risk of having the procedure performed later. One young woman told me dismissively that families who don't circumcise their daughters are just hoping to get resettlement faster. The practice is illegal in Kenya, but Abdi said that whenever he called the police for help in stopping FGM, he was told there was nothing they could do.

In the student paper, *The Dawn,* in April 2008, one male student wrote about a visit of agencies fighting FGM to his camp, Hagadera:

> *At block J1, the* [anti-FGM] *team met violence from a small number of ignorant youth who tried to jeopardize and stop the activities. The activities stopped for about half an hour as the violent youth threw stones and sand at Agency staff and incentive workers because of the effect that the campaign was having. This was seen by the big number of women, uncircumcised girls, female youth and male youth participating in the campaign. Ultimately security personnel were called . . . to make sure the activities were carried out successfully without violence.*

CARE employed one strategy that Abdi could not go along with: it designed a T-shirt to be worn by men that said, "I would marry an uncircumcised girl." The T-shirt created conflict in the community. Abdi felt that it stigmatized girls who were already circumcised but still unmarried, thereby replacing one form of stigmatization with another. One young woman told me she found the T-shirts offensive and wasn't convinced, in any case, that the men who wore them believed in the words. "When the time comes, they will marry a girl who is circumcised," she said with assurance.

For both sexes there were other equally pressing medical concerns in the camp. Measles, cholera, Rift Valley fever and tuberculosis swept through the compounds regularly. Malaria is something every student expects to contract despite the mosquito net and spraying programs designed to prevent it. "It's not a big problem," Siyad says. "You just take the medicine." Chloroquine and quinine had long been used in the camps for children. When Siyad contracted malaria, the health clinic gave him Coartem, which has since become the first line of treatment for uncomplicated cases. Siyad admits that the disease can be hard on the very young, "especially the cerebral kind, because it goes to the brain and kills you." When I asked Muno if she'd ever contracted malaria, she answered in a polite but almost dismissive tone, "Yah, why not?"

German Technical Cooperation, GTZ, ran the health care facilities during the years the students were in the camps, but it was never able to match the needs of the sick. UNHCR reported that in 2008, on average, there was one health facility for every 17,000 people. Refugees avoid hospitals when they can, turning to midwives in the camp to deliver babies and using remedies such as camel milk to control diabetes, which is a common disease in Dadaab. Muno said that the hospitals were often out of medicine and that sick people were told to buy their own in the market. Refugees can purchase many of their medical supplies at the markets, but often the prices are too high or involve a difficult trade-off in their lives. Girls can buy sanitary pads at the market, for instance, but a box of ten pads costs the same amount as a family spends on food for the whole day. So girls and women often resort to using rags instead, sometimes getting ill when the cloths aren't clean.

Muno becomes angriest about the health care system in the camp when she talks about the time her infant stepbrother, her only brother, was sick. From the time he was three months old, the infant was in and out of the hospital. The family had no idea what was wrong with him. Although he screamed in pain, painkillers weren't prescribed to him. One day, Muno saw a health worker give her brother an injection and she asked what it was for. No one would tell her, and she wasn't allowed to read the chart. Finally, a Kenyan doctor told her that the infant could not digest food and there was nothing to be done. Muno's stepmother took her son home so he could die with his family. The next day, the family received word that the infant would be sent for further care in Garissa. As Muno walked back to the hospital, her brother died in her arms. "It was not his death that's painful," she says. The greater pain comes from the memory of carrying that weak infant making horrible noises in her arms and being helpless to do anything for him.

After hearing all the stories of the restrictions and the pain experienced in Dadaab, it is hard to believe that anyone could ever miss living there. But the students, checking in for their first flight, knew they would. The missing was already there under the layers of clothes for Canada, under the layer of excitement of the freedom to come. They would miss their parents and siblings, of course, but they would also miss the jokes and the stories told in between the compounds, gossip about neighbours, older women talking about husbands, old men reciting Somali tales. They would miss wedding celebrations where any groom worth his salt would supply the meat of one camel, if not two, and they would miss watching soccer matches with friends in the hotels. They would miss walking down the laneways in the camps knowing everyone they passed and knowing they were known.

Only one of the eleven students leaving that night for London did not share the same history or the same regrets as the others. After four years as a refugee, Dilalesa felt no nostalgia for Dadaab. To him it was a prison that still held his friends. Almost five hundred Oromos remained in the camp when he left.

Dilalesa was flying out of Nairobi, however, with gratitude for the protection he'd received in Kenya and with gratitude for one UNHCR officer in particular. When he and his teaching colleagues made that decision to walk across the border from Moyale, Ethiopia, to Moyale, Kenya, in the spring of 2004, they turned themselves in to local police for protection from the Ethiopian government, which was cracking down on both students who had protested against the mistreatment of Oromos and the teachers it accused of inciting those demonstrations. Six hundred Oromo students had also crossed the border that spring along with the ten teachers. The

Kenyan authorities had set the students up in a temporary camp of tents, but the teachers remained in police custody. Days later, Ethiopian authorities demanded to take the teachers back to Ethiopia. Article 33 (1) of the Convention and Protocol Relating to the Status of Refugees states: "No Contracting State shall expel or return ('refouler') a refugee in any manner whatsoever to the frontiers of territories where his life or freedom would be threatened on account of his race, religion, nationality, membership of a particular social group or political opinion."

Dilalesa feels certain that it wasn't a clause that saved him and his fellow teachers from being sent back, but the presence in Moyale of Rossella Pagliuchi-Lor, then assistant representative for protection with UNHCR in Nairobi. She had come to the remote border town with a team to process the Oromos in the temporary camp. Pagliuchi-Lor will say only that she is aware that Ethiopian authorities requested the teachers be returned and that the presence of her team made a difference to their future. But Dilalesa remembers how on May 15, 2004, she took the teachers from their cell to a truck that drove them to Dadaab under escort. He is convinced that on that day she saved his life.

The students moving through the airport with Dilalesa called him Dereje, not knowing how much he hated that name. It was a name he had used since primary school, one he never carried comfortably. He started school in 1987 during the dark days of the Mengistu regime, a time of slaughter and fear in Ethiopia, a time when ethnic Oromos felt marginalized. On the first day of school, his teacher had teased him about his given name: Dilalesa, the name of his grandfather, a hero among the local Oromo people. Stunned by the teacher's derision and the laughter of the other pupils, he ran home and told his parents he would never go to school again. To get him to go back, his parents gave him a more acceptable name in Amharic, the language of those who controlled Ethiopia: Dereje. He became Dereje Guta Dilalesa. He had attempted to change his name back to his original name when he grew up but couldn't figure his way around the legal system in Ethiopia. And then, as a refugee, he was worried that any confusion over his identity might affect his status or interfere with his application for the scholarship. In Canada, he hoped he might find a place where he could become his old self, a place where he would not have to choose between his name and an education.

Just before midnight the students moved from a waiting room on the second floor of Jomo Kenyatta Airport to the inside of the plane. Through an airport window, Aden could see the British Airways aircraft on the tarmac and was surprised to find himself walking through a hallway directly into the interior. Inside, there was no dividing line between men and women. Halima, Muno and Marwo stuck together as they moved down the aisle to their separate, assigned seats. When he got on board, Hussein thought he had merely stepped into yet another waiting room until he heard a voice advising him to fasten his seat belt. On takeoff, Aden felt the shudder and the sensation of his body pulled backwards. He was frightened until the airplane levelled off and the flight became smooth. He admired the way the pilot controlled the aircraft in the sky and decided he liked flying. Being a pilot would be a fine career choice after all. Once in the air, Abdi knew he was finally leaving the refugee life behind. On the map on the screen in front of him, Hussein watched as the tiny drawing of an airplane moved away from a dot marked *Nairobi* and left the continent of Africa—left its turmoil, its warmth and its beloved people behind.

PART TWO

Welcome to Canada

CHAPTER THREE

A Citizen of No Country

TWENTY-THREE HOURS LATER and more than twelve thousand kilometres away, a crowd was forming in the sparkling clean international arrivals area of Terminal 3 at Toronto's Pearson International Airport. On the electronic board that spanned high above the doors where arriving passengers exited, yellow letters spelled out the expected arrival times and the status of incoming flights from Port of Spain, Amsterdam, Newcastle, Seoul, Moscow and Paris. At 14:53 on August 20, the board announced that British Airways Flight 093 had arrived. The Dadaab eleven had landed on Canadian soil, no longer refugees but residents of a country they'd never seen.

A few of the students gathered in the circular hall pointed at the sign and cheered. The more seasoned among them, those who knew the ins and outs of the paperwork for Customs and Immigration and the delays it involved, nodded and continued to talk at a volume that the wide-open spaces and excitement seemed to invite. Some began waving Canadian flags. Others held up bristol board signs that read, "Welcome Muno," "Welcome Mohamed," "Welcome to the 2008 WUSC Students."

Across Canada, other students were still drawing their welcome signs, decorating dormitory rooms, setting late-night snacks of cook-ies, fruit and juice on bedside tables and planning tours for the new arrivals. They were all members of World University Service of Canada's Student Refugee Program. Through student levies, fund-raisers, faculty and staff contributions and the willingness of univer-sity administrators to forgo fees, committees at universities across Canada had raised enough money to bring refugee students to their campuses and pay for everything the students would need for at least their first year. In Brandon, Manitoba, Brandy Robertson was part of the team getting ready to welcome Aden, just as she had welcomed students in previous years. "I think it's very bittersweet when they come here," she said. "That's just the kind of sense I get from them. We take them up to their residence room and we usually have it decorated, like it says 'Welcome Aden,' a bunch of Canadian stuff and a bunch of Brandon stuff, and they're always so happy when they see that and are overwhelmed to be here. But there's always a sense of sadness you can see."

World University Service of Canada grew out of a European group started after the First World War to supply students with their basic needs. Canadian students joined the movement to help another generation of students in the Second World War. In 1948, WUSC began international seminars to expose Canadian students to devel-opments beyond Canada's borders. And then, in 1978, it created the Student Refugee Program, the program that brought the Dadaab eleven to Canada.

The idea and the opportunity to bring students to Canada emerged in the period when Canadians witnessed and were moved by the plight of Indochinese refugees fleeing Vietnam, Cambodia and Laos, the so-called "boat people." The Private Sponsorship of Refugees Program that came to the fore in that period, and that still thrives today, allows church groups, civic groups and individuals to bring refugees to Canada if they promise to support them financially for a year and help them settle in to their new country. For its part, Citizenship and Immigration Canada (CIC) checks out the refugee status of those selected and puts them through security clearances and medical checkups in their asylum countries before granting them permission to come to Canada. Sponsored refugees enter Canada with no need to apply for refugee status when they arrive, with no need to attend hearings or wait for a determination. They arrive as permanent residents who can apply to become Canadian citizens in three years. While the International Organization for Migration arranges the travel for the refugees chosen for resettlement, it is CIC that lends them the money to cover those expenses. A family of refugees might receive a loan of up to $10,000, which must be paid back during those first crucial years of getting established in Canada.

CIC's director of refugee resettlement, Debra Pressé, says the WUSC students have many advantages over most sponsored refugees. First, they come with a minimum of a high school education and a facility in English, which help them integrate more easily. Second, they receive additional financial aid to cover the travel loan and a year of university education— "and they're arriving with no dependants. They're young. They're bright." Their status as permanent residents also means that after their sponsorship ends, they can apply for student loans to finish their degrees, like any other domestic student.

The eleven arriving from Dadaab were the luckiest among the lucky. Fewer than 1 per cent of the world's refugees were sponsored through private organization or government resettlement programs in 2008. About 20 countries have resettlement agreements with UNHCR. Out of those 20 countries, 9, including Canada, take the bulk of resettled refugees. Canada accepted 10,807 refugees that year, just shy of the 11,000 Australia accepted. Only the United States has consistently taken more refugees for resettlement. In 2008, the U.S. took about 60,000 refugees. James Milner, who has advised WUSC through the years, said the organization doesn't do enough promotion of its role in resettlement. In a presentation on global refugees, Milner demonstrated that if WUSC had been ranked as a country accepting refugees in 2006, it would have come in in fifth place, after the United States, Australia, Canada and Sweden, with the more than 50 refugees it sponsored that year, ahead of Spain with 45 and Brazil with 30.

In 2008, the Canadian government, relying on UNHCR referrals, directly resettled or brought to Canada 7,295 people. Private sponsors brought in 3,512 more, about half through groups of 5 permanent residents of Canada seeking to bring particular individuals, and half through one of the 84 organizations that have sponsorship agreements with the federal government. WUSC brought 55 students to Canada that year.

It takes eighteen months from the time the WUSC-sponsored students are selected in their camps to the time they land on Canadian soil. The process, which normally spans several years, is quicker for them than for most sponsored refugees partly because WUSC has partners on the ground, such as Windle Trust in Kenya, to get paperwork in order. It's also because WUSC has had such a long history with CIC that the department understands the need to get the students to Canada for the start of the university term.

At Pearson Airport that August day, there was the buzz of a homecoming among the crowd of students and faculty who'd come to take students back to universities in southern Ontario. Some of the students standing with signs of welcome had arrived on flights just a year or two earlier. Other students and university staff members had met at annual WUSC assemblies in Ottawa. They shook hands, slapped each other on the back and hugged. Everyone in the crowd sought out one woman: Asnaketch Mekonnen, known simply as Asni. As senior program officer for WUSC's Student Refugee Program, Asni spends much of her year at the Ottawa headquarters assisting local committees, matching sponsored students to universities and evaluating how students from the previous years are doing. But the key part of her job is deciding who will come in the first place.

For the past six years Asni had visited camps in Kenya, Malawi and Thailand to sit on panels that selected students based not just on their essays and their grades—a minimum B+ average for young men and, as encouragement for girls to stay in school, a minimum C+ average for young women—but also on something she calls "not very scientific," an instinct that a young individual would have the tenacity to survive alone in a strange, new environment. She knows she always leaves behind capable students, but, in her pragmatic way, she keeps herself going with the knowledge that each year WUSC gives a handful of students the opportunity of a lifetime. "The difficult part," she says, "is hearing people's stories. I don't know why young people have to go through all the atrocities. It's beyond understanding."

In orientation sessions in the camps Asni tries to prepare the chosen students as best she can for the shock of entering a foreign nation, knowing what pitfalls they face. Often she feels like a parent unable to get through to an adolescent child: "I told them, 'You guys, the boys, learn to cook. It's going to be very difficult.' And they started giggling and I said, okay, and I said, 'Make sure you have all your music. You are going to miss it.' And they started to laugh." In her soft voice, she tells the scholarship students they will have to adapt to a faster pace than they are used to; they will have to learn to ask for help; they will have to let go of their past and go forward; they will have to invest in themselves before they can help their families back in the camp. "I said, 'When you come to a new country, it brings new difficulties. It's not 'the grass is greener,' as we always think when we are overseas.'" Perhaps they listen to her more closely because she emigrated from Ethiopia to Canada twenty years before, but it's unlikely. Asni knows that most of the information she gives the students won't make any sense to them until they go through the experience of relocation themselves. Nonetheless, she accepts that they will somehow cope with an easy confidence. "They're young," she says.

Arrival day is Asni's biggest day of the year. Until she sees the students on the ground with her own eyes or learns from her colleagues in other cities that they have landed safely, she shares the same kind of anxiety that Abdi felt before leaving—that gnawing worry that something could go wrong. "When I see them here, I say, okay, this is good. Now we have given them the opportunity. It's up to them how they use it." Of the fifty-five students coming to Canada in late August 2008, thirteen were young women. One of the students would be the one thousandth student WUSC had brought to Canada in the last thirty years.

For four of the Dadaab students, Toronto would be their final destination. The seven others would be escorted to Terminal 1 to wait for Air Canada flights to cities across the country. After almost an hour's wait in the arrivals hall, expectations built. Two young women from the University of Toronto's Mississauga campus, Zaynab Ahdab and Saaliha Malik, said they couldn't wait to meet Muno. They had decorated the walls of her residence room with posters, covered her bed with a pink and green comforter, found her dishes and pots and pans, and set up her desk with stationery and some paperbacks because they knew she loved to read. Saaliha had bought Muno a book called *Betty's Book of Laundry Secrets* to help her in the laundry room. Zaynab, a Muslim of Lebanese background, had picked out a prayer mat for Muno's arrival at her new home. They were most excited about the cake they had waiting for her, chocolate with chocolate icing to celebrate her twentieth birthday, decorated with "Welcome Muno" in green icing. The two Somalis standing with the young women—Abdinoor, who had come from Dadaab as the previous year's student, and Ibrahim, who'd gone to Innis College downtown the same year—nodded, never letting on that birth dates are often arbitrarily chosen among the Somali refugees for the forms they have to fill out, or that Somalis do not celebrate birthdays in their culture. Muno's family had, in fact, lost all their records in the war. Her father knew the year Muno was born but not the date. Muno herself had chosen August 20 out of the air because she didn't want to be like so many others who simply wrote down January 1 because it was the first day of the year in which they were born.

Eager students pushed their way to the front of the hall with their welcome signs. Some jumped on railings to hold flags and signs high enough to catch the eye of arriving passengers. The WUSC committee members were outnumbered by other people waiting for passengers, but in terms of sheer energy, they took over the place.

In the end, the four students emerged in rapid fire, catching their sponsors off guard. First spotted was Mohamed, who came down the ramp wearing a green windbreaker over a white shirt buttoned to the neck and dragging a blue suitcase wrapped with IOM tape. He seemed to be about as exhausted as anyone could appear and still be standing. He stood, rocking slightly with a tight, fixed smile, while old friends from Dadaab and members of the committee from the University of Toronto's Scarborough campus surrounded him. His eyes were glazed, his glances around the too-bright hall unfocused. He had forced himself to stay awake on the flight from Nairobi to London and again on the flight from London to Toronto. He had been afraid to fall asleep in case the plane crashed, even though he knew his alertness would make no difference. His friend from primary school, Ibrahim, wearing a short-sleeved summer shirt and the relaxed look of someone who knew how to eat and sleep and get

Ibrahim (right) greets Mohamed (left), his
old school friend from Dagahaley, at Pearson Airport.

around in this strange place, hugged him warmly. The welcome from someone he knew, from someone back home, seemed to do little to raise Mohamed's energy level, but it did bring a first, real smile.

In the chaos, Abdirizak somehow connected with his group from the University of Toronto's University College. And faculty adviser Mark Franke and student Angela Salamanca found Abdi for the two-hour drive to Huron University College in London, Ontario. Both Abdirizak and Abdi looked remarkably alert compared to Mohamed. Abdirizak had the same calm, inscrutable expression he'd had in the camp, and Abdi's voice rang high in excitement as he greeted Ibrahim and others who had come in the years before him.

Saaliha and Zaynab missed Muno's appearance altogether. They found her in the middle of the hall, dressed in a soft, black hijab, encircled by old friends from Dadaab. When they reached her, they hugged her and handed her a small Canadian flag. "You are going to love your room," one of them said. "We have put so much stuff in it." Muno smiled and said quietly, "Too much."

Saaliha Malik (left) and Zaynab Ahdab (right) from the Mississauga campus of the University of Toronto welcome their sponsored student, Muno (middle), August 20, 2008.

On the way to the parking garage, Muno asked the others if it was warm outside. They told her it was, and when she got in the car she said she was hot. "No wonder," Saaliha said. "You've got a leather jacket under there." Under her hijab she wore not just a leather jacket, but jeans, a T-shirt, a shirt and a scarf—armour against the cold she was told she'd find in Canada. As they drove on the fast highways to the Mississauga campus, Muno was so hot, so tired, she thought she would be sick, but there was nothing in her stomach to bring up. She had eaten little of the odd-looking food on the plane or the strange chips the young women had sent Abdi to buy in Heathrow Airport. Expecting potato chips, they bit into the corn chips and spat them out. How could anyone not know that corn was for cooking and potatoes were for chips?

On his drive to London, Abdi, knowing he had made it to Canada at last, relaxed enough to start absorbing the new world around him. He stared out the window at the green countryside of the farmland west of Toronto, at the big cars and the complicated highways, trying to make sense of it all: "You see highways passing down under other ones. And the way the traffic works here is different. In Nairobi there are traffic police. Here it is like it is being managed automatically."

Upstairs at Pearson's Terminal 1 the students bound for other cities waited at one end of the terminal in the seating areas near the gates for their flights. A soft, early evening light streamed in through high windows on three sides of the terminal. Dilalesa and Abdikadar had been escorted to the waiting area for their flight to Saskatoon; Hussein to the area for the flight to Edmonton. Near the gate for Vancouver, Siyad sat alone with his IOM bag in his lap, looking years older than he had days before and confused by the brightness of the sky. He wondered what time it was, certain it should be nighttime and dark by now. Even though all he could see of Canada were walls of clean glass and the well-stocked restaurants of the terminal, he found it very beautiful. Marwo sat with several Sudanese students in another area. One of them, Mary, would be going to the University of Victoria with her. Marwo had lost the sparkle she'd had in the camp. Her ears were plugged and she couldn't hear what the other young women were saying. Her body was aching and her head was pounding after the long journey, and she appeared despondent. She was missing her aunt terribly. Aden, dressed in a grey suit with a tie loosened around the collar, joined her. He still had a flight to Winnipeg ahead of him and a night in a hotel there before the drive to Brandon the next day. But he was ready for it all, ready to see more.

Just before seven, Halima boarded Air Canada Flight 620 to Halifax. With two Sudanese students headed to other universities in Nova Scotia, she walked down the aisle, and without hesitation connected the number on the boarding pass with the number above the row. She wore a white and black patterned headscarf over long, flowing clothing and the requisite warm leather jacket for Canada. After takeoff, she used her flexibility and a black cloth to turn herself into a covered ball on her seat, sleeping that way for most of the trip to Halifax.

When the plane landed, she walked straight down the corridor, hesitating a moment before following the sign with a picture of a suitcase. She hesitated again at the top of the escalator but then stepped on, looking down to make sure her feet were safely on the tread. Escalators were nothing new to her by then—the students had used one at the Nairobi airport and several more at Heathrow. As she descended, cheers rose from a group below holding welcome signs, and her tense face broke into a wide smile of relief. As if she had rehearsed the moment, she rushed to the group and stiffly hugged each person in turn.

It was the first time a group from Mount Saint Vincent University had greeted a WUSC student, at least as far back as anyone could remember. Paula Barry, a staff member with the long title of International and Exchange Student Advisor, stood behind a row of students. It was her job to help international students adjust to a Canadian university. She had volunteered to lead the WUSC committee on campus. An attractive woman with long black hair and bangs, her style was professional with a side of funk, a style that translated into a casual but firm manner with the international students she advised. It was a style that said she was young enough to relate to the students from China, Europe and the Caribbean but old enough to steer them toward the best choices. She was nervous that night, though, not certain she could meet the needs of a young woman from such a harsh setting who was leaving her parents behind indefinitely. She had dealt with homesick students before—she just didn't know how much greater Halima's homesickness would be and how she would help the young woman through it.

Mount Saint Vincent is a small university of about five thousand full- and part-time students, with a history of education for women and an emphasis on attracting international students. About 10 per cent of the student body is from other countries. Eighty per cent of the students in undergraduate programs at Mount Saint Vincent are women, almost 20 percentage points higher than the national average. It was no accident that the committee from the "Mount" had picked the only female as their scholarship student from the list of four names Asni had offered them.

All the students who had accompanied Paula to the airport were female. Three of the students with her were in Canada on student visas from Malaysia, China and St. Lucia. The government of St. Lucia had sponsored Loyan St. Omer to study hospitality. In exchange, it expected her to return to the island and work for five years in the tourism industry there. During the school year, she would be the resident assistant in the building where Halima would be housed.

Only one local Halifax student had come that evening for Halima's arrival, twenty-two-year-old Sarah Chan. "I've always felt that just waiting for the person to come off the plane," she said, "whether they're a close friend, a parent—it's never really comfortable and I think a lot of us were kind of worried for her. We just tried to imagine—we couldn't—putting ourselves in her place. So we were not just thinking of our excitement, we were trying to jump to the other side and think how it might be for her."

Sarah had bought a piece of cardboard and, with help from the Google online search engine, decorated it with Halima's name—in English and Arabic—and the flags of Somalia, Kenya and Canada. She was working full-time that summer and knew she wouldn't be able to help with the orientation but was thankful she'd taken the time to make the sign because it gave her an instant connection with Halima.

Sarah is a small woman who was dressed that night in blue jeans and a red T-shirt with a logo for Beerlao, a line of beers brewed in Laos. When Halima saw a young woman shorter than her, she expressed surprise at finding someone younger there. Accustomed to having people assume she was young because of her short stature, Sarah told Halima that she was a year or so older than her. "How do you know that?" Halima demanded. Sarah explained she'd remembered Halima's birthday from the information they'd received. "That was neat," Sarah commented later, looking back at that exchange as a glimpse of the young woman she would get to know well in the months to follow. "She's incredibly sweet and she's spicy, too. She can snap back and say something and tell you exactly how it is."

Halima poses for pictures at Halifax International Airport, August 20, 2008, with strangers who will become friends. Paula Barry stands on the left and Sarah Chan on the right.

Sarah had become involved with WUSC in 2005 when a few students and Paula Barry got together to talk about how they could sponsor a refugee student at Mount Saint Vincent. "I do remember thinking, I wonder if one day I will meet this person, because we were just at the beginning and we knew that goal couldn't be achieved that year or the next." Sarah spent two years away from Halifax travelling and studying on an exchange program. By the time she got back, she learned, the university had organized a referendum and the student body had voted 93 per cent in favour of a levy to sponsor one student a year for one year. For each course the Mount's students enrolled in, they paid 90 cents, up to a maximum of $4.50, to support a sponsored student.

Sarah had learned that the committee had picked a young woman from Dadaab to be their first student. In her last year at the university, Sarah would meet the young woman who had been only a concept at that first meeting. She thinks the vast majority of students supported the WUSC levy because the program brings a real person to their university: "The idea that one student can come, the idea of an individual, appeals to everyone."

Before the group moved to collect Halima's luggage, a Somali woman stepped forward to speak to Halima. Farhiyo Barkedle had travelled from Kakuma one year earlier on a WUSC scholarship. Tonight, she had come to the airport with a group from her university—Acadia University in Wolfville, less than two hours' drive from Halifax—to greet one of the newly arrived Sudanese students. "At least you are going to a city," Farhiyo said. "I am in a small town." Halima had little time to consider her words or talk to a male Somali student from Acadia before the two left with a promise to connect her to Somalis in Halifax.

Paula led the group to a van she had rented to transport the international students who would all be arriving in the next few days. The airport parking lot offered a poor first impression of Halifax. With construction going on all around, it was an odd maze of concrete barriers and wire fencing. Halima sat in the front seat of the van beside Paula, and the other young women took the two rows behind her. As Paula negotiated her way out of the lot, the others tried to talk to Halima in the front seat. But when the van picked up speed and communication from the back to the front seat became difficult, they began to talk among themselves. Halima sat, still and quiet, in the front seat, staring straight ahead, turning neither to look out the window nor to speak with the other students. Once the van got onto the highway, she saw only the white lines on the asphalt ahead of her and the occasional yellow beams of headlights from passing cars. To each side of her there was nothing but the darkness of the forests on the long drive to the city. She still had no idea where she had landed.

Mount Saint Vincent is on the outskirts of Halifax on the highway between the city and the town of Bedford. After Paula turned onto the Bedford Highway, she pointed out the ocean to their left. "Well, the harbour," she said. At eleven at night, there was nothing to see but a black emptiness, rimmed by lights. Halima had never seen an ocean before and could not imagine what she was seeing now. As the van drove up a hill to the residence, one of the students in the back yelled to Halima, "You have to climb everywhere here." There are buses that go downtown, but "you have to walk down the hill and back up again." That is why they call the university the Mount, the young woman added. "But the view of the harbour from the top is beautiful," another student assured Halima.

The van stopped in front of a green house, one of several buildings around a circular driveway with a pond at its centre. In the front seat, Halima stirred with determined resolve. She looked out the window at her new home with the words "BIRCH 5" on it and jumped from her seat into the cool night air, hurriedly moving to the back of the van to get her bags. The other young women insisted on carrying them in for her, so she walked through the doorway holding only her handbag.

Inside, the hallway was fluorescent bright, a shock after the half-hour drive in darkness. By the half stairway to Halima's room there was a cutout of Garfield the cat with the word "Welcome" and a poster warning against "extreme drinking." Her room was around the corner, past a washroom with a toilet and a sink and another with a bathtub and a sink. To the women around Halima, the building was already ordinary, just another Canadian dormitory. To Halima, each thing in it was something she'd have to get used to. The young women directed Halima to her room with gleeful anticipation of her reaction to the personal touches they had guessed would make her feel at home: a striped comforter, a set of pink flannel pyjamas, an alarm clock, a purple teddy bear and a yellow Gerbera daisy in a pot, as well as a basket of snacks and pamphlets of information she would need in the following days. Halima invited the women in, and when they didn't join her because they thought she might be too tired, she seemed surprised. Paula stayed and asked Halima if she wanted to pray. She pointed to the windows and said, "It's that way." Halima nodded and searched for her blue prayer mat from Kenya with the compass attached to it. She could figure it out herself.

After giving her time for her prayer, Paula came back and found Halima had changed, not into the pink pyjamas, but into a red cotton one-piece outfit from Africa. With her hair uncovered, Halima looked even thinner and frailer than she had under her layers of clothing, the puffiness of fatigue around her eyes more apparent. Paula showed her a calling card they had bought for her and asked if she wanted to call home. Halima said she was too tired, that she would call in the morning. Halima covered her head with a hot pink pashmina after Paula said she would quickly take her around the residence before leaving her for the night.

Paula showed Halima how to turn the lights on in the washroom and how to use the toilet and the shower, warning her to take care with the temperature in the shower because it took the water a few minutes to get hot. She took her to the house's kitchen to show her the appliances, pointed to the room where she would do her laundry and told her these were all things she would learn to use in the next few days when she was not so tired. Then she guided Halima back

107

to her room and showed her the window she could open and close. Halima wanted the window closed and the curtains tightly drawn.

Paula left, and Halima began the first night in her life that she had ever spent alone. The university was in a woodland setting far away from the traffic of downtown Halifax. Birch 5 was quiet and virtually empty. Only Loyan was staying there that night somewhere in the building. For Halima, the silence, the unknown and as yet unseen world outside her closed curtains, the absence of a sister in her room, the distance between her and her family added up to a night of utter loneliness.

As darkness moved across the country, the students all faced the first nights of their new lives. In London, Ontario, Abdi was alone in his room in a beautiful, old stone-and-red-brick building at Huron University College. He had expected that the room would be cold at night but figured the building had some way of conditioning the air to just the right temperature. Though the room was smaller than his sleeping house back in Dadaab, he was pleased with it. It was carpeted, with a built-in wooden desk and shelving, and it was spacious enough. Most importantly, it was a single room. He was not afraid to sleep alone—he had done it often enough. But he was thinking of his relatives back home and was anxious to connect with them. Once he called home to make sure they were all right and to let them know he was safe, he would be able to sleep through the night.

In Scarborough, Mohamed, who had not slept at all on the journey, fell asleep exhausted, oblivious that first night to his loneliness and his narrow quarters. But in the following nights, he would wake up and, remembering his home, find himself unable to fall back to sleep again. On one of those nights, he went on his new computer and found his friend Ibrahim online. When Ibrahim asked him why he was still up and Mohamed told him he was thinking of home, Ibrahim advised him not to remember, to put home out of his mind.

It was a coping technique that Abdirizak, in his room in the stately Whitney Hall on the campus of the University of Toronto, learned to use as well. From his window he could see the streetlights and the mammoth shape of the Robarts Library. On a dresser beside his bed were two new wooden picture frames left by the students who had prepared his room. Behind the glass of each frame, the manufacturer's black-and-white photograph showed an anonymous, fit white man in shorts running on a beach. The students had left Abdirizak with the choice of whether to put pictures from his new life or his old into the frames. On those early nights, however, he felt that he was "a citizen of no country." He was no longer a refugee, had never been a Kenyan and did not feel at home here. To move forward, to find a new identity, to sleep through the night, he consciously blocked memories of Dadaab, because "to remember was to get stressed."

For Muno in Mississauga, Ontario, it was only the memories of home and the daily phone calls that got her through her first few nights. She taped photographs of her mom and dad to the wall above her bed to feel their presence, but then moved them to another wall so she could see them when she woke up.

In Edmonton, Hussein's first night came as a relief. He was just grateful to be safe and off the streets after the inexplicable ways of the world he'd seen on his journey and the terror of his arrival. At Heathrow he'd found the airport washroom baffling. He'd had to watch two people before he could figure out how to dry his hands with the box that blew out hot air. And he couldn't understand why a man speaking a language he didn't recognize had admonished him for putting his feet in the sink. He had been trying to do his ablution, the washing required before his prayer, but even though he didn't understand the words, he could tell from the man's tone that he was doing something wrong.

As his Air Canada flight approached Edmonton, Hussein comforted himself with the thought that he would soon be in a place where he could rest and be himself. But when his flight landed, a half hour before its scheduled arrival, there was no one there to meet him. He looked for a welcome sign with his name on it or someone straining to look for him, but everyone ignored him. His local committee from Grant MacEwan College had heard the plane was delayed and had lingered downtown to prepare for their first WUSC student. Hussein stood in the arrivals area too frightened to move. Finally, he asked some young women how to get to the college, and when they told him he would have to take a car downtown, he decided to collect his luggage and wait. He sat with his bags by a poster of the University of Alberta thinking someone would have to remember him; someone would have to show up. Finally, he heard a voice asking, "Are you Hussein?" and was "overwhelmed, like a mother who has found her baby." When the rest of the students arrived to greet him they brought food—halal chicken, and bread—which he gratefully, hungrily ate right there at the airport.

For Marwo, the first nights were not the worst ones at all. She stayed in an apartment in Victoria with Mary, the Sudanese student from Kakuma, until her residence opened. She missed her aunt and siblings in those first days and called home often just to imagine herself home. "When I talk to them," she said, "I feel relaxed." She found everything around her strange; she couldn't even open the doors. She missed the warm sunshine of Dadaab. She moved through the streets of Victoria surprised at how many white people lived there, aware of the way people stared at her. If she could have, she would have willingly gone back home that instant. But at night she had company, and that helped keep the sadness at bay. It was only when she moved into a room of her own that she went through an experience similar to that of some of the others: the loneliness of sleeping alone.

That first night in her new room on campus she felt afraid and woke up repeatedly to look around and see where she was. She thought of herself as she had been in the company of her brother and sisters and aunt back home and of who she was now in that single bed, a kind of stranger she didn't know. And she wondered if she would feel like a stranger forever.

On all the campuses, the days before classes were set aside as a time of adjustment for the WUSC students, a time to take care of business.

The committees in different cities had a number of tasks to accomplish. Students needed to register with the government. They needed to make final course selections and get university identification. They needed bank cards and groceries or university meal plan cards. They needed to learn their way around their campuses and their cities. They needed to know how to wash their clothes and how to turn on stoves and how to handle cash. There were other things the students themselves saw as priorities. They wanted to know how to call home, how to find cellphones in Canada, how to use buses to get around—and, for the Somali students, how to pray in an environment where you couldn't trust the sunsets and sunrises to stay the same.

The first thing Halima wanted to do on her first full day in Canada was call home. When Paula arrived at the dormitory, Halima had not touched any of the strange food in the basket. She wanted to eat something familiar, but first she wanted to call her family, something she regretted not doing the night before. At the pay phone on the ground floor, Paula showed Halima how to use the calling card. On the second try, Halima tentatively said, "Hello?" in a quiet, flat voice before smiling and talking excitedly in Somali. She spoke to her mother and father, and after ending the call picked up the receiver again. She became frustrated when she couldn't get through to her sister in Nairobi until one of the international students stepped in to help her. After she hung up from her second call, she didn't seem relieved. All her family had been worried about her, especially after they'd heard news about a plane crash. The Spanair plane had crashed after taking off in Madrid on its way to the Canary Islands. One hundred

On her first morning in Canada, Halima calls home.

and fifty-three people on board had died. The only thing that Halima's family had understood was that she was on a plane somewhere and a plane had crashed. If she had called the night before, she could have spared them the anxiety.

After the phone calls, Paula drove a group to breakfast at Cora's Breakfast and Lunch, a restaurant near the university. Cora's is enough to startle anyone's senses, although Halima seemed too distracted to notice the walls painted in bright shades of yellow and blue with red trim. The place was busy, packed with men, women and children. There was no separate room for women here. And no simple choice like the one hot meal prepared daily in the hotels in the camps. The waitress handed Halima a laminated menu that folded out to three pages of meal choices with pictures of plates of food piled high with eggs and pancakes and more fruit than a family in the camp might see in a year. Halima stared at the menu with incomprehension, and after she was told a crepe was a thin pancake—perhaps like *anjera,* she hoped—she ordered crepes that came with two eggs, potatoes and toast.

She was more decisive in her choice of beverage. When her black tea came in a glass carafe, she quickly tried to turn it into something resembling Somali tea. After pouring the tea into her mug and adding milk, she turned the glass container of sugar with a small hole over the mug and held it there. "That's a lot of sugar," Ashley-Jane Chow, one of the WUSC committee members, a student from Malaysia, said with surprise. Halima stopped for a moment to listen to her and then added more. Ashley complimented Halima on the henna design on her hands and forearms. Halima seemed pleased and said she had done the artwork herself and that it would last about two weeks, depending on how often she washed.

Before the breakfast came, Halima picked up the paper placemat from the table and examined the artwork—a map of Canada, a photograph of Cora, the restaurant's founder, in one corner and dots of sunshine where all her restaurants were situated. In each region of the country were drawings of Canadian icons: a tractor for the prairies, mountains for British Columbia, Mounties and the CN Tower in Ontario and, for the Maritimes, a giant red lobster sitting in the ocean. Those meant nothing to Halima, but she ran her fingers over the busy map trying to place herself on it and figure out where her friends, Muno and Marwo, had landed. When her breakfast arrived, Halima ate the eggs, some of the potatoes and a bit of the crepes. She had no trouble using the fork. Her father had known how to use cutlery and had taught her, a skill that added to her ease now.

Later in the day, Ashley took Halima on a tour of campus, showing her the library and the computers she could use there, the cafeterias and the buildings with classrooms. There was no way Halima could remember the Byzantine way the different levels of buildings were arranged on the hill after just one tour. She was more interested in seeing a real laboratory where she would do chemistry and biology experiments. That was her dream, after all, why she had come. Ashley found the laboratories, but they were all locked and there was no one around with a key. Halima peered in through a door's small window at the desks and the rows of shiny faucets.

In the afternoon, out in the van again on a sightseeing drive, Halima got her first look at the city in daylight. Most of it was just a blur; she would not even remember later the places she saw that day. As Paula drove, someone told Halima how Halifax was changing, becoming more multicultural as people from Saudi Arabia, Lebanon and the United Arab Emirates moved to the city. But Halima was intrigued by the puzzling details of the new physical world around her. Looking at the trees, she asked if Nova Scotia had a lot of forests, and she wanted to know what the containers in the port were and what the field with the row of standing stones was. It was like looking at the world through two sets of eyes. "It is very beautiful," Halima said. "It's your city now," someone responded.

The group stopped at a small grocery store called House of Halal. Ashley and Halima were going to cook a meal together that evening so that Halima could learn to use the stove, and Paula knew Halima would want to cook with halal meat as her Muslim faith required. *Halal* literally means "permissible." In dietary terms it refers to meat from grazing animals other than pigs, and birds other than birds of prey that have been killed under religious supervision by cutting the throat of the animal to allow all the blood to flow out. No halal meat can come into contact with pork, which is completely *haram*, or "forbidden." But Halima found the House of Halal almost as foreign a place as Cora's. The store was filled with Middle Eastern halal food, most of it unfamiliar to her. She had never seen any of the spices, bottled sauces or canned goods before. "How can you choose when there is so much you don't know?" she asked. "It's so complicated." If even the places that were supposed to be familiar were not, how would she ever feel comfortable here? Eventually, she picked a bag of frozen ground goat meat and another of chicken breasts, as well as two packages of frozen samosas, the only convenience food she recognized, a dish eaten to break the fast during the holy month of Ramadan.

If the halal grocery store was complicated, Sobeys was confounding. On her first visit to a Canadian grocery chain in search of food to accompany her meat, Halima gravitated to the familiar, to the individual baking potatoes that looked like the potatoes at home, to the cooking onions, the green onions, the carrots and the bananas. She could not even look at the abundance of strange foods around her and wanted only what she knew she needed. Ashley guided her to the aisles where she could find tea, sugar, rice and pasta. She was not sure which jar of tomato sauce to pick from the long row of different brands. She tried sniffing the bottles but that didn't help, so she picked the simplest one she could find, a tomato sauce with basil, although she had never heard of basil. In the dairy section, in search of milk, Halima stopped in front of the yogourt. "It's dairy," Ashley told her. "Does it have protein?" Halima asked. When Ashley answered that it did, they picked out a peach yogourt, although Halima had never tasted a peach.

Ashley was craving rice for supper that night, but she recognized Halima's need for food that would seem normal to her. They cooked a pasta dish, spaghetti mixed with a sauce made with the tomato sauce, potatoes, green pepper, onions and carrots, as close to a home-cooked meal as Halima could create.

Email from Siyad in Vancouver, Friday, August 29, 2008:

Hi Debi,

Am really doing well praise be to Allah [God].

I had a rough and boring time in the first four days but now adapting little by little. The city is so nice when u are not feeling stress of loneliness. U know it is very hard for one who has been living with extended family to live in a house alone. The other reason that contributed to the stress was cooking food. I never cooked food back home and am suspicious of the foods in the market whether it's halal or haram. Otherwise now am ok. I was shown where halal foods are available and I was promised I will get a dining card, a perfect way to reduce the stress.

———

In that first week of orientation, many of the students walked through campus tours and offices and the streets of cities in a daze, unable to articulate their feelings over the alterations happening in their lives, unable to see the world sharply but through a kind of haze that the grieving feel.

In Victoria, Marwo was frustrated with how little she could do for herself. She didn't know how to get cash from the bank or how to travel to the bank by herself. She didn't even know how to pay for things in stores. She could do none of it alone. "I was just wondering how do these things go. Are you going to know them, or are you going to be like this forever?" In the camp, when she worked for FilmAid International, she'd been part of a team educating people on diseases such as malaria and cholera through films projected on the sides of white trucks. In the camp, she had made money and contributed to her family's well-being. She had been a young adult who knew her way around the blocks and the laneways. Here she felt like a helpless, dependent little sister.

One week in, Dilalesa and Abdikadar had still not moved into their residence, a tall apartment building just off campus where they would have kitchens to do their own cooking. They spent their first three nights in the home of one Canadian and the following nights in that of another. Abdikadar, unsure of the food, had eaten only vegetables. He still didn't have all of his belongings. Air Canada had lost one of his suitcases and he had been filling out forms to get it back. He had discovered that there were not many Somalis in Saskatoon. Dilalesa, for his part, had not been able to find the Oromo he had heard lived in Saskatoon, which was his one disappointment. Neither of them was seriously bothered by the small setbacks. They were in a place where they could get on with their education, and although they came from different cultures, they had taken the same journey from the same place and now were going through the adjustments together. They spoke warmly of their Canadian hosts. "They gave us all that we required so that we could feel at home," Abdikadar wrote. "Canada is such an amazing country that I loved it from the bottom of my heart," Dilalesa wrote. "Hope everything is gonna be fantastic in the near future."

In Edmonton, Hussein was able to push away some of his loneliness because he was cushioned initially from the shock of his new situation. He had come to a city that had a large Somali community. Edmonton's 107th Avenue, which had been known as the Avenue of Nations because of all the immigrants who had settled there, was now called Little Mogadishu by some. Before school started, Hussein had enjoyed the company of several Somali friends from the camps, students at other universities who had come to Alberta for summer jobs. He was happy when they took him to the shops for halal meat and to the Somali restaurants just blocks from his residence. They showed him the mosque and the direction for his prayers and gave him a calendar so he could pray at the right times.

He was less interested when his friends took him to West Edmonton Mall so they could go skating on an indoor rink before they returned to their universities in other cities. Hussein watched from the sidelines while the others skated. There was a roller coaster inside the world's biggest mall, but he wanted nothing to do with that either. "It is very dangerous," he said. "Those wires and electricity can just go." He had walked from Somalia to Kenya as a child because he'd had no other choice; he had lived in a camp with bandits because he'd had no other place to go; but he saw no reason to ride a roller coaster, a danger that was optional. "When I see the roller coaster and people who were going there in Canada," he said, "I see this is the most dangerous thing in life. Taking myself up there? Why risk my life?"

In late summer, the city of Edmonton was warm and the trees along the river were beginning to turn colour, but Hussein had explored little of the city other than the West Edmonton Mall and the blocks around his residence. And he saw no reason to move beyond the familiarity of mosques and Somali cuisine, to move out of that comfort zone. He was there to learn, after all, not to change.

Email from Aden in Brandon, Manitoba, Friday, August 29, 2008:

Hello Ms. Debi,

Hi, how are you?

Am fine and all is well in Brandon. I find Brandon good so far. It is a small city and easy to walk around; you can't get lost in it. In spite of the strangeness and the unfamiliar food I met here it is a good place to live. Am lucky I was welcomed so well and my sponsors are kind to me. Am lucky too to meet a Muslim professor in the university who picked me up in his van and took me to a nearby mosque [worshipping place] and from there he introduced me to some Muslim brothers. I really felt so happy that it eradicated some loneliness in my heart but one frustrating thing here is that I have no Somalis in Brandon, so if I am to see them I have to travel to either Winnipeg or Regina. But all the same I have some good friends here at least not to feel lonely. They are kind. Oh about the journey. I really enjoyed the flight. I enjoyed flying, I tell you.

After travelling by bus across the green, flat, beautiful prairie from Winnipeg the morning after his arrival in Canada, Aden found himself on the small campus of Brandon University, a campus not much bigger than a city block. In the waning days of summer it was a quiet campus, too, with very few students living in the dormitory for friendly Aden to befriend. There were no other Somalis in Brandon for Aden to turn to, no halal stores or restaurants where he could buy meat. He worshipped in the town's small mosque with about fifteen other Muslims and survived on pizza and on vegetarian sandwiches from Subway.

His local committee had been welcoming and generous and had arranged tours and activities for his arrival. He felt such gratitude to them for bringing him out of the camp, for giving him the opportunity to study at a university, that he didn't want to complain or try to explain the differences in their worlds. He told them nothing of missing home or longing to see his mother. Instead he went online and complained to his friends that he was lonely, that he was the only Somali in Brandon, that he wanted to transfer somewhere else.

In Toronto, Mohamed said he had met Somalis, "up to here," hitting his chin. Muno had found she had a Somali cousin living in the city. She tried joking online with Aden—"I tell him why don't you come to Toronto if you want to meet Somalis. I meet hundreds of Somalis every day. I tease him." But she also understood that having Somalis around would not be enough to ease his sadness. "Marwo says I don't care about Somalis. I left my Mom [aunt]. I won't see my Mom for years."

Throughout the first week, the students compared notes on who had to cook their meals and who had a meal plan, who had a laptop computer and who had a desktop computer, who had a cellphone and who had a room phone, who had an apartment and who had a roommate. The dissatisfaction they felt often had little to do with their actual circumstances. The vague envy they felt for each other's situation had more to do with their confusion over why they did not feel happy, why, when they had achieved the future they had worked so hard for, they couldn't enjoy it.

High-rises, subways, kettles, toasters, vacuum cleaners, elevators, revolving doors, tea that came in cardboard cups, machines that made coffee, machines that washed clothes, machines that cut lawns, daylight at 8 p.m., loonies, toonies, five-dollar bills, white people, lots of white people. Each new object took mastering; each new strange sight, time to absorb. Exhausted after the emotion of their farewells and all the strangeness of their long journey, the students often retreated in those early days, closed the door and played their music—if they'd taken Asni's advice—or spent evenings reading email or talking on the phone or, for a few, looking at prized photos they had brought from home.

Just a week after arriving, Mohamed took the ferry to the Toronto Islands for a picnic organized by the WUSC committees from some of the various colleges at the University of Toronto. The summer weather seemed to have disappeared overnight, replaced by a premature cold and dampness. By the time the group found a suitable area on the island, Mohamed was late for his prayer. He rushed to the water's edge and pulled off his shoes to wash with the lake's cold water. He was still getting used to the prayer times, which changed so frequently in Canada. He never knew where he would be when he had to pray. There were calendars of prayer times for North America that he could consult, and software programs he could download on his computer, but it all took getting used to. The regularity of his days in Dadaab was gone, lost not only to the changing light but also to the hurried, erratic pace of life here.

He had also discovered that he had been praying in the wrong direction during his first days in Canada, that Mecca was not north of Toronto as it had been in the camps. His friends relying on the mats with the compasses, he said, were praying in the wrong direction too, since the compasses on the mats only pointed to north and were useless for any travel out of Africa. Looking out at the lake, he asked Jennifer Cabell, a member of his committee, to point out the direction for New York City, which would also be the direction to Mecca. Jennifer pointed south at the lake, and then to the left for east. Jennifer knew little about the Muslim faith, but she was learning. She wanted to be helpful to Mohamed but was nervous about the boundaries between females and males in his culture. Others had warned her she'd have difficulty, and she found herself wondering if it was okay for her to sit on his bed when she came to his room to discuss financial arrangements with him. She'd discovered after a few days of knowing Mohamed that he was a great deal more easygoing than people had led her to believe. "Mohamed was such a kind fellow. "I don't think anything bothered him."

Wrapped up against the cold in fall jackets and blankets, the ten or so who had braved the cold for the trip to the Toronto Islands ate sandwiches of tomatoes, onions, cheese slices and halal pressed meat and then played soccer on the open lawn beside their picnic table. The Sudanese student who had come from Kakuma to Trinity College stood with headphones over his ears, not to listen to music but to keep his ears warm. Mohamed stopped playing twice, frustrated at the damage the wet grass was doing to the white sneakers he had bought in Africa. He took time-outs to sit on the bench and furiously wipe the stains off his shoes with paper towels and water. A young woman on his committee watched his efforts with sympathy and told him there was a polish he could buy to keep his shoes white. Something else to learn.

Mohamed was still trying to block out memories of his mom and his siblings at night when he was alone and most vulnerable to nostalgia. During the day he was grateful for the distractions provided by the WUSC students. And he took heart in knowing there were so many diverse cultures in the city. Someone had told him that 51 per cent of people living in Toronto had been born elsewhere, and he found it comforting to know they had experienced the same dislocation he had. Adjusting, then, was a normal part of life here.

Muno did not make it to that picnic for the Toronto students. She was in her room in a townhouse on the Mississauga campus with a cold, caused, she said, by the change in her environment. She shared the top floor of a townhouse with an Asian female student who was rarely there, leaving her full use of the kitchen and the living room. Zaynab had shown Muno how to clean the floor with the vacuum cleaner and how to use the stove and refrigerator. Now Muno used the stove mainly to make Somali tea. She tried to make it as similar as she could to the tea they had at home, crushing cinnamon and adding it with black tea to water on the stove before pouring in the sugar and the milk, guessing the measurements as the liquid heated up.

In her first week she had ridden subways, eaten at a barbecue and shopped at an electronics superstore, but now that most of her orientation was over, she felt little desire to explore the campus or the city around her or even to be outside with people who misunderstood her English. She was content to stay in the apartment with the windows shut and to go outside only when she had to. In the camp

Muno takes her first subway ride in Toronto.

she had thought of herself as cheerful and friendly, as someone who enjoyed meeting friends in the market and laughing with other young women in the laneways, but here she found she didn't want to be around many people or talk with anyone unless she had to.

She might have found some solace listening to the cassette of Somali music she'd brought from home, but no one she'd met in Canada had a cassette player anymore. What surprised her most was how, now that she had books to read in her apartment and bookstores and libraries full of books close by, she had lost her appetite for reading, her ability to concentrate on the stories of others. Instead of reading, she stayed up late into the night reaching out to those she knew online.

Soon after his arrival, I sent Abdirizak an email inviting him for the drive I had promised him when we'd walked together on Ifo Highway. He answered back saying he "would appreciate a drive on Toronto's puzzling streets." On that sandy laneway in Ifo, as we'd passed thorny bushes and a dead goat lying on its side, I'd had an image of driving him in a convertible—even though I don't own one—up the Don Valley Parkway on a summer evening cooled by a lake breeze. But when I picked him up at his residence at the University of Toronto on a Saturday morning, he wanted a far more practical drive.

For the outing, he was dressed impeccably in a stiff, off-white shirt and dark dress pants. Outwardly, he appeared to be the same proud Abdirizak I had met in Ifo camp, the serious leader the others looked up to. But he admitted that here, he felt lost. To rid himself of that disorienting sense of bewilderment, he wanted to master the confusing details of his new life ASAP. He had a list of errands he wanted to do that day. He wanted me to drive him to the registrar's office so he could get his course selection in order, but that plan was thwarted when we discovered the office wasn't open that day. He also wanted me to drive him to a Fido store on Spadina Avenue. He didn't like the cellphone plan the WUSC committee had arranged for him, with its charges for incoming calls. He had tried to change his phone the day before but had gone to the store without the proper identification.

We drove down Spadina Avenue until he recognized the Chinatown Centre, where he'd been the day before. At the Fido booth on the second floor, the salesman suggested a promotional deal with a $17.50-a-month plan. But Abdirizak stood firm and pointed at the phone that Omar, a student who had come years earlier from Dadaab, had advised him to get: a $30 phone with a $30-a-month plan. Abdirizak respected the advice of former students and felt more comfortable putting questions to them than to the Canadian students who didn't understand how complicated everything was for him.

He handed over his one-time entry visa and a paper with a brand-new social insurance number for identification. It was all he had until his permanent resident card arrived in the mail. The salesman searched a computer for a credit rating with Abdirizak's identification, clearly ignoring the fact that the one-time visa was dated a week earlier. When he couldn't find a rating, he told him he would have to pay an extra $50 as a deposit, which he would get back in a year. Abdirizak

Abdirizak on Spadina Avenue in Toronto with his new cellphone.

had brought cash with him but not enough to cover the deposit. Before taking the phone, he had to find a bank machine on Spadina Avenue and pull out some extra cash to pay for the transaction, using the bank card the students had recently helped him get. After, on the street, he relaxed for the first time that morning. He walked holding his new phone open. To test it, he called my number. I answered, ready to play the old game of talking on the phone when it wasn't necessary, but Abdirizak hung up immediately. He had proven his phone worked. He was satisfied.

By her fourth day in Halifax, Halima was feeling overloaded. With Paula's help, she had picked the courses she would take that term: chemistry, biology and, at Paula's suggestion, an elective in Canadian studies. She had stood on a boat in the harbour, listened to a fiddler and seen bagpipes for the first time. She had passed her first dogs on the street. She had gone to the home of a white Canadian student, tasted ice cream by the ocean, learned that kettles were just for heating water, not for all the ingredients for Somali tea. She had watched Paris Hilton on television and, certain America would never let a black man win, had watched Barack Obama announce his running mate. She had met at least a dozen new people who were all very nice to her but not remotely like her.

On Saturday morning it was the turn of another WUSC student, Zhao Meng, from China, to show Halima more of the city. The orientation itinerary that had blocked out the past four days for Halima called for a visit to the Saturday-morning market. The young women arrived later than planned and the market was already packed. Meng and Halima moved slowly through the crowds together, stopping whenever Halima showed interest in anything. Halima sniffed at pots of herbs, hoping, without luck, to find a smell she recognized. She pointed at yellow squash and asked Meng what it was, but Meng didn't know the vegetable either. Halima tried a wild blueberry that a vendor offered her but turned away from him with a look of sour shock on her face. She took a sample apple but after one small bite

Days after arriving in Canada, Halima finds the products and produce in the Halifax market bewildering.

carried it around with her until she could find somewhere to throw it out. She showed interest in rose-coloured quartz balls with candles glowing inside them, the racks of handmade jewellery and counters of fur-lined slippers, but looked at everything else half-heartedly. She walked by stalls with mounds of late summer vegetables, stopping only to buy small ears of corn and then a cellophane bag of lentils, saying, "I know those; we have them in Africa." There were a few other blacks but no other woman wearing a hijab in sight. Those around her knew how to greet each other and knew what to buy. In the market of Ifo they would have been lost. Here, Halima was.

She said she had not eaten that morning but couldn't see anything she wanted until she came across a table with a sign that said "Brown Sugar Fudge." She tasted a sample and bought two pieces. Meng took her outside to a bench, where Halima ate one piece of fudge. She didn't look at the old Halifax buildings, at the people passing on the sidewalk. She made no attempt to smile or talk to Meng. She nibbled at the confection, letting each sugary bite comfort her.

CHAPTER FOUR

One Day I'm Going to Be Normal

IT WAS SEPTEMBER BEFORE loneliness really hit Hussein, but when it hit, it hit him hard. Classes had started and the weather was changing in Edmonton, getting colder than any weather Hussein had known in Dadaab. Just that day it had been nine degrees in the morning and he'd found it hard to get moving, making him wonder how he would manage in the winter ahead. His friends from other universities who had come to Edmonton to work for the summer had left, gone back to other cities for their new terms. He still had a Somali community, the stores and the restaurants, and the mosque nearby where he could find other Somali Muslims. But that wasn't enough anymore. His new life in Canada was nothing like the one he had imagined.

His courses came closest to his expectations: chemistry, calculus, statistics and economics. He had always loved the beautiful logic of numbers. And numbers didn't shift their meaning or change their shape from one continent to the next. Sometimes he did have trouble understanding the accent of a professor, and already he could tell the workload would be heavy, but he was confident that the internal drive he'd come with—the desire for a good job so he could help his family—would keep him on track. He had met enough of the Somali refugees in Edmonton, the ones who came without scholarships, to see the menial work they did in the restaurants, in the industries and driving cabs. "If you quit school," he said, "you won't get a good job and you will just work hectic. Doing manual work is hard." Hard and not well paying. He knew he would need his university degree to earn the kind of money that could help his family in the camp or bring them out of it.

The academic work was easy to understand compared to the social life on campus and in the residence. He wanted nothing to do with parties, where there might be alcohol or something *haram* in the potluck dishes. On Saturday nights, he could hear the students who had been drinking and were carousing in the hallways. He stayed in his room. He had made no new friends. "I really feel lonely here. Up to now I haven't been able to interact. Most of the students here are not Somali. I just know the WUSC students and they are always busy learning. Most of the time I just come and lock myself inside and read."

His room was in the biggest residence in Western Canada, a mammoth building of red and yellow blocks and glass sitting in a field in downtown Edmonton. It was a strange and isolating home after life in the small family compound. He lived on the eighth floor and found being so far away from the earth disturbing. At home, he used to eat sitting on the ground, he used to pray on the ground and, when he washed, he watched the water soak into the sandy soil of Ifo. The first time he'd cut his nails in Canada, he didn't know what to do with the clippings. At home he used to bury them in the sand. He'd called one of his friends, a student from Dadaab who had been in Canada for two years, a man who must have trimmed his nails many times. "What do I do with the clippings?" he asked. The other man laughed and told him, "Just throw them in the garbage." Sometimes Hussein would go outside and sit on the lawn, just to feel the connection to the soil. He would watch the sun set and feel a little more at home.

There were things he appreciated in Canada, things that made his life easier: the washing machine that cleaned his clothes so fast, the stove that heated up so easily and the refrigerator that kept his food fresh for so long. But by now he knew that Canada was not the land he'd supposed it was, a place where right away you could get everything: "That's what we thought in the camps. If a brother comes here, he is in banks of money. When you come here, you realize that is not true."

He had known he would miss home, had cried when he hugged his mother goodbye at the bus stop, but he could never have guessed how much the loneliness would hurt. "When I was in the camps I was working hard to leave and to come to Canada but when I left I'm saying, 'Why did I leave my family?'" He knew that if someone offered him a ticket back to Kenya, he would be tempted to take it, if it were not for the responsibility he felt to make his family's life better: "Something has changed now, and I have to accept it."

When I visited Hussein in the middle of September, halfway through the Muslim holy month of Ramadan, I found a young man suffering from alienation. I had gone to Edmonton for my job and had emailed him beforehand on the off chance he might be able to see me on my one free evening. When I didn't hear back from him, I was not surprised. I assumed he would be breaking his daily fasting for Ramadan with Muslims in the city. And he had seemed the most distant student in the camp, the one who had shown the least interest in our conversation. I did finally hear back from him when I got to the city. He told me he would welcome my visit.

It wasn't hard to find his residence. All through the day in Edmonton, from various locations downtown, I had seen the tall towers of Grant MacEwan. They were like something out of *The Lord of the Rings,* angled concrete structures looming above all the other buildings around them. To get to Grant MacEwan in Edmonton, all you have to do is walk toward the towers.

Grant MacEwan College took its name from a former lieutenant governor of Alberta, Dr. J. W. Grant MacEwan. A large portrait of

Dr. MacEwan hangs on the main floor of the college, beneath the portrait a quotation from his personal creed: "I have tried to leave things in the Vineyard better than I found them." There is another phrase from his creed that suggested he would have been pleased to know his college was trying to make the life of a refugee better: "A fundamental concept of Good consists of working to preserve all creatures with feeling and the will to live."

When Hussein took me to his room, I could see Tupperware containers of food on a small table against one wall that indicated he had already broken his fast, alone. He showed me the dates that he'd eaten—the traditional first food after the sun has set. I was more impressed by the rest of the meal in the containers, evidence that he had some cooking skills. His mother had just one daughter, a young girl, so Hussein had helped his mother with the meals. In Edmonton, he had tackled his food management with the skills of someone trained in home economics. Each week, he told me, he cooked enough of the "soup"—a sauce of meat, tomatoes, onions and spices— for the week. An open plastic container on his table was filled with several *sambusas*, triangular pastries filled with spiced meat, another traditional Ramadan food. They looked like the perfectly formed samosas that I often ate at Indian restaurants in Toronto, and I assumed his were ready-made. But one *sambusa* in a store cost a dollar, he said, and he knew he could make them for less. Luckily, his private room had a small kitchenette—a countertop with a stovetop built into it, a microwave and a refrigerator. There was no oven, but he didn't seem to miss one because he didn't know what an oven was. He showed me the egg-roll sheets he had in his refrigerator that he used for the *sambusas*, and the oats he had in the cupboard and the Shreddies he ate with boiled milk. He showed me the Lipton tomato vegetable soup, which he found "salty and a bit complex," and the dried kidney beans he had tried soaking overnight but could never get soft even when he cooked them for hours.

I congratulated him on how well he was managing, but it didn't take long for me to see that managing is not the same thing as doing well. He talked to me about the sadness of his first Ramadan alone. At home, his mother woke him up before the sun rose to give him tea. In the evening after the sun had set, the family broke the fast together. In Edmonton there had been evenings during Ramadan when he had forgotten to eat and mornings when he'd slept until the sun was up and had to forgo food and water for the day. Once, he had gone through a twenty-four-hour period without anything to eat or drink at all. He talked about how other students had invited him in the past weeks to go for coffee after class but he hadn't been able to join them. "I tell them I can't, so it's a bit lonely."

He talked about how he sat in his room and remembered his family: "I just feel at home when I'm thinking about Mother, being with those boys, my brothers. I can't say, let's forget about them, because the moment I forget about them I will be thinking negatively. I can't forget, so I just think that I'm with them always." He talked about his plans to go back to see them when he had his degree and Canadian citizenship in three years. He talked about his hopes that his family might get resettlement in the United States before that. He talked and he talked.

As I listened, I noticed his room was sweltering. I asked if he found it warm. He was wearing a lined nylon jacket over his shirt and pants but said he found the temperature comfortable. He did admit that he was having trouble sleeping at night, that it was so hot he'd had to kick the sheet away. I got up and discovered a thermostat on one wall. It was set at 30 degrees Celsius. When I pointed it out, he said he had no idea what a thermostat was or that the air of the room was not naturally heated like the air in Africa. He was grateful when I showed him how he could turn the heat down for the night.

I realized I had been there for two hours and apologized for staying so long. But he thanked me for my visit and said it had helped to talk to someone who knew the person he was, who had seen his home. He insisted on walking me down to the street where I waited for a taxi. It was dark outside by then and the air was cool, a sharp contrast to the sauna-like atmosphere in his room, but he waited with me. He seemed to want to reassure me that he would be fine. Beyond the wide field and across the street we could see the lights of a Tim Hortons. Hussein told me that in his first few days in Canada he had not been able to figure out the traffic signals to cross the busy street. Now he could, though. And when Ramadan ended, he would drink tea with others and start to make new friends. "One day," he told me, "I'm going to be normal and get adapted to this." When the cab arrived, Hussein made no attempt to reach his hand out to me as some of the other young Somali men did, making a point of showing they accepted the Canadian custom despite the belief in Islam that unrelated men and women should not have any physical contact. I nodded goodbye to him and promised to visit again. I stepped into the cab and watched as he turned to enter the vast loneliness of his residence.

In that first semester, across the country, others were coming to the realization that life in Canada could be complex and hard. If pushed, they might have admitted that they should have listened more carefully to Asni's warnings. The pace of life was faster here, and the university schedules required new organizational skills. They were nothing like the regular routines they'd grown used to in the camps. Here they had to stay on top of things or get overwhelmed by appointments, irregular class times and copious assignments.

The young Somali men, who had depended on mothers and sisters to wash their clothes and magically make meals appear, found that when they had to pile domestic chores on top of their school assignments, just getting through the day became all-consuming. Catching buses to stores and then shopping and, worst of all, cooking meals in strange kitchens involved a steep learning curve that left them exhausted. They didn't know how other students managed it all so easily.

In a townhouse on the Scarborough campus of the University of Toronto, Mohamed had filled his shelves in the communal kitchen with an odd collection of cereal, pasta, bread and hot sauce. For dinner, he usually ate spaghetti with a sauce of tomatoes and potatoes, because cooking spaghetti was easier than cooking rice. In the morning, he often didn't have time to make tea even though there was an electric kettle that would heat the water quickly. "Waking up early in the morning was the hardest part," Mohamed said. "I had a class at eight. Sometimes I would wake up exactly at eight and I had to go directly to class. I didn't eat anything. I had to cook, so it was difficult." He now appreciated his mother in a way he never had before.

Mohamed missed his old transistor radio as well. He had loved to listen to soccer matches and news in his Dadaab house. Jennifer Cabell, the young woman on his wusc committee, bought him a radio so he could listen to the news again. He followed the fighting in Somalia, and the American presidential campaign. He listened with concern when people called Barack Obama a Muslim as though that were a bad thing. And he listened with pleasure when Republican Colin Powell said that there were graves of American soldiers with the Islamic symbol of the crescent etched on their tombstones and that there was nothing wrong with being a Muslim.

Mohamed was grateful for all the help Jennifer had given him. Since there was no money in the wusc budget for a computer, she had arranged for her father's insurance company to donate one to him. She'd also invited him to her home, where he had enjoyed meeting a Canadian family and discovering that not all adult children in North America lose their connections to their parents, as he had believed.

But both Mohamed and Jennifer found some things baffling about each other. Jennifer and her boyfriend accompanied four of the Toronto wusc students, including Mohamed, to a baseball game at the Rogers Centre in downtown Toronto. Mohamed could not eat anything until after nine at night, Jennifer remembers. She says that during the game, he told her he had to pray near a body of water. He told her the washroom wasn't appropriate, that he needed something like a fountain. Jennifer had to persuade a befuddled security guard to let them out in the middle of the game.

Mohamed says the Blue Jays won the game easily that day. He didn't believe he'd ever like baseball as much as he liked soccer, but he admitted he didn't understand what was going on the field. "It didn't make any sense because I didn't know the rules."

The differences between them made it hard for Jennifer and Mohamed to move to a closer friendship. Mohamed turned to his Dadaab friends, who could understand him, and joined a Muslim association on campus.

The WUSC program at the Scarborough campus offers students a combination of part-time work and part-time studies in the first year. The committee pays for two courses each term and arranges a job in the admissions office so the new student can earn some money while acclimatizing to academic life in Canada. Mohamed registered for economics and calculus in the fall term, but he found the courses difficult without the prerequisites that the Canadian students in the class had taken in secondary school. He was determined to get grades high enough to qualify for any program he wanted to take in the second year and for scholarships to help with his expenses. When he had trouble with the curriculum for his calculus course, he became more and more anxious that he wouldn't do well. "I HATE CALCULUS!" he screamed online to everyone on Facebook. He dropped the course before the mark could go on his record.

At the University of British Columbia, Siyad had chosen three of the hardest courses so he could get them out of the way: calculus, chemistry and physics. When he started the classes, he found that it was not the mathematics or the scientific principles that tripped him up, but the cultural references used in the examples: "There are a lot of things that people know, obviously, and I wonder, 'How do they know these things?' For example, when we do labs for physics, we simulate the speed of a normal car in Vancouver and the distance between downtown and UBC. [The Canadian students] have been living here and driving. They ask me how many minutes does it take to walk from UBC to downtown. I have never done that." Once Siyad realized how demanding the courses would be, he started studying in the library. That way he wasn't tempted to spend hours talking online or reading friends' comments on Facebook.

At the University of Toronto, Abdirizak picked four courses at the beginning of term: Swahili, calculus, a management course and economics. Under his WUSC program he was only supposed to take three courses, so he gave himself the first week of classes to decide which course to drop. That became easy when he attended his first lecture in economics: "Everybody came in excited. The professor was excited. The students were excited. So the professor began asking questions and people are laughing and you don't get why. You feel embarrassed. You feel like the odd one out." Even though he had done well in English back in the camp, he couldn't understand the professor's accent and decided to put off economics for another time.

During the fall, most of the students joined Facebook as a way to connect with each other and with friends and relatives around the world. The list of friends on the Somali students' pages looked like a study in the diaspora, with names from Kenya, Australia, South Africa and Saudi Arabia, from across Canada and from Kansas, Minnesota, Pennsylvania, Texas and Oregon. On their pages, the students posted videos about Somalia and rap singers, joined anti-poverty and Muslim groups and philosophized about life. In the cyber-cafés in the Dadaab markets, they had paid $2 an hour to use the slow Internet services. At their universities, they had free access to the Internet, and they took full advantage of it.

In the camp, Dilalesa had been worried that his lack of knowledge about computers would hold him back in Canada, but by the end of the first term even he had a Facebook page. He seldom wrote on it, though. Neither did Abdikadar. The others complained that the two students at the University of Saskatoon were not communicating and didn't respond to online or phone messages. "The Saskatoon boys have gone silent," one noted.

The Saskatoon boys had buried themselves in their work. Abdikadar was taking four courses that term and planned to take five in the winter term. He wanted to get through twenty courses in two years.

It was all part of his plan to become a doctor. He knew that getting a medical degree would take years, and he could not afford to waste any time along the way. He turned twenty-three that fall and wouldn't be able to marry or give his family the real help they needed until he finished his studies.

Dilalesa had not decided on his career path yet. He was content to be studying philosophy again and trying a variety of social sciences. But he was starting to worry about life after university. He knew he would have to pay back the student loan he would inevitably have to take on, and people told him it was not that easy to get a job with a degree in philosophy. It was something he had to think about as he tried to negotiate the intricacies of university courses on a Canadian campus. In his free time, he pursued two activities that he hadn't been able to pursue in the camps. He joined a karate class so he could finally learn to master a martial art, and he started the paperwork to legally change his name, wanting to leave the despised name Dereje behind forever.

On Thanksgiving weekend, my family invited the Toronto-area students to our home. We served a roasted halal goat leg along with rice, flatbread and a sweet, hot tomato sauce that Muno had told me how to make. Abdirizak, thanking me later in an email, said the dinner was "almost similar to a traditional Somali dish."

Both Abdirizak and Mohamed, perhaps unsure of the dress code for dinner in a Canadian home, wore suits bought in Africa, so new that the cloth labels with the manufacturer's name were still sewn on the sleeves of their jackets. They both looked slightly uncomfortable when they saw that Ibrahim, who had come to Canada a year before them and had been to our home several times, was dressed far more casually, in a black T-shirt and slacks. They took many of their cues from Ibrahim, sitting on the couch in the family room when he did, talking English as he did when we were around. But when Ibrahim asked after our dog, Schmidt, whom we'd sent away for the evening to make the visit easier, they seemed surprised that he regretted the dog's absence.

The goat took longer to cook than we'd expected, and while the students waited on the couch, Ibrahim used the remote to turn on the television and search through the channels before stopping at an extreme fighting program on Spike TV.

Muno, dressed in a brown hijab from Dadaab, sat at one edge of the couch, looking bemused and a little bored. When my daughter, Jane, invited Muno to see her room, Muno rose quickly to follow. I had introduced the two young women soon after Muno had arrived in Canada. By then, Jane had met several of the Dadaab students and, as a Canadian who had always taken education and the basics of life for granted, she was awed by their stories of struggle. But with Muno, things were different. The two were students of English literature and aspiring writers. At their first meeting, they discovered that they were both studying Virginia Woolf that term and, as they talked about the author's mental illness and suicide, they realized that a love of books and words could bridge myriad differences. If the two had been strangers in a classroom, it's unlikely that they would have come to that realization; their shyness and their assumptions about each other would have prevented it. It's unlikely that Jane would have seen past the hijab, unlikely that Muno would have thought she had anything in common with the red-headed student whose skin was paler than she thought skin could be. But after that first meeting, they chose to get together on their own for tea and talk as friends.

When the goat was finally cooked, we gathered around the dining-room table. The Dadaab students fiddled with the waxed red maple leaves that decorated the table and checked in on each other's lives. They compared cellphone plans—who had call display and who had voice mail and calling cards, which ones gave the most minutes—and the frequency of their calls home. Muno said she had to call every two nights or she would have trouble sleeping the third night. Abdirizak and Mohamed said they were now calling just every two weeks. Ibrahim said he called home only every two months or so. The first year, he told the others, the connection is with Africa: "You are always calling and asking about so and so, but in the second year the connection is more here." They listened to him as if they found it hard to believe.

Ibrahim warned the others that in their first year they would "be treated like kings living in a palace" but in the second year they would be on their own. He was managing with a scholarship and a loan and said he was comfortable enough. The others sipped the Somali tea that Muno and Jane had made in the kitchen and stared at him again, perhaps wondering how much more difficult life in Canada could become. After a few moments, Muno looked around the table at the others from Dadaab. "Can you imagine," she asked, "how difficult it would be to go through such a big change if the people weren't friendly?" There was silence around the table as if the thought was something best not imagined.

Throughout the fall the situation in Somalia and, by extension, in Dadaab was deteriorating. In Somalia, fighting continued between Ethiopian troops and Islamists. The Ethiopian troops had gone into Somalia in late 2006 with American backing to oust the Union of Islamic Courts (UIC), which controlled Mogadishu at the time and had brought the greatest sense of order to that city since the civil war began. The Ethiopian military fought on the side of the transitional government formed in Nairobi in 2004, which had never been able to get its footing in Somalia. There may have been a united desire in Somalia to get rid of the Ethiopians, a traditional enemy, but there was no agreement among the Islamists on how the country should be run once they ousted the foreign troops. Moderates in the UIC wanted to negotiate a deal with the transitional government, while its more radical youth wing, al-Shabab, wanted nothing to do with any such deal. Ideas of how to lead Somalia were once again causing factional wars, this time between different religious elements.

A measure of al-Shabab's cruelty came to light when a young girl named Aisha was stoned to death for adultery in Kismayo after she informed authorities that three men had raped her. Amnesty International reported that Aisha Ibrahim Duhulow was thirteen years old when she died on October 27, 2008, at the hands of fifty men who threw stones at her in a crowded stadium. She had disappeared from her parents' home in Dadaab's Hagadera camp months earlier.

Muno only realized that she had known the girl when a reporter from the *Toronto Star* came to the Mississauga campus to talk to her about Hagadera. Muno was saddened to hear of the fate of a young girl who had been her student for a few months in the camp. She didn't remember Aisha well, only as a student who struggled with her classes, who "didn't look mentally fit. She was always in trouble with students, teachers. She was just a child." To the world, Aisha became a symbol of the dangers of extremism. But she was also a symbol of the desperation of life in Dadaab. She was a thirteen-year-old girl, after all, who thought running away, alone, to the city of her family's memories had to be better than staying where she had no prospects for the future.

That same month, October, *The Economist* called Somalia "the world's most utterly failed state." But while thousands of civilians were dying in the fighting, the world's media cast its spotlight on the coasts of Somalia, where pirates had demanded more than $100 million in ransom for ships seized in the Gulf of Aden. Suddenly, people were talking about Somalia again. Siyad, in his job as a courtesy clerk at a Safeway in Vancouver, found that as he pushed carts through the parking lot, people for the first time were recognizing the name of the country of his birth. "Oh, the place with the pirates?" they would ask him.

With no end to the violence in Somalia, more and more people were trying to get out any way they could. Hundreds drowned in the Gulf of Aden attempting to make the dangerous trip to Yemen in small boats operated by people smugglers. And it was getting harder to get into Kenya to claim refugee status there. In October 2008, Human Rights Watch concluded that by closing its borders in 2007, the Kenyans had violated international refugee law, which prohibited the forced return of those seeking asylum. The organization said the closure of the Kenyan border had driven desperate people to pay bribes to police or hire smugglers to get them across the border.

Despite the challenges, that same October, more than 6,000 new arrivals made it to the Dadaab camps looking for plots of land that didn't exist. By early November, there were 224,000 people in the camps, 15,000 more than had been there the day the students left in August, just three months before.

UNHCR expressed concerns about the aging water infrastructure, the poor sanitation and the lack of shelter, all of which could lead to major health concerns during the rainy season. The organization warned that if people continued arriving, there could be food shortages by January. The students in Canada heard from their families that the new arrivals were driving up the costs of goods in the markets and introducing to the community new, dangerous thieves.

At the same time as they were hearing frightening reports from Africa, the students were witnessing an economic downturn in North America, an event that changed their perception of Canada as a place where they could easily find financial security, if not wealth, for themselves and their families. In September, the worse news seemed confined to the United States, where it appeared that greed and a lack of regulations were devastating financial markets, toppling banks and driving families to bankruptcy. "I know where Wall Street is," Abdi said, trying to understand the dramatic headlines of the crisis spreading from corporations to average Americans, "but where is Main Street?"

The smugness that Canadians felt over their regulated banks and their declining debt vanished in October when talk of a recession in Canada passed the lips of economic pundits. The news left the students from Dadaab bewildered. They were just getting over their realization that not everyone was wealthy in Canada when they had to come to grips with the reality that jobs could be hard to find in the future even if they had a university degree. They had all heard, in particular, about the booming economy of Alberta and had assumed they could go there to take their pick of summer jobs if they were so inclined. Other students from Dadaab had gone to Edmonton,

Calgary and Fort McMurray in the past, and word had spread about how lucrative the pay was in those cities.

But as the days got shorter and the recession deepened, even the possibility of easy wages in Alberta seemed less likely. The combination of the news about Dadaab and the fragility of the economy had a sobering effect. Most of the students started a process that would continue into the winter and the spring: they began re-evaluating their choice of courses and the degrees they sought. A practical choice with a guaranteed job at the end of a degree was looking more attractive all the time. For Siyad in Vancouver, that meant considering engineering, a program that wouldn't take as long as the degree in medicine he had dreamed of in the camp. For the young men studying economics, it meant looking more closely at practical courses. For Halima, who had wanted to be a biochemist, it meant considering something more saleable, like nursing or a career as a dietitian. For Marwo, it meant considering nursing as well. For Muno, who'd wanted to study English and become a writer, it meant questioning whether her choice was a selfish one, a choice that would satisfy her own curiosity about all those books out there but not one that would ultimately benefit her family.

In the fall, Abdi was keeping his options open. He had ambitions and he wouldn't let them go. He wanted to do a master's degree. He wanted to study French so he could be a bilingual Canadian. He wanted to move out of London, Ontario, someday and live in Montreal, a city he'd never been to but one he'd read about, because of its excellent university, McGill, a university he thought might be more suitable than Western for a master's degree in science. He knew that, like a tightrope walker, he had to keep his balance, keep his head up. He had heard of other WUSC students who had come before him to Huron University College but had dropped out in the second year. He was not going to let that happen to him. Friends and family from home called him all the time. Most of the students across Canada were inundated with calls and emails requesting help, since everyone back home thought they were rolling in money. Abdi sent home what he could to his closest relatives, but he believed that if he was going to help his uncle and other family members in the camp in any real way, if he was to search for the half-sisters and -brothers who might still be in Somalia, he had to concentrate on his studies. He couldn't look away, couldn't take his eyes from the textbooks for too long. That focus would keep him moving in a straight line toward his goals.

On the first weekend in November, several of the students had their first opportunity to see another Canadian city and to catch up with each other in person. They had come with their local committees to WUSC's sixty-second annual assembly at the Crowne Plaza Hotel in downtown Ottawa. Mohamed and Abdirizak had come from metropolitan Toronto; Abdi had come on the train from London. In Toronto he'd had time to wander through the streets downtown. "I saw Bay Street," he said. "Someone told me it is supposed to be the Wall Street of Canada." Aden, the only Somali in Brandon, had flown in from Winnipeg, and this time he'd requested a window seat so he could see what the earth looked like from up in an airplane. Halima had flown in from Halifax and Marwo from Vancouver. Now that they were WUSC members themselves, their committees paid their way to Ottawa, the fee for the conference and the hotel accommodation. They joined hundreds of students, professors and WUSC employees for sessions on the assembly's theme of "youth action and civic engagement." They were pumped about a weekend of exploring the capital and having some fun after the first two months of the university grind. "Two months and seventeen days," Abdirizak corrected.

On Friday, the first morning of the conference, the lobby of the Crowne Plaza Hotel looked like a junior United Nations. Young people from Africa and Asia mingled with students born in Canada. As Halima lined up with two other female students from Mount Saint Vincent to register at the hotel desk, she scanned the crowd for one person she knew would be there: Marwo. She had hoped the weekend would be a reunion of the three young women from Dadaab who had grown so close during their year of preparation and the journey to Canada. But Muno was not coming. Her committee had not made any plans for the assembly, and Muno was content to stay in Mississauga.

As Halima's group moved toward the elevator with room keys in hand, Halima spotted Marwo. The two young women hugged and laughed in the lobby. They were both dressed in colourful headscarves. Halima wore a shiny lime green scarf over a flowing piece of material reminiscent of the dull colours of the Dadaab hijab; Marwo wore a flowered scarf over a cardigan sweater and long skirt. While they talked, the elevator came and the other students from the Mount waited, not wanting to interrupt Halima's moment of joy. By day's end, Halima and Marwo had convinced their committees to adjust the sleeping arrangements so the two of them could share a room and talk together into the night. They caught up on life back home and their new lives in cities at opposite ends of the country. Halima had been to Cape Breton for Thanksgiving weekend. She'd found

Old friends Halima and Marwo meet again
at wusc's annual assembly in Ottawa.

the red leaves of the trees amazingly beautiful and had eaten her first turkey dinner. "I finished the whole plate," she said. Birch 5, her house at Mount Saint Vincent, had filled up with students from many countries, including China and Sweden. Loyan from St. Lucia, the tough taskmaster in the house, organized potluck suppers once a week so the students could all get to know each other. The WUSC committee had offered Halima a full meal plan of $2,500 to use at the cafeteria or a small plan of $200 with a budget for groceries, but she had worked out a third option with Paula Barry. She now had a meal plan worth $600. That meant she could eat in the cafeteria when she was extremely busy at school and cook her own meals in the Birch 5 kitchen when she wanted to eat something familiar. Halima said Paula had become like a mother to her, and that Sarah, who had met her at the airport, had become her "best Canadian friend."

Marwo said her best Canadian friends were two young women from her local WUSC committee: Serina and Nicola. She was cooking her own meals now in the apartment she shared with other female students, but there were still lots of foods in the grocery store she didn't recognize, so she just took her time and usually just bought the things she recognized, like pasta and rice.

Before the first open session in the afternoon, a workshop on the Student Refugee Program, WUSC's Asni Mekonnen greeted students outside the hall. Sometimes she forgot names or what university students had gone to, but she recognized all the faces of those she had met in the camps over the years. The students who spotted her posed for pictures with her on new cameras and cellphones. But as soon as the students from Dadaab saw each other, they gasped and rushed across the open space. When Marwo and Halima ran into Aden, the three giggled with joy. The faces of the other young men from Dadaab broke into wide smiles. They had all survived more than two months in Canada and were walking around a big Canadian hotel as though it was the most natural thing in the world.

In the workshop, Asni described the Student Refugee Program to the audience of one hundred or so students, most of them already

Aden laughs with Marwo and Halima, overjoyed at seeing each other for the first time since their arrival in Canada.

the converted, young people who were in Canada thanks to WUSC or were students in women's studies or international development programs across the country. Marwo and Halima sat at a table together, suddenly serious as Asni described their world, seeing for the first time the large organization that had brought them out of the camp. They turned to face Asni as she listed the recommendations WUSC had come up with to help girls in the Dadaab camps. Montreal's 60 Million Girls foundation had given WUSC a grant of $100,000 to support girls' education in both Kakuma and Dadaab. With the grant, WUSC planned to focus both on "community mobilization," in an attempt to convince parents it was worth sending their daughters to school, and on remedial classes for girls. "By the time WUSC does its selection," Asni said, "it is at the level of finishing high school and most of the girls are not able to get to that level, so what we have to do is to bring them up first so that by 2015 their numbers will be equal to the boys in the program."

Throughout the workshop, students took notes. They scribbled facts about the program: the cost of a full year of sponsorship: $17,000 to $25,000; the number of local committees that provided multiple years of sponsorship: 27 per cent; the number of participating universities that had student levies: 90 per cent; the highest levy: $12, at Abdi's Huron University College in London; the lowest levy: 50 cents.

For the Dadaab students, there was no need to take notes when the third speaker stood up. Mohamed Mursal had come from Dadaab to Canada two years earlier, and as he told his story of his life as a refugee student from Dadaab, he was telling their story. "I don't think anyone in my Somali society thought that we could accept living in the conditions, even the environmental conditions, provided by Dadaab camp. It's so hard. It's so dusty. It's so windy, so hot and above all insecure," he told his audience. "It deletes from your memories that good life, that life of being in a good situation. You are scarred a little bit. You are hardened."

It was difficult to reconcile the place he spoke of, a place so desperate "you feel like committing suicide," with the view from the penthouse meeting room of the Crowne Plaza Hotel. The wide blue waters of the Ottawa River shone in the bright afternoon light of a clear fall afternoon while the glass wall on a nearby high-rise building reflected the majestic Supreme Court of Canada across the street. When Mohamed flicked to a slide of girls in a classroom, Halima knocked Marwo on the arm and the two young women smiled at each other and stared at the familiar setting. "That slide takes me back to the school," Mohamed said. "I'm very familiar with that room. I was actually there for over six years, four years learning and then two years teaching. It's one of the best rooms in my school." Halima got up from her table and moved to take a picture of Mohamed speaking and then sat at another table closer to the front so she could see and hear him better.

The assembly's sessions on refugee life and aid issues inspired Abdi. In the camp, he had been more than a student. He had been a presenter and an advocate for the rights of women, and at the assembly he saw the possibility of using his skills again. Before he went back to London, he hoped to figure out a way to give presentations beyond Huron University College, at the larger University of Western Ontario, on refugee life to raise awareness about WUSC and Dadaab. And he'd decided he wanted to come back to the assembly the following year and speak at a workshop, sharing the knowledge he had on gender issues from his work for CARE.

It was the assembly's keynote speaker, however, who inspired all of the students. His speech made them consider the possibility that not only could they have lives in Canada, they could have great lives. Alfred Orono Orono had come to Canada in 1995 as a WUSC scholar. In his native Uganda, he had been a child soldier during the dictatorship of Idi Amin, and later a conscripted soldier in the Sudanese rebel army. He escaped from Sudan and fled to Kenya, where he lived in the Dadaab refugee camps. Once in Canada, he finished a degree in criminology and a second degree in law at the University of Alberta before going to work for the federal Justice Department. Now, just thirteen years after he'd arrived in Canada, at a Saturday afternoon luncheon in the ballroom of a hotel in Ottawa, he walked to the podium in a well-tailored suit, a crisp red tie and stylish wire glasses as a prosecutor for the United Nations International Criminal Tribunal for Rwanda.

Students who had arrived in Canada after him and who were still deciding where their lives were leading watched the keynote speaker, leaning forward in their seats to get a better glimpse of the successful man. Orono had a rapt audience, and as a speaker, he knew how to use his prosecutorial skills to tell his story of struggle and gratitude.

"Over thirteen years ago, I was living in a refugee camp, in all sense of a refugee camp, without a house, with as little food as possible. There was only one thing keeping me alive. That's hope. That's what kept me alive. You know that feeling: something tells you that against all odds there is something good coming in the future. There are many people who have supported me in this world, to bring me into the position that I am today. When I was at the bottom, they lifted me up. When I was leaning, about to fall, they put their hands out to make me stand." Picking up on the assembly's theme of youth action and engagement, he exhorted the WUSC students to continue connecting to those in the world who needed their help. "What I'm trying to tell you is that to make people like me, it takes a lot of civic action and engagement."

During the rest of the weekend, the new students sought out Orono to be photographed with the man who had lived in Dadaab and was now famous. Aden, in particular, felt proud to meet a man who had lived in his camp: "I was happy to hear he was a refugee like me and he used to live in Hagadera. I was really happy to find someone who came from our place and is so courageous and inspiring. And I'm really hoping to follow in his steps."

Orono chatted with the students and agreed to their requests for photographs, but he did not want a lot of attention at the assembly. After an interview with the *Ottawa Citizen,* he told the conference organizers he would do no more, leaving them confused about his decision. Here was a man who could bring publicity to their organization, a man who had such gratitude for what he'd been given. But he was a man with a complicated past and a sensitive job. Reporters were more likely to question him about his days as a child soldier or his work as a prosecutor than about his life as a sponsored student. Gratitude was clearly something he intended to show but not by talking with reporters.

Showing gratitude was the theme at one unscheduled meeting that weekend. The new students from Dadaab heard about the meeting in emails from Omar Ahmed Abdi, a student taking a postgraduate year in economics at Queen's University in Kingston, Ontario. Omar was a pioneer, one of the first two Dadaab students to come to Canada on WUSC scholarships, in 2004. But he'd been a pioneer long before that.

When schools first opened in Dadaab, teachers taught an informal mix of the Somali and Kenyan system. Then, in 1997, when Omar was in his last year of primary school in Ifo camp, CARE decided to switch one group, Omar's group, to the formal Kenyan curriculum to see how the students did. At the end of that year, CARE arranged for the ten test-case students to travel to Garissa to sit for the examination for the Kenya Certificate of Primary School. When all of the students scored well, CARE expanded the Kenyan system in the camp and sent the ten primary-school graduates to a private school in Garissa for their secondary schooling.

Omar and the others had boarded at the school, where they washed their own clothes and sometimes went without food because there wasn't enough for all the students. When they sat for the secondary-school certificate four years later, two students did well. One of them was Omar, with the second-highest score in the province. The students' success spurred camp officials, including Marangu Njogu, CARE program manager at the time, to search for opportunities at universities. Through Windle Trust in Nairobi, they found WUSC scholarships for the top two students. When Omar came to Toronto in the fall of 2004, there were no Dadaab students in Canada before him to help him through his transition. He credits a caring local committee at the University of Toronto's Trinity College with getting him through that first year, but he made sure those who followed him had someone they could consult.

By 2008, Omar had become a kind of godfather to newly sponsored students. He checked up on them regularly. He was the one who gave them advice on everything from cellphone plans to course selections. In Ifo, he had taught both Halima and Abdirizak, but they would be the last students he knew personally. That didn't matter to him. If they were from Dadaab and now studying in Canada, he would get to know them and any problems they were having. Recently, he'd become one of the founders of Students for Refugee Students. He saw the group as a way for the Dadaab students to stay connected with each other. It also became a way for the students to feel they were doing something for those left behind. Together, they were trying to raise money for textbooks and stationery for the new community secondary schools in the Dadaab camps.

At the meeting, the students from all four years gathered around one round table in an otherwise unoccupied meeting room. Omar suggested that each student who had come out of Dadaab contribute $50 four times a year for the textbook fund. There was already $900 in the bank account, he said, and he hoped there would be $2,000 by the end of the year.

Marangu Njogu, who was now head of Windle Trust, had come to Ottawa to attend the general assembly in his role as a WUSC board director. Omar knew Njogu from his days in the camp and invited him to the students' meeting to give them some advice. Njogu reminded the students that they had all been given opportunities, suggesting that now it was time they showed gratitude by helping others. "There are people who assisted you," he said. "You are the people who know the problems of Dadaab." He referred to the election earlier that week of the next U.S. president, Barack Obama. It was an election that as a Kenyan he took pride in because of Obama's Kenyan roots, but it was also one that made him feel embarrassed for his own country and its disastrous election that had resulted in deadly tribal fighting earlier in the year. He hoped the U.S. election would make Kenyans do better, and he used the name of Obama in that meeting to challenge the students: "Obama called himself 'the most improbable candidate,'" he said, "but he did it." Looking at the students, he said, "Don't be afraid to start something." Asni came into the meeting late and stood beside the table. She reinforced what Njogu had said, telling the students she had been trying for years to persuade them to give back: "When someone has taken a risk on you, and so much help has come from local committees, I don't understand why sponsored students who come with so much support are not giving back."

The new students understood their responsibility, believed they should give back to others. Some, though, felt torn about spending $50 four times a year in their first year. They were already feeling pressure to send any money they could spare to their families or to friends in the camp who pleaded for financial help.

When the students asked how they could turn money they raised in Canada into books in the camp schools, Njogu suggested the group pass on the money to the community elders, who would buy the books that were needed. Omar knew they couldn't send the money directly into the camp. A transfer of $2,000 through a money transfer service was bound to attract attention from anyone monitoring remittances. After 9/11 one of the biggest Somali remittance services, al-Barakat, had been shut down over an American accusation that it had been used to transfer money to terrorists. Omar asked Njogu if he would personally take the money to the elders to avoid any complications. To keep the tracking of the money transparent, WUSC would send the amount collected to Windle Trust, and Njogu would get it to the elders.

Of the newest students, Abdi asked the most questions. He had thought of the idea of helping this way back in the camp, but he had questions about the proceedings and how the group should be run. As someone used to aid meetings in Kenya, he wanted minutes and an agenda and wanted the group to think of bigger plans for down the road.

Like any good conference in Canada, there was time for socializing at the national assembly. Aden made full use of the "networking breaks" between sessions to collect the email addresses of young men and women from across Canada. He was in a big city now, and he wanted to meet everyone around him. Aden might not have known the meaning of the word *schmoozing*, but he had an innate ability for it, smiling broadly, shaking hands and repeating his story. "So, you're a global citizen," one young woman said to him with admiration.

In the assembly's longer breaks, the students were like high school students on their first bus trip to Ottawa. They explored the blocks around the hotel, soaking in their first real views of the buildings and monuments of the country's capital. At night, Aden and Mohamed stared at the glow of the eternal flame on Parliament Hill. In daylight, Halima, Marwo and Abdi posed for pictures in front of the Peace Tower and pointed across the river to Quebec. Halima, already immersed in her course in Canadian studies, wanted to know the names of the people represented by the statues, wanted to find the statue of the first prime minister of Canada, Sir John A. Macdonald, which she was certain had to be around somewhere.

Abdi stands on Parliament Hill gazing across the river at Quebec.

———

On the last evening of the conference, I invited Halima and Marwo out to dinner. Over the weekend I had been stunned to watch how easily they moved through their new world. At the airport in Toronto, Marwo had looked miserable and anxious, but she now seemed like the calm young woman I had met in the camp, a young woman happy to go with the flow of her more exuberant friends. The last time I had seen Halima in Halifax, she had been in Canada four days and had shut down, overwhelmed by all the differences in the world around her. "Everything was so new then," she said now by way of explanation. She laughed as she fearlessly crossed the Ottawa streets on red lights in her green headscarf, jean jacket and long skirt. It had been a warm day for Ottawa in November, but now there was a sharp night wind from the river. "It's so cold," they both said. I said it wasn't quite winter weather yet. "It's not winter yet?" a surprised Marwo asked.

I spotted a Thai restaurant where there would be rice and noodles that they would eat, so we headed inside. They liked the shrimp-flavoured chips the waitress brought us and the pad thai but didn't know what to make of the vegetable spring rolls. Halima wanted the chicken from the fried rice because she was craving chicken and trying to gain weight. Marwo avoided the chicken because it wasn't halal. Throughout the meal they talked about their new friends and where they might go over the Christmas break when their dormitories were empty. Halima said she had met the family of her Halifax friend Sarah several times and might stay there, or she might stay with a Somali family she had met in Halifax. Marwo said she might stay with Serina, who was in charge of her local WUSC committee, or she might stay with a Somali family she had met in Victoria.

I photographed Marwo, who sat across the table from me and showed Halima the image on the camera screen, saying it was a good picture. "It is pretty," Halima said. Then she looked across at Marwo, who was smiling, and said, "prettier than you are." I gasped a little and Halima said that she was teasing, that friends in the camp teased each other that way all the time. She said that for more than two months she hadn't been able to talk to anyone that way, so all that teasing had been building up inside her. She had to take advantage of having a friend in front of her now. I asked Halima if she could tease Sarah, and she said she really liked Sarah but she couldn't tease her in the same way.

In her Mississauga townhouse, Muno was scared of the coming winter. She had been finding it cold since September, and people kept warning her that it would only get colder. The weather was just another thing keeping her from leaving her apartment unless she had to go out.

The MaGrath Valley Residence at the University of Toronto's Mississauga campus looks more suburban enclave than university residence, a place someone seeking quiet might choose. The residence was mainly populated with graduate students who had already shown they took their studies seriously. In August, when other Dadaab students, who had moved into single rooms or crowded houses and huge residence buildings, heard about Muno's living arrangements, they envied her privacy.

Once classes started, though, the townhouse that had seemed grand and splendidly private seemed isolating. Other Dadaab students were forced to socialize, but Muno was not. It took her fifteen minutes to walk to most of her classes or to go to the cafeteria where she had a meal plan, where she would eat a sandwich before walking back to her apartment alone.

The isolated setting mirrored Muno's loneliness. Zaynab and Abdinoor, who had met her at the airport, checked in on her often, but they were busy with their classes now. Muno had not made any "Canadian friends" at university, and she berated herself for having lost her ability to be social. Back in the camp, she had found it easy to talk to people of different nationalities. In the TOEFL classes she had talked to Dilalesa a lot. But here she found herself incapable of making conversations with strangers. At the beginning of the term, Zaynab had introduced her to several Arab students. Muno, confused over who was who and by whether she'd met the person before, chose to avoid conversations rather than face the embarrassment of not remembering someone she'd already met. She had made friends with some Somali young women who were in her class, but they were young women who had lived in Canada most of their lives. Some of them didn't even cover themselves. That didn't bother Muno—she didn't believe it was her place to judge others—but she knew she would never be like them. "I came here when I was twenty," she said. "I'm going to do what I have done all my life. I cannot imagine doing without the hijab. I've been wearing it since I was five." And although her father was an imam, she said she did not feel pressure from him. "My father is religious and strict, very strict. But then, my father is not here now. I still want to keep doing what I did in his prayer house."

Books had always provided an escape for Muno, a portal to worlds beyond the refugee camp. She had marvelled at the cleverness of Sherlock Holmes and cried over the betrayal of a boy in Kabul. She found that books she'd read helped her with some of the strange details of North American life. If it had not been for a book, she would have been horrified when someone handed her a halal hot dog at a barbecue during an orientation week for Muslim students. She might have wondered why someone would suggest she eat dog meat. But back in the camp she'd read a book call *Coming to Birth,* in which a mother bought a hot dog for her child. Muno had looked up *hot dog* in the dictionary and learned a hot dog was beef, not dog.

But books had done nothing to prepare her emotionally for the upheavals in her life. Characters in books were strong and coped with all sorts of disasters. She didn't feel anything like them. She just felt lonely, unable to find her emotional footing and unsure of how her own story would unfold. Before she left the camp, someone had loaned her a book about a courageous young Christian woman who left a good home to do missionary work, but Muno couldn't identify with the main character: "Hers is a more courageous story because she leaves her family and she faces problems because she wants to help. She had to be strong. Maybe I wouldn't have left my family if I didn't need to study."

She had given up reading and rereading every book she could get her hands on. Several books she had started sat unfinished in her room. Now that she had university coursework, she just didn't have the time. And the courses were filling some of that need she had in the camp for intellectual engagement. She had chosen a wide range of courses in the humanities—from religious studies to modern literature. Her Arabic class was going well, but she felt she was struggling in political science, largely because she had trouble understanding the professor. Sometimes she felt like an outsider when the professor cracked jokes that everyone seemed to find funny except her. On one test, fifteen of the twenty questions had been based on the textbook, and she'd been able to answer them, but when it came to the five questions based on the lectures, she felt lost. Even so, she scored 76 per cent.

It was her English course in modern fiction that reminded her why she had come to Canada. She had never heard of the books on the list: James Joyce's *Dubliners,* Virginia Woolf's *Mrs. Dalloway* and Franz Kafka's *Metamorphosis.* But she found her literature professor funny, and his description of *Metamorphosis* appealed to her sense of humour. "It is about somebody who just all of a sudden in one morning becomes a cockroach," she said. "I love that."

Sometimes Muno underestimated her own resilience and resourcefulness, underestimated how her tolerance of others helped her face fearful situations. In late November, we invited her to our house for dinner so she and my daughter could spend some time talking more about the books in their university English programs. I had offered to take Muno and Jane out to dinner because our dog would be home and I knew dogs were *haram* to her. No one in Dadaab kept dogs. Dogs were something people elsewhere used to guard property. None of the students could believe how many dogs there were in Canada. They found it impossible to understand why people would keep dogs in their homes at all. When Halima passed a dog on the street, she would grab the arm of the person beside her and cower. Abdirizak tried not to show his fear, but he said that inside he was "just as scared as the girls."

Muno, however, found the idea of eating in a restaurant where there were strange men present as unsettling as dogs in people's homes. Besides, she said, she had to learn sometime to adapt to the presence of dogs in homes, and she accepted the dinner invitation.

When I pulled into our driveway with Muno, Jane was just taking our schnauzer, Schmidt, for a walk. Jane held onto Schmidt's leash, pulling him away from Muno. But Schmidt was a curious dog who liked to welcome visitors by jumping on them, a bad habit we had never succeeded in correcting. Jane held tight while Schmidt barked and wagged his tail. "I thought they only barked when they were angry," Muno said after I pointed out the wagging tail.

Muno settled on a couch to wait for the dog's return. She said she was such a coward in the camp she had even been afraid of the prowling, skinny cats. When Jane returned with Schmidt, she and I each sat on either side of Muno to keep Schmidt away from her. As

Schmidt tried to reach her, Muno laughed and squealed and said, "I'm such a coward." The dog grew frustrated that he couldn't give Muno a proper welcome and finally made a dash around Jane and up the back of the couch to Muno. Muno admitted that he was clever to figure out the route.

Eventually, Schmidt calmed down and Muno relaxed, staring at the dog as much as he stared at her. Muno wanted to know why the dog panted, how we trained him not to bite, said she had never known that dogs had so much fur. When she went upstairs to pray, we kept Schmidt downstairs. Muno had brought a clean set of clothing with her to wear for her prayer. When she was finished, she came downstairs in her first set of clothing and moved easily around the dog. When she and Jane retreated to Jane's basement room to look at books, it was Schmidt who was allowed to follow, not me, a prying parent. By the end of the evening, Muno went home with one small step of adaptation accomplished. She had met a dog, and she had done it without going against any of her beliefs. "He is cute," she finally said.

During a visit to our family home in November,
Muno gets acquainted with our dog, Schmidt.

PART THREE

A Long Winter of Adjustment

CHAPTER FIVE

Where the Heart Is

THEY GATHERED IN A TIM HORTONS coffee shop on Bloor Street near the University of Toronto, four young men in their winter coats. By now they were well used to the orderly lines at Tim Hortons and knew exactly what they wanted to order: large French vanilla cappuccinos. With its sugar and spices, French vanilla cappuccino was their beverage of choice because it tasted "just like Somali tea."

Abdirizak and Aden had come from the Dadaab camps the previous summer, while the other two, Ibrahim and Abdinoor, had come the year before. Word of a coffee at Tim Hortons that tasted like Somali tea was one of the hundreds of bits of information handed down from the students of one year to the students who followed.

It was January 5, 2009, and the second term of the university year was just beginning. Across Canada the new Dadaab students were finishing the first break they'd had in their studies. While Marwo and Halima had both considered spending the holidays with new Canadian friends, they had spent most of the break with Somali families in their cities instead. Christmas was a strange new holiday; the familiarity of Somali customs was comforting. Before leaving the camp, Mohamed had asked one of his relatives to find out if he had any other relatives in Canada. When he learned he had cousins in Windsor, Ontario, who had left Somalia before the civil war, he phoned them. The family invited him to spend the break at their home in Windsor, so Mohamed took a bus to see them. They were total strangers in one sense, family in another. Although the students didn't like to talk about the clan system that had torn their country apart and, in some cases, destroyed their families, the connection Mohamed made to his relatives showed what the centuries-old clan system had originally been intended for: to protect nomads in the desert. Those who were suffering or had been abused could turn to their clan for help. Mohamed had done what any nomadic ancestor of his would have done when alone and in need: he had sought out clan family members who would offer shelter.

The students who had no relatives to visit or who lived in cities with no other Somalis had camped with their friends from Dadaab. Aden had flown all the way from Brandon to Toronto for the break. The other young men were impressed that Aden's WUSC committee had bought him his airplane ticket. But with no one to visit in Brandon and his residence closed, he needed somewhere to stay, and the trip provided the solution.

Abdirizak stayed alone in his room in Whitney Hall over the break. On the University of Toronto campus, he was beginning to meet students who weren't Somali, but he had not made any Canadian friends yet. His reserve made it hard for him to initiate conversations. "It depends on your personality. What I have come to know about myself is I like to talk a little bit more to people I know than people I do not know. When people meet you, they just start talking. I just kind of sit."

He was, however, starting to feel more comfortable in Toronto, now that he knew how to function in the city. He was a man who did not like to feel dependent. He didn't like it much that he could not go on the subway alone when he first arrived: "I didn't know where I was headed or where I was coming from." Now he could "go anywhere." He dismissed the early adjustments as normal. In his frank way he told me, "I am sure when you were in Ifo, it was clear you were new to the place."

He still found some of the customs in Canada strange, even offensive. And he wasn't afraid to say so. When he and the others were leaving our house after dinner one night, I gave each of them leftover goat meat wrapped in foil to take back to their residences. Later, Mohamed politely told me that he had enjoyed the leftovers that same evening. The package, he said, "did not last the night." But Abdirizak, holding the foil package in his hand, immediately asked me, without the trace of a smile on his face, why I was giving it to him. He said that in his culture, when there was a feast where neighbours and friends were invited, any remaining food would be given to women or children who were not invited, or to the poor or even to the goats, but not to the invited guests. When I explained to him that in Canada we often gave leftovers to guests, especially to university students on a tight budget, he understood that I had not insulted him.

He did enjoy the stories my husband, Peter, told at the dinner table because they reminded him of his uncle, who was a great storyteller. Abdirizak wished he had a record of all the stories his uncle had told him. "There is a saying that you never know the value of the water until the tap runs dry."

Abdirizak had not put any photos in the frames his WUSC committee had left in the room. To him, his identity was no clearer than when he'd first arrived. He knew he was a permanent resident, but he still felt more like a refugee than a Canadian because his connection to Somalia was stronger than his connection to Canada. When I mentioned a story in the news about young Somali-American men leaving Minnesota to return to the fight in Somalia, he claimed the stories were exaggerated, dismissing the media as he often did for their lack of understanding of issues in Somalia. But as long as the collapse of the social order in Somalia continued to destroy people's lives, he, too, would feel an emotional pull to the country.

Even in his classes at the university, the poor country Abdirizak had come from was not far from his thoughts. He was learning that good governance and natural resources were two elements that contributed to a country's prosperity. In the past, bananas had been the main export from Somalia. Now, he joked darkly, it was guns. The good governance that could bring good management to Somalia's natural resources again was still far off. In the years since the civil war, all attempts to establish a national government had failed. Abdirizak viewed any new attempt "with two eyes: one of hope and one of despair."

His disdain for the media deepened with the extensive coverage of pirates wreaking havoc off the coast of Somalia. He said reporters paid little attention to why fishermen had turned to piracy after their harvests had been repeatedly stolen by fishermen in foreign vessels who were taking advantage of the lack of government in the country. Worse, the media ignored the real problems of Somalia and the generation of his peers who had grown up as the "most disadvantaged generation in the world. No education. Not a glimpse of hope. That's why those of us who are able, just a few, who get a chance like we did, that's why we feel overburdened by the problems the country has right now."

That sense of responsibility was why it was hard for him to decide where his life would take him. He wanted to have a life in Canada, but he felt a responsibility to Somalia, especially since he didn't know where his father was or whether he was alive or dead. "Any sane man who is Somali and says he will make a life here is telling you a lie. They may stay here, but that is not where their heart is."

Outside Tim Hortons, Abdirizak threw a loonie to a man sitting on the sidewalk. Abdirizak gave change to the homeless whenever he had some handy. He couldn't understand why in a country as developed as Canada the government didn't make the homeless go to school so they could work. Now that he felt a little settled in his routine, he was starting to notice more about the country he had come to. He had watched the two elections in the fall—one in the United States and one in Canada—and remarked on the differences he saw between them: "In the United States, politics rule the country, but in Canada nobody cares." Abdirizak could tell you the ins and outs of the politics of Somalia—a country he hadn't lived in for years—so it came as a surprise to him that during the federal election in Canada none of the students around him talked about the issues or the leaders. He had even met students who didn't know who the prime minister was.

In the quiet months of winter, others were forming their first impressions of Canada. Canadians, several students discovered, were surprisingly sociable and helpful. "If you don't know something," Halima said, "or you get lost on the street and even if it's your first time and you ask somebody, that person sincerely tells you whatever you want." Halima recalled one time when she was hurrying to catch a bus in downtown Halifax: "I was far from the lights and I crossed the road and there was this guy and he stopped the cars. He was kind to stop the other cars and let me get across. I don't think that would have happened in Nairobi."

Showing gratitude for all the help they had received was sometimes another matter. Some of the Somali students who had worked with aid agencies had come to Canada with the habit of saying "thank you." But it was not a phrase natural to their culture, where those who had money and food gave them and those who were in need took them. It was a cultural difference that sometimes left those who helped them wondering if their gestures had been appreciated.

According to Abdi, gratitude in the Somali culture was not recognized with direct thanks but by acknowledging the deed to others. When you give, he said, "you will find out that that person is telling another person about your goodness. So Debi would give me something. I would tell someone that Debi is the best person, but I would not say thank you." When the students talked about Canadians being welcoming and friendly, in their own way, they were showing gratitude for the acts of kindness they had received.

While they applauded the friendliness in Canada, they did not always feel comfortable with the openness they encountered. Abdi was bothered by the way complete strangers at bus stops would start asking him personal questions about where he was from and what he did. Others were bothered by the physically demonstrative way men and women acted in public and by the way women showed their bodies.

As a young woman in a confined and, for the most part, homogenous society, Halima had known not to touch a male who was not a relative or to walk too closely beside him, and she was always fully covered in his presence. The rules had been clear in the camps. In Canada, women who dressed in summer clothing and touched their boyfriends made her cringe, literally. In Kenya, people had told her there would be "naked" women on the streets of Canada, but she never believed it until she saw a nearly naked one herself, "a woman wearing just brassiere and shorts and she was standing close to a man, and once my eyes saw that I just turned away. I couldn't look at that. I was shocked. I have never seen such a thing. Anyway, it's life here and I have to accept it. But I don't like it."

What disturbed Hussein even more was seeing Somali girls who had grown up in Canada wearing pants and sometimes not even covering their heads. The hijab, he said, "is something God said you must do, and when God says you must do this, it is a must. There are no excuses. There are no exceptions. Women were told they should wear hijab, they should cover their heads, they should cover their bodies. And all that is to avoid temptation from men, so when I see a Somali lady who is not covered, who is not fully covered, I just feel let down. But I don't feel like telling them this is wrong or this is right."

Some were startled at the difference in attitudes toward community and came to think of Canadians as more individualistic than Somalis. They met young people at university who had moved away from their parents before they were married and others who appeared to feel no responsibility for their elders. In the camp, Halima said, children and young people never talked back to their parents, and no one left the aged to fend for themselves. "I was so surprised to see old people—when I went to the mall—who couldn't even walk properly and didn't have anyone to take care of them. Generally people here are individualistic. That's very common here. Nobody cares for whomever."

Dilalesa had come to Canada believing he'd find a country of fairness and tolerance. At the University of Saskatchewan, he read about the history of Aboriginal peoples in North America in a textbook, the history of people with a spirituality similar to his own in its connection to the earth. On the streets of downtown Saskatoon, he witnessed the reality of the homeless Aboriginals he encountered. "Some people in Africa are better off than these people," he said. "These people's life is a piece of shit and they smoke and young boys and girls, they are just in the bus terminal smoking and walking around, wandering in the city. You know Canada is one of the most peaceful countries in the world and one of the most generous countries in the world, but when you come to Canada and you see what is happening here, then you may tend to give less credit to this country."

Before arriving, all the students had feared the cold weather of winter. Walking through air that felt like ice was beyond the comprehension of those who had lived their whole lives with the African heat. But of all their fears, winter turned out to be the one that melted away the quickest. In Toronto, snow started at the beginning of December and continued through the month. If things kept up that way, climatologists said in January, the city would break the seventy-year record for snowfall.

The four young men walking through the streets of Toronto that day seemed nonplussed. To them, winter was a math problem with clear answers: add clothes for outside; subtract them when indoors. With all the studying they had ahead of them, hibernation through the long, dark months would be easy. Abdirizak said "people over-exaggerate. When the real winter comes it feels like, oh, this is snow and you touch it, and it's okay."

In London, Abdi was bothered more by the weight of winter clothing and boots than by the cold. Sometimes he wouldn't take the trouble to put on boots or even socks and shoes but would dash the short distance to his cafeteria in his sandals. Students who had grown up with the cold would laugh at his boldness. In the cold prairie city of Saskatoon, Dilalesa and Abdikadar found they adjusted to temperatures as low as minus 45 degrees Celsius. "We were assuming that you could not even leave your home," Abdikadar said. "But when it came, winter was not so bad. It took minutes to dress well, although the worse problem was when you were going to school in the morning. You need to wake up at seven and then it's dark and very cold." Dilalesa, who had said he'd slept for a week in Nairobi when it was 10 degrees Celsius, found that he got used to winter after the first month. In December, his nose was dry and he experienced nosebleeds for the first time, but "apart from the nose, there was nothing much that terrifying." Both Abdikadar and Dilalesa tried skating and tobogganing and agreed, "Sliding was more fun."

On the west coast, Marwo and Siyad had been told they would have the easiest winters because it hardly snowed at all in Victoria or Vancouver. So they were surprised by the unusually heavy snowfalls in December, weren't prepared, as Marwo said, "to see everything white." Siyad stayed in his room, away from the snow as much as possible, but one night a friend urged him to go out. He slid around on the snowy fields and decided he liked the stuff.

Two of the young women admitted that winter was a terrible season. In Mississauga, Muno hated the cold and the ice she fell on repeatedly. "I wish this winter would go away," she said. Winter became another excuse to stay in her apartment with the windows shut. In Halifax, Halima got tired of everyone asking her what she thought of snow. She hated the snow after the novelty of the first snowfall wore off, and hated the cold. She couldn't understand why any of the others would choose to play outdoors at all.

Paula Barry had witnessed many international students' first Canadian winters. She was worried that Halima's desire to hibernate had gone too far: "There was one week when it was frigidly cold and she didn't leave her house for four days. I was like, 'Halima, you can't do that, you have to go outside.' So that's a huge adjustment, although I have to say she doesn't complain much."

On their winter walk through Toronto, the four young men passed the old buildings of the University of Toronto and turned south on Spadina Avenue. Along the way, Aden snapped pictures with his new camera. The young man from Hagadera who had dreamed of owning a camera now had one, thanks to his WUSC committee, and he used it constantly. He held it at all angles, snapping shots left and right, up and down: shots of the sky, friends, the CN Tower, whatever caught his fancy. They were pictures he would show back home in Brandon, evidence that he was fulfilling his hobby of travelling. But he had other pictures on his camera that showed his connection to his new home. There was one of a blond woman named Brandy Robertson who worked at the university and volunteered on his WUSC committee. She had been particularly helpful, he said, in getting him settled in.

Aden's natural curiosity and friendliness had helped him bounce back from his initial loneliness. He had an ability to take joy in the things that came his way and to shrug off things that weren't happening as he'd hoped—it was how he had carved out a life for himself in the camps. Even though there were no other Somalis in Brandon, no friends like the ones he walked beside now, he had found African students who understood where he came from and Iraqi friends who understood his faith.

There was a detail beyond the winter coat and the camera that looked odd about Aden that day. It was his cellphone, or rather, the absence of a cellphone. In Hagadera, he was always carrying his cellphone in his hand or holding it up to his ear. He relied on his phone with its Jamaican "bob" ring to keep him in constant touch with his friends and his family. But after Aden had returned to Brandon from the annual assembly in Ottawa, he'd received a bill for $182. He hadn't realized that the calls he was making and receiving in another city involved long-distance charges. "If you are not careful and have no knowledge on how it goes, you are screwed." He knew he had to find a way out of a two-year plan with a cancellation fee. He told the company he was new to Canada and didn't have the money. He made them a deal: he would return the phone, which was practically new, and he would pay the bill. After that he decided he didn't need a phone in Canada. He began to rely on calling cards and his computer for all his communications.

Online, however, Aden had taken on a somewhat chameleon-like character, changing his name several times. In January, his name on Facebook had become Jimmy Romeo Love. He said he chose the name for fun and to confuse people. It worked. Abdirizak said he couldn't figure out who "Jimmy" was when he first came across the name. Aden laughed and said he'd taken his picture down from his site to confuse people more. Joking on Facebook was common. Some of the young men showed their status as "in a relationship" or "married" even when they were not.

I learned from some of the students that they used email as a way of staying in touch with beloved ones left behind. They would talk to me about those relationships only anonymously.

In the camps, young people often told each other how they felt, careful always to make sure they kept their attachments secret. It would not do for their affection to become public in the closed world of the camp, where little escaped the gossips. A young woman's reputation was at stake—the only thing she possessed in the camps was her virtue. Couples could not express their love physically without great dishonour to the young woman and her family. It was up to the young woman to maintain the morality of the community. It was up to a young man to control his desires, even if it meant fasting to strengthen his resolve. Young couples could not marry, not without their parents' permission and, in the case of the students hoping to go to universities abroad, not without risking a scholarship available only to the single. So words were all they had then. And emailing was all they could do now.

Some had cut off their relationships before leaving, believing it was the kinder thing to do. Unless they were married before leaving, there was no way they could bring their beloved ones to Canada. But that didn't stop them from searching online for any bits of news.

Online social networking served another purpose: staying connected to what was happening back in the camps, where families still lived, through sites for Hagadera or Ifo. UNHCR reported that in January 2009, the population of the three camps of Dadaab had reached 244,217, almost 40,000 more people than had been there when the students left. The problems in Dadaab were not going away; they were getting worse. None of the students could deny that they were lucky, and that made them feel worse for those left behind. On the Ifo site, Abdi started a discussion board to continue the advocacy work he'd done in the camp. The topic: "What is your stand on FGM? How has the fight against it been successful in Ifo camp?" It was mostly young men who wrote on the board, mostly from North American homes and mostly against the practice. They suggested that young women take part in the discussion, but despite the invitation, throughout the winter, no women did.

That was not surprising. Back in the camps, young women had seldom discussed FGM publicly. One told me about a session where the topic was debated and where whenever young women spoke against the practice, young men shouted them down and called them feminists.

Sometimes, on Facebook, the students made political statements, but more often than not they used the site, as most students do, as a distraction from their studies when they sat alone in their rooms on dark winter evenings. The quizzes they took added up to an online identity search: the "full personality evaluation quiz," the "What is the first letter of the person you will marry?" quiz, the "How Somali are you, REALLY!!" quiz, the "Where should you live?" quiz and the "What were you born to do?" quiz.

The two young men in Saskatoon—Dilalesa and Abdikadar—shied away from posting regularly on Facebook and from contact with the others. On top of their studies, they were both now working part-time as stockroom employees. And Muno had not joined Facebook at all. She was content to communicate with those who knew her email address.

As Ibrahim led the three students down Spadina Avenue, one of them would stop from time to time to look at two-for-$10 shirts on racks outside the stores, although Ibrahim had already told them about Honest Ed's, the source of all things cheap in downtown Toronto. Abdirizak was feeling the cold. He had gone shopping on his own and paid more than $100 for his stylish black nylon coat before discovering it did little to guard him from the winter winds. He didn't want to spend more money to get another coat, so he wore layers underneath it.

The sun that day took the edge off the January cold. Ibrahim and Aden walked bare-headed down Spadina Avenue past the Chinese fruit markets and grocery stores before turning west on Dundas Street. The north side of the street was lined with shops offering hair-cuts for as low as $5. Abdirizak had learned about the street from Ibrahim, who had learned about it from Omar, the first of the Dadaab students to settle in Toronto. Today, they'd all brought Aden here so he could get a cheap haircut before going back to Brandon, where he had to pay $19 for the same service. They stopped at one $5 hair-cut place. Inside, the seats were filled with young Asian males. A woman wielding an electric shaver above one young man's head said it would be at least a half-hour wait, so they continued on.

Farther along the street, they found a shop with neon green walls and a sign offering cuts from $6. The shelves in the shop were lined with hair products and the stations with swivelling chairs. All that was lacking were customers. The lone Asian stylist—a woman with long, straight hair and an excess of pink lipstick and black eyebrow liner—said unenthusiastically that she could cut Aden's hair. The young men consulted with each other and decided that the stylist should shave Aden's hair "a one on the sides with a two on top."

With the shaver set at one, the stylist sheared off most of the hair on the side of Aden's head. Sitting in the chair, watching himself in the mirror, Aden looked like an actor in an opening scene of a movie about marines, while the stern-faced stylist played the role of the uncaring drill sergeant. When a freshly shorn Aden stood up, Ibrahim said he thought the cut could have been better, but Aden seemed happy with the results. He was ready to go back to Brandon, knowing it would be a long time before he needed another $19 cut.

As they approached the middle of winter and the halfway mark of their first year in Canada, the students moved through the motions of their Canadian days with greater confidence, managing bus routes and bank accounts, running washing machines and their own lives without the support of family and friends they had back in the camp, retreating to their rooms and their computers when they'd had too much. But for some, at night, in their sleep, feelings of limbo often caught them off guard. In their minds and during their days, they were in Canada; in their hearts and at night, they were at home.

In Vancouver, Siyad dreamed of hanging out with his friends on Stress Corner in Hagadera camp. On the quiet Scarborough campus, Mohamed sometimes woke up feeling out of place. "Sometimes you wake up in the middle of the night and you say, no, I can't believe I am here." Dreams of life in Dadaab left Mohamed more frustrated than sad: "I don't feel unhappy or anything. I just say, no, that was a long time ago. It was all those things that happened before. Why are you not forgetting about it?"

It wasn't that Mohamed didn't miss his family or worry about them back in the camp. He didn't phone home as much as he used to, now that he was busy with school and his part-time job at the university. But he did call to check up on his mother from time to time, and once a month he sent her $100 through the Dahabshiil in Scarborough, a money transfer business that had blossomed after the post-9/11 closure of al-Barakat. All that his mother had to do was go to the shop in Dagahaley and say who she was and who had sent her the money, and she had the cash to help her cover the rising costs in the camp. Across the country, students had managed to find the easiest way to send money home. In the larger cities they could use the Dahabshiil. In smaller cities they could use Western Union to send money to someone they trusted in Nairobi, who would get it to their families in the camps.

Mohamed worked at blending into his new life while holding onto his old one. When the male students in his townhouse dormitory stared at the traditional *ma'awis* he wore around the house, he explained it was part of his culture. But he never wore it outside, where people might point at a man in a skirt. He used a spoon when he ate with other people rather than his hands. He still preferred Somali meals, but he'd tried new foods like Jamaican patties and halal hot dogs. He adjusted his prayers to his schedule of work and classes, but he used the prayer room on campus to stick as closely as he could to the required prayer times.

In his second term, Mohamed was taking economics, and environmental pollution as an elective, and starting calculus again, certain that this time he'd crack it. On Facebook he announced that he wanted to kill calculus.

Mohamed didn't like the dreams that pulled him back to the camp and tore him away from his new life. He believed that all the terrible things that had happened to him had led him to a university in Canada: "If there had not been that war, maybe I would have always been in the bush looking after animals. Dadaab's a camp, but I got a good education there and now it's through my education here that I'm getting to know other people and getting to know the world better. It was a blessing for me in disguise, a blessing the hard way."

On the other side of Toronto, in Mississauga, Muno's dreams reminded her of just how lonely she still was when she woke up every morning: "The first two months I was always dreaming about home every night. It was good. I was happy in my sleep and once I woke up and found myself in my room it was bad. I told my sister: I'm not dreaming of you anymore." But now, in the winter, her dreams had started again. "The whole of this week I dreamed about them every night. This morning I woke up hugging my mom. I tried to go back to sleep. When I wake up, I become disappointed."

Her classes, especially modern fiction, kept her mind occupied through the winter. She was reading Franz Kafka's *Metamorphosis* and was struggling with the topic she had chosen for her essay, a question about what the book had to say about modern alienation. Muno had so many ideas on the topic she didn't know where to begin. She was starting to believe that it wasn't her own immersion in Western culture that was alienating, but Western culture itself: "I think even someone staying in Western culture can get alienated because people get lonely here and there isn't much interaction. We don't usually get alienated back home."

The reading that inspired her was sophisticated and eclectic. She described *White Noise* by Don DeLillo as the funniest book she had ever read, Khaled Hosseini's *A Thousand Splendid Suns* as one of the saddest. She liked to talk about the authors she was discovering, even if they had beliefs opposed to her own. When she told her Hagadera friend, Abdinoor, a student of science, about Virginia Woolf, who had killed herself by walking into a river with stones in her pockets, and Ernest Hemingway, who had shot himself, he said, "You keep on learning this and you're going to commit suicide." Books had always made her feel a little different from her friends. But when she read about other lives she came to understand them: "Woolf says there's no God. There's nothing to believe in, but even then you have to be good just for the sake of being good and that gives more hope than anything else."

She liked to reflect on something Mahatma Ghandi once said: "I want the cultures of all the lands to be blown around my house as freely as possible. But I refuse to be blown off my feet by any." Muno had her own version: "If I lose my Somali identity or my Muslim identity or my African identity, I don't believe I can understand Western culture. If I can keep my identity, I can look at the other things from other cultures and understand them."

———

175

In February, I had lunch with Abdi in TG's Addis Ababa Restaurant in downtown London, Ontario. The Ethiopian restaurant with its gold-coloured walls made Abdi feel like he was back in Africa. The Ethiopian injera that came with our meal was thicker and spongier than the Somali version, but it was African, and the closest thing to *anjera* he'd had since leaving the camp.

The sun poured in on Abdi and me at our table by the window, creating an illusion of African warmth. We were the only two customers left in the restaurant, but the waitress didn't seem bothered by how long we lingered over our lunch. We talked about Somali politics. Abdi had become more hopeful after the Ethiopian troops pulled out of Somalia in January and an agreement for a unity government was reached in Djibouti. The agreement called for increasing the size of Parliament to include members of the Union of Islamic Courts who had controlled Mogadishu before the invasion, with members of the transitional government, whom the Ethiopians had gone in to support. In early February, thousands cheered in the streets of Mogadishu when a moderate Islamist cleric, Sheikh Sharif Ahmed, was selected in Djibouti as the country's new president. But, as expected, the militant wing of the Islamists, al-Shabab, which had built up support during the presence of the Ethiopian troops and taken control of much of the south of the country, continued fighting against the compromise. Despite the worries over al-Shabab, Abdi felt hopeful that this time peace could be forged out of the chaos. He believed that the elders of the various clans, who supported peace, would rein in the youth of al-Shabab. He saw another hopeful sign in the actions of President Ahmed, who had shown that the country could rise above the issue of clan. The president, who was from the Hawiye clan that had brought down the government of Siad Barre, had selected as prime minister Omar Abdirashid Ali Sharmarke, who was from Barre's Darod clan. "Maybe these two guys can bring something," Abdi said.

We also talked about religion and, more specifically, about how the laws of Islam fit into the laws of Canada. He said that even though according to Islam men were required to marry four women if they could afford to take care of them equally, the religion also required men to respect the laws of the country they were in, "to live in harmony with other people."

Abdi was always open to discussions about the inequalities toward women in Somali culture, inequalities that led to domestic violence and early, sometimes forced, marriages. In fact, Abdi preferred talking about social issues, politics and religion to talking about anything personal. He did admit that he found the total commitment he had to make to school hard. There was always something he had to read or an exam coming up, so that he had little opportunity for leisure. He missed the times he had had in the camp when he could meet friends. But he chose to describe the loneliness of student life through someone else's story. He said he was "seeing a girl on Facebook" who was a Sudanese-sponsored student at another university. "She was saying student life is hell. She says she misses going out with her friends in Nairobi. She says she cannot adapt to this lifestyle."

When I drove Abdi back to his residence, the sun had already dropped behind the buildings of downtown London. The winter afternoon light now had a depressing, flat quality that made the sky and city a dull grey. The air had become damp and chilling. But Abdi said he liked the weather in London. He preferred it to the heat and the dust of Ifo. "The dust of Ifo." He said the phrase with vehemence.

Abdi knew his way around the streets of London and guided me to a store where he wanted to buy a calling card. Back at his residence he would stay in for the evening and study. But before that, before he opened the textbooks again on another lonely winter's night, he wanted to call home. Talking to those who knew him, who shared so much of his past, would give him the strength he needed to carry on in this world.

CHAPTER SIX

Girls Are Not Equal

On a Saturday morning in mid-winter, Halima sat at her white desk in Birch 5 dressed in a red and white cotton African dress and a matching scarf that loosely covered her hair. Her bare feet didn't reach the floor. As she watched video clips of the new Somali president on her computer, she rested one foot against the pull of the desk's bottom drawer.

The room around her at Mount Saint Vincent had evolved since the night the WUSC committee had picked her up at the Halifax airport. Above her head, three wrinkled balloons, still partly filled with helium a month after her birthday, hugged the ceiling. On the table next to her bed was a pile of snapshots—some from Canada and some from home—beside a stack of books and the copy of the Qur'an she had placed there shortly after she arrived. Above the table on a bulletin board she'd pinned a yellow lei from an event at the residence around a photograph of her parents from the day she left. On the wall beside the bulletin board she'd stuck a black ribbon for "cutest Hallowe'en costume" from another residence event. Someone had posted a picture on Facebook of Halima bobbing for apples with the red wings of her ladybug costume sticking out behind her, but she had pulled it down. She was nervous about people posting pictures on her site, pictures that could be seen by anyone, although there was nothing inappropriate in the way she was dressed on Hallowe'en. Nothing but some red wings over her proper clothing.

The poster that Sarah had made of Halima's name in Arabic and English hung beside the bed, and the purple teddy bear the students had bought sat on the dressing table surrounded by lotions, creams and makeup—some that had come from Africa and some purchased here.

Outside her closed door, Birch 5 had evolved into a comfortable home for a young woman from another continent. Shortly after Halima moved in, the other rooms had filled up with international students from China, the Caribbean, Finland and Sweden, students more comfortable in a residence where they could cook their own meals. The resident assistant, Loyan, from St. Lucia, ran a tight operation. In the kitchen, she'd labelled all the shelves of the refrigerator and the cupboards with each student's name. On one cupboard door she'd taped a poster to get her message of good order across: "Your Mother Does Not Live Here! No One Else Wants to Deal With Your Mess! Please Clean Up After Yourself." But Loyan also brought a spirit of family to the house through events, birthday parties and organized meals.

Paula Barry describes Birch 5, with its residents from as many as ten cultures, as "a little experiment," with constant misunderstandings and mediation. "It's a really positive environment to be in when you are trying to figure things out." She found the residence that year particularly remarkable: "I've never seen a group like this in Birch 5 before. They have a big potluck every Sunday. And they're really, really tight." Halima had come to depend on Loyan, whom she was beginning to think of as a sister. In her adjustment to her new environment, Halima had suffered from frequent colds and flus in the fall and had turned to Loyan when she was feeling vulnerable.

Halima had midterms the next week in biology and chemistry,

and she was supposed to be studying. She had been planning to go to the library to study with a friend, a young Somali woman named Mariam who had grown up in Canada, but she was two chapters behind in her biology textbook and had to catch up. When her sister called to give her news of progress in Somali politics, Halima put aside her book and went online to find the video of a meeting in Djibouti where the new president spoke about the unity parliament that he hoped would finally bring stability to the country.

Peace in Somali was not just a wishful fantasy for Halima, a mere matter of ethnic pride. Her concerns were far more concrete and personal. She had another sister, a married woman, who had left Dadaab and now lived in Mogadishu. The constant escalation of violence in the Somali capital left her sister in constant danger. And that violence also put more pressure on her family in the camp, as the number of refugees increased. More than ever, Halima was worried about her father. His condition had worsened in the months since she'd seen him; his diabetes had left him unable to walk. She felt panicked at the thought she might never see him again and tried to get her head around the finances and the logistics of a trip back to Dadaab in the summer or during the following winter break. She wanted to record her father's stories from his long life while she still could and, like Abdirizak, she regretted she hadn't taken the time to write them down before she'd left home.

Her concern for her father was also forcing her to reassess her program at the university. She was considering the possibility that she might have to transfer away from the Mount. In the camp, when she'd allowed herself to dream, she had seen herself as a doctor, and in August, she'd arrived in Halifax keen to study biochemistry. A degree in biochemistry would be a first step to her dream. But everyone told her how many years a degree in medicine would take, and she knew there was no way she could study that many years before she had to earn a living and found a way to help her family. And she no longer believed that an undergraduate degree in biochemistry alone would be enough to guarantee her a decent job. She had decided that a degree in nursing was the answer. She could transfer to Dalhousie University in Halifax, if she could get in there, or she could try to go to Alberta, where there were programs and perhaps a wider range of jobs available once she'd completed a degree in nursing. At the annual assembly in Ottawa she had talked to students from the west, and she'd come to think that moving there, to a city where there were more Somalis, might make her feel more comfortable in Canada.

Paula Barry counselled students from her sunny office in the main administration building. She'd advised Halima not to rule out bio-chemistry and graduate school yet, to talk to all the professors and to keep all her options open. She noticed that Halima, more than the other international students, had an "ability to self-advocate and talk to faculty. Halima was someone willing to do what she needed to do and figure out things for herself."

That Saturday morning, though, Halima was set on nursing. There was an impatient quality to her thinking, a need to make decisions and move on. She was already figuring out how to make the change to the nursing program. Her science courses would count as credits, but her elective in Canadian studies would not. Her first set of marks had been good, an average of B+, but she wasn't happy with them. Now she felt more pressure to get higher marks so she could be competitive when she applied for nursing. This term she felt more settled, ready to work harder.

Paula Barry often witnessed homesickness among the international students she advised; some of them couldn't afford to go home during the five years they were in Canada. She didn't find Halima's home-sickness any worse than others', but she did notice that Halima's concern for her father strongly affected her emotions in the first term: "I think that weighs on her, her dad being older and not being well. So she went through a little period where I would say she was probably feeling quite depressed and overwhelmed."

She started seeing an improvement in Halima when she became friends with Mariam and then, by extension, became close to Mariam's Somali-Canadian family. One evening Loyan had called Paula because

Halima was ill. "She seemed quite sick and I thought it was digestive," Paula said. "I wanted her to drink some Pepto-Bismol, and she did. She was supposed to have gone for dinner, so I had Loyan call Mariam's family and the older women came. Having the community has really changed things for her, and it's a connection to home, and I think that's really helpful."

Paula did worry about Halima's eating habits. Sometimes she'd find Halima in the cafeteria at four in the afternoon eating her first meal of the day, a meal consisting of nothing but french fries. Paula noticed Halima seemed more tired than she had in the fall, so she took her to a doctor, who said Halima was deficient in iron and other vitamins. The doctor talked to Halima about nutrition, but Halima seemed more concerned with putting on weight than with eating healthy foods.

As the Somali president spoke from Djibouti on her computer that Saturday morning, Halima expressed surprise at the women sitting among the men in the audience. She had strong, sometimes confusing and somewhat changing views on how women should behave. She had fought hard for her education and believed that all girls had the right to go to school. News stories that fall of men throwing acid at the faces of schoolgirls in Afghanistan horrified her. "Where is it stated in the Qur'an that no woman should be educated?" she asked. She accepted the prophet Mohammad's teaching that women should stay home if their husbands could do everything for them and there was no need for work, "but if I don't have anybody to take care of me, I have to take care of myself. If a woman is not educated, who is going to take care of her?" Even with an education, though, a woman should behave modestly and look up to men, in her opinion. The women in that audience in Djibouti should have sat apart from the men, she believed. It was what the religion required.

Accepting religion did not mean she accepted what was going on in Somalia. Far from it. She deplored the extremist actions of the Islamist group al-Shabab—not just the violent incidents against women, such as the stoning of the thirteen-year-old girl, but also the

183

erosion of women's freedoms in their daily lives. In the regions of the country al-Shabab now controlled, the insurgent group had prohibited women from walking with men who were not their relatives and had told them they could no longer run businesses. "Women are more educated in Somalia today," Halima said. "Daily life is managed by women. Some men are drugged, some of them have died in the war, so how could you say no women can do business?" At the store in Halifax where Halima bought her calling cards, she often talked to the shopkeeper about Africa: "He said, 'Halima, do you feel happy with Somalia now that they are stoning girls?' I told him, 'No. I really don't.' I don't think that was according to the religion."

During my visit to her room, Halima lowered the volume on her computer so we could look at pictures together. The president's low male voice continued to fill the room as she told stories of her friends and relatives in the shots. "Oh, I miss those guys." She moaned a little over the picture of her and her mother on the day of her departure. "I can't imagine that. It is right outside my compound."

Then Halima looked at the pictures on my camera of the other students across Canada. This had become a routine in my visits with the students. They liked to sit and press the button that brought their friends from Dadaab to life. Photography was one of the first ways I had connected to them. They welcomed having their pictures taken, sometimes directing me to get their whole bodies in the shot as I focused in on a close-up, sometimes asking me to photograph them by fountains or cars or, in Muno's case, shelves of books. After each visit, I would email them the best of their pictures. Some would send a message of thanks back; others would complain that I hadn't included every picture. If I happened to be slow sending the photographs, a couple of them, including Halima, would email to ask where they were. Halima paused at a picture of Marwo on the University of Victoria campus. "I heard they had rabbits there," she said pointing to a well-fed and tame bunny on the grass at Marwo's feet.

Throughout that morning I sensed that Halima was feeling more anxious than the last time I'd seen her, at the annual assembly in

Ottawa. She had asked me to bring her copies of the photographs from the assembly, photos that I had already emailed to her. She flipped hurriedly through the four-by-six glossy shots before stopping at one. "You know this picture caused problems back home," she said. In the photograph she was standing with Aden and Marwo. It was from the first day of the assembly, when they all had been so thrilled to see each other. As the three of them had leaned to get into frame, Aden had touched Halima. Without thinking, she had forwarded my email with all the photographs of the assembly on to her family. To me, the picture of three friends was quite innocent. But to Halima's brother it was not. I asked Halima if her brother was concerned that she was losing her way, but she didn't really answer the question. She mumbled "yah" under her breath and moved on to another photograph. Later, she told me that her family had faith in her but people in the camp believed that young women who went to the West were bound to change and that belief led to vigilance on the part of their families. The three women who had come from Dadaab checked up on each other and warned each other if one of them was not behaving in a totally acceptable manner.

When we went to lunch that day at Cafe Istanbul on Spring Garden Road, Halima wore a grey hijab like the ones she'd worn regularly in Ifo. She seemed to enjoy her chicken kabob, but she acted more reserved than she had when we had eaten together in Ottawa. There she'd been happy to have me photograph her in her pretty green headscarf with tables of diners around her. Here she would not let me take her picture in front of the colourful mural that illustrated scenes of Halifax until there were no other customers—no men—in the restaurant.

In our discussions, Halima forcefully reaffirmed her commitment to her culture's beliefs about women, as though it was me she had to convince of her steadfastness. "Girls are *not* equal," she said. Women, she told me, could never be presidents. It didn't matter if they were capable of being leaders, even more capable than men, they couldn't be presidents. "Of course, I believe it. It is in the religion," she said, sensing my Western skepticism. But hadn't she cheered in Ottawa when I told her polygamy was not legal in Canada? She admitted that she didn't want to have a husband who had other wives but said there was nothing she could do if her husband chose to marry more than one woman. "I am my husband's property."

Halima, dressed in the traditional Dadaab hijab, poses for her picture in an empty Halifax restaurant.

As firm as Halima was in her beliefs, she was open to debate on women and religion. She eagerly welcomed arguments with Paula and her friend Sarah Chan. After Halima went back to studying in her room that Saturday, I met Sarah in a small Greek restaurant in the north end of Halifax where she lived. Sarah is the kind of cosmopolitan Canadian student often attracted to WUSC. She has travelled to Asia and Haiti, and has a profound desire to see more refugees admitted to Canada. Dressed in a tweed jacket that could have been vintage and a blue scarf that looked Asian, she sipped hot chocolate from a diner-style mug and recalled the complexities of her relationship with Halima. Sarah wanted to understand Halima's beliefs, not condemn them with a knee-jerk reaction, even if she found some of the details horrifying. The two had talked for hours about the role of women and about relationships between men and women and had come to no conclusions. But they left each argument, each visit, respecting each other.

Like all friends, they came to know what mattered most to each other. Halfway through the year, Sarah had heard about Dadaab so often she could imagine the place: "I could see different roads and where her school was. Even though it's not real, it's my own confection, but to me it's no longer a refugee camp. It's a society that she had and a home and a community, and things were really settled because no one ever thought they'd be there that long."

Being able to visualize Halima's home helped Sarah understand the depth of Halima's dislocation: "There was one night I asked myself, 'What are we doing, why are we doing this?' We're taking them away from everyone they know and they're so isolated and it seems incredibly unnatural and severe. I don't know if I've told Halima this, but I don't know how many times I remember her specifically and it puts my whole life in context, any struggle that I have."

On Sunday, I visited Halima again between her study sessions. Paula had advised her to concentrate on her studies that term and look for a summer job later and, as far as Paula knew, Halima was following that advice. So I was surprised when Halima wanted me to drive her to a Canadian Tire gas bar so she could drop off her resumé. She wanted a part-time job now, so she could start to earn more money to buy things and help her family. At the gas bar, she approached a young guy behind the counter who said the manager wasn't in but would get the resumé the next day. It was all very quick and very polite. Walking away, Halima said she'd made a point of speaking slowly because people told her she talked too fast.

I assumed she would want to go back to her residence to study after that, but Halima had other ideas. Halima's requests came so spontaneously, were often so out of the blue, that it took some time to get used to taking them as they came, one by one. It was easy enough for me; I was there to visit her, but I did wonder how her friends handled her requests. Now she wanted me to drive her downtown, to the harbour, so she could have her picture taken with the ocean behind her. The sky was losing light fast when we parked by the boardwalk. She stood shivering while I hastily snapped a few photographs, and then she said, "Let's go." We drove home the long way, looking for a Tim Hortons that was open late on a Sunday afternoon. On the way, Halima recognized the name of Sarah's street, Moran Street, and, of course, wanted to stop. So she called Sarah and told her we were coming.

Sarah opened the door to the clapboard house. It was pitch black inside as we made our way up the stairs to her apartment. When we stepped inside the apartment, Sarah, dressed in a pink sweater and red toque to ward off the cold, explained that she and her roommates were doing an experiment. They had taken the light bulbs out of all the fixtures and were trying to live naturally with the movement of the sun and a few candles. "As you did, Halima," she added.

Halima wanted to pray her evening prayer in Sarah's room, but as we stood in the small kitchen a young man emerged from the darkness of another room and Halima hesitated, saying maybe we should go. What had seemed to her like a good idea was now, in the gloomy apartment with strange males, making her anxious. But the young man left, and Sarah assured Halima she could pray in her room with a candle. After, Halima didn't want any of the jasmine tea Sarah offered her and seemed eager for me to finish mine so we could leave. She had adjusted to many new people and things in her few months in Canada, but even now when she felt confused by a situation, in the dark about what was happening around her, she quickly and quietly left. On the way back to Birch 5, we stopped at a Tim Hortons and she ordered a French vanilla cappuccino, wanting to see why the others liked it. "Yes," she said, sipping it in the car, "it does taste like Somali tea."

The next morning, in Halima's chemistry class, the topic was kinetics. The professor's first slide read, "In kinetics we study the rate at which a chemical process changes." Thirty or so students, most of them young women, sat in the tiered lecture hall, writing in notebooks, watching the screen, whispering to each other. Halima and Mariam sat at the front—the only women with their heads covered. In the Ifo classrooms, where Halima had attended school and later taught, girls had always been in the minority and all of them had worn hijabs. As the chemistry professor explained how the presence of a catalyst speeds up reactions, I couldn't help wondering how such an intelligent young woman would ultimately respond to the social catalyst of her new surroundings.

On another wintry Saturday morning, I found Aden in his dorm room across the country at Brandon University. He had slept in after a late WUSC party the evening before. He answered the door in shorts, a white T-shirt and sandals, and invited me in while he put on warmer clothes so we could go for tea. Scrunched-up clothing, empty juice bottles, books, a microwave, a small refrigerator, computer equipment and two beds filled the cluttered room. Aden had a Canadian roommate who often stayed the night elsewhere, so Aden had the room to himself most of the time.

His room was on the eighth floor of Brandon University's McMaster Hall, the building at the centre of his existence in the cold prairie city. There was no need to go outside for tea. Aden had only to ride down on the elevator to the ground floor and walk through a link to the cafeteria. For many of his classes, he could walk through another link to the science wing. And if he had a question for his WUSC adviser, Brandy Robertson, he could find her in her office on the first floor, where she worked in a clerical job. Sometimes the closed environment gave him a false sense of what winter in Brandon was like. Earlier, he'd been fooled by the sun streaming in through the windows of McMaster Hall into thinking it was as warm outside as it was during his first days in Brandon. When he'd walked straight outside from the hall without a coat, he'd come to a new appreciation of what cold felt like, and he'd never made that mistake again.

When he gave me a tour of his campus, the cold didn't seem to bother Aden. It was cold enough that I was bundled up, but he wore a light jacket, unzipped, and a New York Yankees baseball cap. He had no gloves. He showed me around the residence, the sports facility and the library. He told me about the election campaign he was running to become the science commissioner at the university. It would be a way of getting involved with campus life and making new friends, he said. The Student Union would give him money for the meetings he attended and the reports he wrote. "And if there is a scholarship, you'll be the first considered," he said. Aden thought he had a good chance of winning the election that week. He just had to do well at the "bear pit" session, where people would question him on his ideas.

As we walked across the small campus, Aden waved at most of the people he passed and stopped several times to introduce me as his "guest from Toronto." Everyone we spoke with was a white Canadian, and most were female. There were some blacks on campus, Aden said, including the former WUSC students he knew. But Aden seemed at ease with everyone he met. He asked questions about their studies and their families, and he listened. It was clear that those who received his attention were charmed by his open, friendly manner.

Aden's big personality was probably the best thing he had going for him in coping with the isolation of his situation. He was too social a person, too curious a person to hide himself in his room for long. "That's my biggest fear when they come here," Brandy said, "that they are going to sit in their room and be lonely."

Aden attended plays and concerts on campus and often accepted the WUSC committee's invitations to events off campus. "I can socialize with anyone," he said. And it was easier for him in his jeans and T-shirts to blend in with the crowd than it was for the young women of Dadaab dressed in hijabs. He was a quick study, too, in the ways of young people. Listening to all the women talking about their boyfriends—something no Somali young woman in the camp would have done—he quickly accepted it as normal and sometimes told others he had a girlfriend even though he didn't. Aden had become Jimmy Romeo Love online, after all, a guy who liked to trick people about his identity. Having different names for different aspects of his personality was nothing new to him as a Somali. In Dadaab, each child grows up with a variety of nicknames that define something about their age, their physical appearance, their character or even their relationship to a specific person. By March, Aden had changed his online alias to Anwar. In Arabic, Anwar means "bright" or "light." His mother had given him the nickname when he was a boy to describe her "happy son."

His natural ability to connect with people helped Aden out in practical ways. When he missed a chemistry class, he borrowed notes from a woman who was studying in the cafeteria. She was a nurse who had decided to take some courses that would help her get into medicine. He had talked to her about his own wish to be a doctor, and she'd given him some hope. She said schools were looking for candidates who weren't white. She taught Aden the value of the word *diversity.*

Aden tried to balance his social need to fit in with his fidelity to the basics of his religion. He felt conflicted about socializing at university parties when there was alcohol served. Sometimes he went anyway just to dance, play pool or talk to friends. "There are other things you can do if you are not drinking. But most of the time I don't go."

While his loneliness had eased since this arrival, he still longed for some Somali companionship in his day-to-day life. He didn't think he wanted to wait through all his years of education before getting married. He had an image of cooking with a wife in an apartment in Brandon, of sharing a life together, of never, ever being lonely anymore. Although he imagined his future wife as Somali, he said he didn't care what country she was from as long as she was a Muslim.

On our walk on the campus, Aden wore his backpack with a Brandon University crest and posed for pictures by a bronze statue of a bobcat—the mascot for the sports teams—and the university's stone marker. He knew the university's history and took pride in it.

But it was the small university's respected record of bringing refugee students to Canada that impressed him most. In twenty-five years the university had sponsored twenty-six students through the WUSC program. Two professors at Brandon, Christoph Stadel, who has since moved to Austria, and John Everitt, now retired, started the program with donations from faculty members in the early '80s. Over the years, they persuaded alumni to contribute money and university administrators to waive tuition and room and board for a year. Student involvement came after a referendum was held to establish a levy. "Everyone who gave money and was involved saw it as something they could do," Everitt said. "In Brandon there is not much you can do to help the world. But the refugee students were a visible symbol of helping. You'd done something."

Toward the end of his tenure, Everitt suggested that the last referendum contain two questions: one asking for support to increase the levy, and another asking if the students would support indexing the levy against inflation ensuring future costs could be met. In 2007, the students voted in favour of both questions, and by the time Aden came, the levy to cover his travel expenses, clothing, books and supplies, welcome budget and monthly allowances was $4.08 per student.

Brandy Robertson, who both works and studies at Brandon, is at the centre of the current WUSC program. Each year, she reads the dossier of the selected student and makes it a point to learn about his or her country of origin, lifestyle and religion so she can help the new student fit in. "We don't want to assimilate them into our culture. We want them to be themselves in our culture." She believes that one of the ways of integrating students like Aden was dropping the "refugee" label as soon as possible. "We try to focus on the fact that they're here and they're here because they want to get an education. And then kind of forget about the whole refugee status."

Despite her loyalty to WUSC, she was unaware of a tragic twist in the Brandon connection to the organization's history. In 1986, when Brandy was just a toddler, the success of the Brandon program had brought Windle Trust's Hugh Pilkington to the city. One winter morning, the tall white Kenyan was on an early morning run along the highway when a pickup truck hit and killed him. Without any knowledge of the man from another continent, Brandy sat in the cafeteria at the university more than twenty years later and echoed his creed: "Education should be a right," she said. "And the fact that all students aren't privy to that is quite sad, so if we can help one student a year then it makes a difference."

On Saturday evening, I took Aden out to Joey's, a restaurant in a strip mall where we could have fish, which is naturally halal. Aden seemed surprised at how long it took for our orders of salmon and rice to arrive at the table. In the camps, the "hotels" served the food immediately, because there was little selection. When the waiter finally brought our dinners, Aden ate quickly and asked why there was no bread with the meal. He seemed hungry, so I ordered some garlic bread for us. Even though the bread arrived soaked with butter, he spread more butter on it. "More butter on the garlic bread?" the waiter asked as he passed the table. "May I take it you are new to Canada?" Many would have found the comment insulting, but Aden took it in stride. "Six months I've been here," he said. The waiter noticed the Brandon crest on Aden's white T-shirt, and the two young men found common ground talking about the university where they both studied, ending their conversation with "Good luck" on the waiter's part and "I'll see you around" on Aden's.

When I got the bill, Aden peeked at the total and was horrified. He stated decisively that for the rest of the weekend we would eat in the cafeteria. And he never budged from that position. I always got the sense that Aden genuinely liked women. He speaks fondly of his mother and sister and he has never made a single harsh judgement on the habits or characteristics of Western women, but he has a sense of chivalry toward women that most young Canadian males no longer possess or don't show. He would not allow me to pay for what he saw as expensive meals and, while the other Dadaab students called me by my first name, as I had invited them to do, Aden always used the more formally respectful "Madame."

Throughout the weekend, he was a generous host. I remembered how his mother had prepared sugary tea with milk and some of her cookies for my visit to his compound. As Aden saw it, I was now a guest in his home in Brandon. At lunch the next day, he insisted on using his meal card to pay for our food. I said I was happy to pay for lunch, but he would not accept that. When I picked out a salad, he said it wasn't enough and I must get something from the grill. I added a grilled cheese sandwich and a coffee to my tray, and we sat at one of the large, round tables. He said I didn't have enough food on my tray and I should get more. I told him I was older than he was, that I had to watch my weight, which he finally accepted.

That evening he wanted to give me a tour of the city. Brandon is the second largest city in Manitoba, a fact that makes it sound bigger than it is. With fewer than fifty thousand people, it is fifteen times smaller than the largest city in the province, the capital city of Winnipeg. It lies in agricultural land that gives it both its sobriquet and its purpose. The "wheat city" serves as a hub and a trading centre for the region.

Fresh snow was falling as I followed Aden's directions in my rental car. He had me head down 18th Street, the main artery that leads to the Trans-Canada Highway. The roads were slippery, and although I warned him to tell me ahead of time where to turn, he often left it to the last moment.

I asked about his family in the camp, and he told me things were getting bad. The Kenyans had closed the border to goods coming in from Somalia. When the goods, which originated in the Emirates, arrived in Dadaab via businesses in Somalia, they were cheaper than when they came through Nairobi merchants. So now prices were going up. Each month he tried to send $100 home through the Dahabshiil in Winnipeg because his family was missing his teacher's pay.

We turned in at a darkened mall and I wondered what he wanted to show me. "We only have one Walmart in Brandon," he said as we sat in the idling car. Then he suggested we turn around and head back through the town. As we drove, Aden said he really wanted to learn to drive and asked how much cars cost. After I explained the prices and the added cost of car insurance, I reminded him, perhaps to soften the blow, that he'd wanted a camera in the camp and now he had one. Maybe someday he'd have a car too. "In three years I will have a car," he said. It was hard to doubt his confidence.

I couldn't make the right turn he wanted because I was in the left lane at a red light, but he said to never mind, there was another Tim Hortons farther along the road past all the restaurants and malls. Of course there was.

Even though it was a snowy Sunday night, the parking lot at Tims was packed with minivans and pickup trucks. Inside, there was only one free table. Aden agreed, reluctantly, that I could buy the hot drinks while he grabbed the table. When I brought his French vanilla and my tea over, he had squeezed into the small corner table. The coffee shop was full of white people, mainly male and mainly older. The motto of the town's newspaper, the *Brandon Sun,* came from a poem by John Donne about the connection of all humankind: "No man is an island, entire of itself." But in the Tim Hortons that night,

Aden on a winter's night in Brandon, Manitoba.

Aden stuck out like a black island in a sea of white. The other customers glanced at him with curiosity. If they felt any hostility, they kept it to themselves. But Aden had lost some of his boldness. Usually he sat with his legs stretched out and an arm wrapped around the back of a chair. Although it was physically impossible for him to sit like that in the tight space he had, I could see there was more to the way he'd pulled himself in.

We sipped our hot drinks in silence. Outside, the snow fell, lit by the Canadian Tire sign across the way and the spotlights over the pumping stations. Finally, I asked him if, back in the camp, he could ever have imagined being in a place like this. The question was awkward and illogical. Aden just looked around the Tim Hortons and said so softly I could hardly hear him, "I'm sure these people have seen an African before." I assured him they had, and we let the matter drop.

I didn't know if it would help Aden to let him know he was not the only WUSC student who had ever found himself in a small community where he stood out. I thought of Ruth Mathiang, a Christian Sudanese woman who had lived in the large cities of Khartoum and Nairobi before ending up in Charlottetown, Prince Edward Island, in 2001. There were no noisy markets outside her window, no *matatus*—the packed minibuses that honked their way through the congested, polluted streets of Nairobi. There were only a few cows grazing in a green field.

And I thought of Ajmal Pashtoonyar, who, in 1998, left the crowded Peshawar area of Pakistan, where he had lived with his exiled Afghani family, to come to the small Newfoundland fishing community of Burin, with "one gas station, one bank, one grocery store and a Sears outlet, which was also a post office." Even after Ajmal left Burin to continue his studies at Memorial University in St. John's, he was still the only Afghani in the province.

Both Ruth and Ajmal endured, finished their degrees and found careers in bigger Canadian cities. Not only endured—they blossomed, in part because of the effort they had to exert to find their way in their strange environments. They became attached to those places more strongly than if they had lived with others from their cultures in larger Canadian cities. Even when Ruth came to live in Toronto so she could work with immigrant women, she remained an "Islander" at heart who missed the church and the families who had welcomed her there. And Ajmal, now a lawyer who has travelled the world for humanitarian agencies and has worked with Canadian federal departments in Ottawa, jokes that he is still an Afghani-Newfoundlander with a deep love for the ocean: "Now I am attached. I have to see it every six months." He came to believe that those first lonely months in rural Newfoundland shaped him as much as any other experience in his life: "I think isolation brings in the natural instinct for survival to some extent."

Despite Aden's feelings of awkwardness in the Tim Hortons that night, I expected that he would endure and succeed as Ruth and Ajmal had. But I knew he had to figure that out for himself.

Our tour that evening was not complete until Aden and I returned to the cafeteria for movie night. Back on his home turf, Aden relaxed and took charge again, insisting we have a late-night snack. While we were walking to the cash, Aden stopped the middle-aged woman in charge and went into schmooze mode, asking if she had received his application for work. She told him she needed someone who had experience. "No problem," Aden said. "I can learn fast." The woman hesitated and said she needed a cashier on Monday nights. "I can work any evening," Aden said. Again the woman looked a bit dubious but told him he could come for training the following night. "I have psychology class on Monday night," Aden said. "Now, see, there's the problem, you just said you could come in every night," she said. The frustrated woman must have expected Aden to give up but he continued, calmly adding, "I can come any other night." She relented and told him to come Tuesday evening for training.

The movie that night was *High School Musical 3,* playing on two large monitors in the darkened eating area. On the monitors, skimpily clad teenage girls and rich teenage boys cavorted in a lavish-looking school and drove around in expensive cars. I couldn't imagine what Aden would make of it all. "School is fun in Canada," was all he said before growing tired of the movie and returning to his room to study.

The next day, before I left (and before I assured Aden I didn't need a meal for the road), we were walking in a hallway in McMaster Hall. He was dressed in his favourite T-shirt that read "Girls only want boyfriends who have great skills." He was late for his statistics class when he suddenly said, as if to answer my confusing question from the night before about relocating, "From Hagadera to Canada. I'm so happy."

PART FOUR

What Lies Ahead

CHAPTER SEVEN

So Scared of the Transition

SOMETIMES, FOR MUNO, the books she read were a way of leaving the reality of her loneliness behind—all those characters with all those stories to entertain her. But sometimes, reading was simply a means of procrastinating, a way to avoid thinking of the personal choices she felt she had to start making. This was her "transitional term," she said near the end of the winter semester, a term when she would have to start considering some tough decisions: where she would live the next year and how she would pay for her rent, food and tuition. Other students, born or raised in Canada, had a better understanding of the mechanics of finding jobs and comparing costs of rental units than she did. At twenty, Muno had always lived where there had been few opportunities for work and no choices in homes. And back in the camp, she'd had her parents for guidance in any matters she did have to consider; but they were far away from her now and, in any case, they wouldn't understand the options facing Muno any better than she did.

Muno's WUSC committee at the University of Toronto Mississauga campus had made many of the decisions about her first year in Canada long before she'd even arrived. They'd arranged where she would live and how she would get her meals, and they'd taken care of all the costs. She could count on financial support until the next sponsored student arrived in late August. The deadline for applying for student loans for second year was months away, and the WUSC committee would help her with the paperwork long before that. In March, she still had almost half a year of breathing space, but Muno had an active imagination and it was filling her empty moments with dread. She'd read enough books to know that life can take disastrous turns.

When she wasn't studying or procrastinating, she mentally listed all the steps she'd have to take to become self-sufficient by the end of summer. She knew she should be getting out of her apartment more often now to hand out resumés at nearby stores and restaurants if she wanted a job by spring. Wendy's Restaurant had offered her a part-time position, but because there was pork on the menu and it was *haram* for her to even handle that meat, she had had to turn the job down. She had gone to another interview where a Muslim woman, waiting to be interviewed as well, had advised her that she'd have a better chance if she took off her hijab. But no job was worth that to Muno.

Then there was the question of whether she should live alone or find a roommate in her second year. She knew she couldn't afford the privacy and the proximity to classes that her residence offered if she had to pay the fees herself. And moving in with her cousins didn't seem like much of an option either, considering the long commute from their place in Toronto to the Mississauga campus. She had talked to a Muslim woman in the cafeteria who rented a basement apartment for a reasonable price, but her friend Abdinoor had discouraged her from that choice. He had told her basements were cold in the winter and hot in the summer. Muno wasn't sure what a basement was. All she knew was it was just another new thing to worry about, among the many unknown problems that lay ahead.

All of the eleven students faced transitions that could, ultimately, affect their career choices down the road. Across Canada, both the level of financial support and the approach to the Student Refugee

Program varied from university to university. In evaluations with sponsored students, WUSC's Asni Mekonnen finds that right from the beginning of the year, one of the biggest complaints she hears is the disparity of support students receive: "They start to email and they compare what each other has, so that has been a bone of contention—like how come this person when he came was provided with a laptop and I was not."

Glen Peterson, faculty adviser for the WUSC committee at the University of British Columbia since 1994, says there has not been much discussion within the larger WUSC community about the differing levels of support across the country because each university cobbles the money together in its own way. He says that even before students arrive in Canada, they are often intensely aware of the differences at universities because local committees send letters to the students outlining their programs, although WUSC Ottawa discourages the practice.

There are also philosophical differences among universities. Some committees operate on the belief that it is better to fulfill the basic requirements of private sponsorship—twelve months of financial support, bringing one or more students every year—in order to get as many students as possible out of refugee camps. Others believe that it is important to provide some continued support to the current students to give them a better chance at success.

On top of that, the way each committee is organized can affect the level of practical support the sponsored student receives. Committees run entirely by students, by nature, have a higher turnover than committees with staff and faculty involved. In student-run committees, once graduates leave the university, new volunteers take over, often unaware of any past problems that could be corrected and unfamiliar with the former students who might still appreciate moral, if not financial, help past their first year. Peterson says that even at UBC, where the program has been running for years, faculty members still need to be reminded of what WUSC is and what the Student Refugee Program actually does.

Throughout the year, WUSC administrators in Ottawa send out checklists for committees that they should be following to guide the student through the seasons. The April checklist suggests helping the student with income tax returns, with summer housing and with applications for financial assistance for the second year if needed. But WUSC headquarters is not sponsoring the student. Each local committee is, and each can decide how to raise its money, how to spend it and how to help its student.

Financially, there was no advantage to Halima to continuing her studies at Mount Saint Vincent. In her second year she would have to pay her own tuition and living expenses, so it didn't matter where she attended university—either still in Halifax or somewhere in the west. Paula Barry and the students on the committee tried to figure out ways they could ease the transition if Halima did stay at the university. Paula told Halima, "If you find yourself in a situation next year where you need a root canal or you're hungry or you need your rent paid, you can come and see me. We have some money in the second year to support you. But at the same time I feel very strongly about bringing a student per year." Halima, who was now a member of the committee, agreed with that approach. How could she expect more when so many students were left behind in Dadaab?

The Brandon program would not cover Aden's tuition or other costs in his second year either. But the committee did have money to smooth out the transition. "Usually they move out of residence because of the food," Brandy Robertson said. "It's difficult for them because they want to be able to cook, so we help them find an apartment. We pay their first month's rent. We furnish their apartment if they need a bed or a desk or a bicycle. We help them apply for student loans. We help them find a job. But other than that, their financial assistance ends basically once we've got them settled—unless there's an emergency."

Aden didn't know yet how he would manage in his second year, but he knew he would. He didn't think the financial situation would alter his desire to become a doctor, although he knew it would make it harder. He had lived through war, made it to Dadaab, succeeded in finishing secondary school with marks high enough to win a prized scholarship. In his few months in Canada he'd already found a job at the cafeteria and, after successfully handling the "bear pit" session, had secured the position as the science commissioner for the student body at the university. Figuring out how to support himself would be a challenge to be sure, but it was doable.

Siyad and Abdi would find the transition to second year financially easier than the other students. As one of largest universities in Canada with an established levy, the University of British Columbia collected close to $100,000 in the 2008/09 school year. The university sponsored three students in 2008, including Siyad. The money raised by the levy paid the students' living expenses for the first year only, but the university gave the students free tuition for their first degree at the university as well as an annual allowance for their textbooks.

The program at UBC started in 1981 when students, unsure how they would pay for even one whole year, brought a young man from Eritrea to the campus. Glen Peterson says the program at UBC and others across Canada have become institutionalized since those early years because of the "dogged effort" of local committees and faculty members who got agreements for stable funding.

At Huron University College, which has only about 1,200 students, Abdi would also get free tuition for his undergraduate degree. Mark Franke, an assistant professor at Huron's Centre for Global Studies, was the faculty adviser to the WUSC committee from 2003 to 2009, during a time when the university did some soul searching over its responsibilities to sponsored students. He says he's always found the Student Refugee Program to be an "amazing educational program," but not one without flaws. Over the years, he's seen students struggle to adjust to the Canadian university environment without families, without anyone close they could turn to. And he's seen students arrive with severe health problems and psychological traumas that made focusing on studies hard. Of the nine students who were at Huron during his years as adviser, he watched one struggle for years at his studies and two others "kind of drift away."

Franke decries an attitude he has perceived among some committees that the Student Refugee Program is charity work: "I've heard so many times from members working in local committees and administrators at universities who are supportive of this idea that, my gosh, we give them a whole year of support and then it's up to them to pull up their socks and get to work." Franke said what's wrong with that attitude is that it supposes the sponsored students are on the same footing as students who were born in Canada.

Franke believes that the attitude stems from a lack of awareness of the difficulties immigrants to Canada face and a lack of awareness of the ethical responsibility of the program at large: "There is a huge thesis within WUSC of human development through education, and the whole carrot WUSC holds out to people in Dadaab and Kakuma is, come to Canada, take advantage of this program and you'll have a chance to get a university degree, and they come here and they may get decent support for the first year and then it's, 'Okay, go ahead.' They are pointed toward the financial assistance office and told, put yourself forty, fifty thousand dollars in debt and try your best to make a career with that debt load, with no credit history and no Canadian work experience. And deal with all the stresses of being a student in this country." In the last three years in his role with WUSC, Franke started to notice a sharp turn away from that attitude and toward greater responsibility to the students. "Thank goodness that's being addressed. But that's been a hard one."

At Huron, the committee worked hard to convince the student body and administrators of their ethical responsibility to the young person they've brought to the campus and to make them see the program as a social responsibility that meshed with Canada's international obligations to take the plight of refugees seriously. The new commitment resulted in an increase in the student levy from $4 in 2003 to $8, and then in 2007 to $12, "by far the highest levy" in Canada, Franke says. Two years before Abdi came to Huron, the administrators agreed to the proposal to make the sponsored students' tuition free for up to five years.

While Abdi didn't have to worry about his tuition costs, he still had other decisions to make, and he was already starting to think about them in late winter. He knew he would have to pay for his living expenses and planned to apply for a student loan. But he hoped to work in the summer to supplement the loan and leave himself with enough money to send to his relatives back in the camp.

Abdi would have to find a place on his own, and he'd have to learn to cook. In the cafeteria he'd survived on rice and spaghetti, and fish when they had it, so he was looking forward to eating meat more regularly. In a kitchen of his own he would be able to store halal meat in the freezer. But where would he start? How would he learn his way around a kitchen?

Abdi was even less confident about finding a summer job. London is a small city with few jobs Abdi could do at the best of times. As a student of economics, he knew the recession would make matters worse. Mark Franke says that finding summer jobs is always tough for refugee and immigrant students: "The vast majority of Canadian students have someone to go to, a family friend who says, you can work for my uncle putting in swimming pools or something like that, and they [refugee students] don't even have that. They're just lacking the social connections."

As I drove Abdi through London one day, he picked up a mis-shapen penny from the cupholder in my car. An edge had been cut away from it, forming a sharp, spiral shape. My daughter, Jane, like many university students before her, had learned about Vector Marketing on campus and had worked during the summer selling Cutco knives. The sliced penny had been part of her sales pitch, and now it lay, rather useless in its present form, in my car.

I started to explain what it was, but Abdi already knew. He had seen someone cut a penny with scissors in a Cutco demonstration, and he planned to join the Cutco team for three days of training the next month. The company representative told him that even if he didn't sell any knives, he would earn money for each presentation. Abdi thought this was a great opportunity: maybe he could make more money merely trying to sell knives than working in a store that paid minimum wage. My daughter had been able to build a list of potential clients through her friends and the friends and colleagues of her parents. I couldn't imagine where Abdi would start. I warned him about all the calls and follow-ups Jane had done before getting into homes to do her presentation, and how she'd earned more the summer before, working in a hardware store. But it was when I asked Abdi how he'd feel if a homeowner he was visiting owned a dog that he said he might decline the training and rethink his summer job options.

Abdi was still haunted by the horror stories of sponsored students who buckled under the stress of second year. A couple had given up on their degrees, and he wanted to make sure that didn't happen to him. He was doing well in his courses. He'd got 24 out of 25 in a calculus midterm and had yet to figure out where he'd made a mistake. He received 90 per cent in biology and 88 in economics midterms. He planned to take two summer courses that year so that he would have 4.5 of the 20 credits he'd need to graduate. Then he would take five courses and maybe six the following year. He hoped to finish in three or three and a half years, to rush through it before the difficulties of getting by on his own got to him.

He still wanted to go to graduate school, but he wanted to make sure he was working toward a practical career. "I am still undecided. My mind changes every two months," he said. One possibility was business. The other was pharmacology, which would give him the opportunity to do research on new drugs: "It's working in drug companies where there are good jobs, and it's interesting, learning how chemicals react when they are injected in the body. You can do research and contribute." What he wanted to figure out was which skills were more marketable, especially in the current economy.

In 2007, WUSC wrote a study about the students who had come to Canada through the Student Refugee Program. By that time, the program had brought almost 900 students to Canada. WUSC prepared a survey and tried to reach as many students as it could by emailing it to 283 participants who had arrived prior to 2004 and posting it online as well. The organization received a total of 111 responses. Of those who responded, 96.8 per cent were either pursuing or had completed their post-secondary program, in fields such as social sciences, applied sciences, engineering and medicine. Almost half of the respondents said they were "somewhat or completely integrated into Canadian society; 85 per cent claimed that "enrollment in a college or university upon arrival was a key factor in the integration process."

It's anyone's guess what became of those who didn't respond to the questionnaire. Paul Davidson, executive director of WUSC from 2002 to 2009, says the organization just doesn't have the resources to come up with complete data. In late 1990, after some bad real estate decisions, the non-profit non-governmental organization asked the Canadian International Development Agency for an advance on funds. When CIDA refused, WUSC was forced to file for bankruptcy. Later, CIDA did come up with bridge financing and WUSC worked its way out of receivership in a year's time—but it took almost another decade to pay off the debt. Then, in 2002, CIDA, which had been a core partner in the Student Refugee Program, announced it would stop its contribution of $250,000 that covered the administration costs of the program. "That left a big hole," Davidson says. "I guess for me that was part of the lesson on how hard it is to do refugee work in Canada, because a quarter of a million dollars for a lot of organizations is not a lot of money to raise, but we started knocking on doors with the foundation community, with the private sector, with individual donors, and it proved to be very difficult to raise money for refugee issues." Several foundations did come through with short-term grants, and the WUSC board agreed to carry a deficit until administrators could find a new business plan. In that plan, each local committee sponsoring students agreed to pay an annual fee of $2,500 to cover all the expenses of the selection and preparation process.

In Ottawa, administration costs have been kept low. After the financial collapse, WUSC returned to its two-storey building on Scott Street in Ottawa, the building that it had been trying to sell so it could move into a larger space. Only a handful of people, including Asni Mekonnen, work full-time on the Student Refugee Program. There has been little time or money for in-depth research. But based on the tracking Davidson has seen and his visits across the country, he believes that "most of our students complete undergraduate education, most of them are employed in their field of study, most of them remain in Canada." He says that virtually all students complete their first year of studies, although there have been "some very rare experiences where the culture shock and the post-traumatic shock" prevented that. In those cases the local committee continued to support the student for the year, but "that's sort of the end of their academic career."

John Everitt, one of the founders of the program at Brandon University, has kept track of the more than twenty students that program brought to Canada during his years at the university. He says that about half the students who came to Brandon University graduated from that institution. Most of the others, he adds, finished their education elsewhere. Some wanted programs Brandon didn't offer; some just never felt at home in the small prairie city. There were those who struggled, Everitt admits, usually because they didn't have enough English or, in a few cases, because they had problems with alcohol "after the traumas they'd been through." He recalls two who moved away to Calgary to find work.

At UBC, Glen Peterson says he knows about twenty-five students who have come through the program there, and, of those, four or five didn't finish their degrees. "My experience," he says, "has been if somebody comes and they have huge problems at the outset, they will drop out after a year. If somebody can persevere through the first two years, then they will likely make it." Among the graduates of their program, some have gone to high-profile positions at places such as the United Nations and the BC Cancer Agency. Their first student, who came from Eritrea in 1981, went on to work in refugee issues before becoming executive director of Mosaic, an immigrant and refugee support centre in Vancouver. Peterson has encouraged students to look beyond the obvious careers in law and medicine and build on their refugee experiences and knowledge of the hardships of life instead.

Pascaline Nsekera, a former WUSC student who graduated from UBC, did just that. During the civil war in her native Burundi in the '90s, Pascaline was completing a degree in environmental chemistry when it became too dangerous for her to continue her studies. She was half Tutsi and half Hutu, caught in the middle of the deadly power struggle between the two. She fled when she learned she was on a list of people who would be killed at the university one night. When she finally made it to UBC in 1997, she picked up her studies in sciences, changing her major to earth sciences. But her graduation from UBC coincided with profound post-traumatic stress that left her questioning her career choice. Although she jokes that she no longer wanted to be a geologist because it was too cold in Alberta where the jobs were, she knew she had to find a way to help others who had lived through the horrors of war. So she took more courses at UBC—this time in social work—and found employment with La Boussole, a public agency for francophone immigrants in Vancouver. There she developed a storytelling project called The Illustrated Journey, which allows youth of all languages to "tell" their stories through the universal language of comic-book art. She doesn't like the expression she sees in the literature to describe people like her: the "wounded healer"; but she realized she had become one.

Referring to the 2007 evaluation, Davidson points out that WUSC-sponsored students become heavily involved in Canadian life. Of those who responded, 92.9 per cent are active in community groups and associations; 65 per cent vote in federal, provincial and municipal elections. "There is a pervasive sense in Canada that immigrants— and refugees in particular—are a drain on Canada and a burden, but when you look at the social capital that students have brought to Canada, it's real." Davidson points to a new program at Citizenship and Immigration. CIC created an internship so that former WUSC-sponsored students could bring their experience as refugees to the department. "People are now looking at our former sponsored students as resources," Davidson says.

Even those who find work in the university disciplines they first chose in Canada often find a way to help others. Irene Kyompaire, who became a refugee from her native Uganda, studied commerce at St. Mary's University in Halifax in the '90s. After graduation she found a job with the Business Development Bank of Canada in Toronto, a job that has allowed her to build a good life for herself. But over the years she volunteered at the Toronto Rape Crisis Centre because she had heard so many stories of rape from other refugees. And she volunteered at a hospice for people dying with AIDS. She saw that as a way of giving back to Canada for the help she received, and also as a way to pay tribute to the suffering in the country of her birth: "I've lost family and I'm still losing family. It's real. So me helping someone in Canada, a place I now call home, in a way brings the comfort of saying: I wasn't there, but at least I'm helping this family here."

Mark Franke of Huron University College says the success of the WUSC program should not be measured solely by how many students complete university: "One of the great things refugees try to obtain is just an agency, being able to realize the right of self-determination, and I think that's one of the most important parts of the program. When I was adviser of the committee here, I said we should not be aiming to make these students stay in school and get a degree. That's up to them. We should make it inviting. All the advantages are here. But the main thing is to support them so they can calm down a bit in their lives and make good judgements about themselves."

Sultan Ghaznawi is an example of the good judgement that Franke describes. Ghaznawi came from Pakistan to Canada as a WUSC student in 1999, leaving behind his family, who had fled from oppression in Afghanistan during the Soviet–Afghani war. He began his courses at the University of Toronto and discovered he had a high aptitude in computer science. But after the attacks of 9/11 and the war against the Taliban, Ghaznawi's fear for his family's safety in Peshawar overtook his need to finish his degree. He became a part-time student and a full-time employee, working as a software designer. Within a year he was able to prove to the Canadian government that he earned enough income to personally sponsor the seven members of his family. Today, he measures his success not by his own education—he still has not completed his degree—but by the improved lives of his brothers and sisters, who were able to go to universities in Canada without the kind of pressure he had experienced.

As they neared the end of the winter term, none of the Dadaab eleven could imagine dropping out of university. They had fought so hard and waited so long for this chance to study. And while the Somalis worried about the escalating violence in their homeland and the degradation of conditions in the camps, they believed their families were relatively safe there—better to help them out in the small ways they could and finish university so they could bring greater changes to their lives later. All of the students who had come before them through WUSC from Dadaab had stuck with their studies, despite the need to pay their own way and the pressures from home. None of the Dadaab eleven wanted to be the first to break that record or disappoint their families.

In their anxiety over how they would get by, none of them talked about quitting. Instead, they talked about how they could afford to stay in school, how they would work, take out loans, seek out scholarships and bursaries, sew together whatever patchwork of financial support they could to get them through. But for Muno, as the reality of being truly on her own came closer, her fears of the unknown challenges in her second year deepened, unrelieved by the assurances of others: "Transition, transition. Everybody is like it just happens. You don't have to worry about it. I'm just so scared about the transition."

CHAPTER EIGHT

Things You Can Never Forget

ON A COOL EVENING IN APRIL, Halima stood outside the Birch 5 residence at Mount Saint Vincent University in Halifax. A light fixture by the door illuminated the backs of a huddled group that watched as a cab driver threw several large suitcases into the trunk of his car, pulled them all out again and tried to rearrange them to fit. One of the owners of the luggage, a blond young man named Henry, threw smaller bags into the back seat and tried to help the driver, perhaps concerned that his luggage might be destroyed before his real journey began. Henry was heading home to Finland.

The rest of the bags belonged to Gabby, who was going home to Sweden. Neither Gabby nor Henry planned to come back to the Mount, and it was highly unlikely Halima would ever see these two new friends again. The international support group that had helped her through her first year of university was breaking apart.

Dressed in a black and white jacket, a long skirt over her jeans and a blue pashmina wrapped around her head, Halima stood back and watched as Gabby and Henry hugged other friends goodbye. "I just met these people and now they are going," she said. "I can't believe how fast the time has gone." The evening brought back the intensity of emotions that had swirled around her departure from her home just eight months earlier. "I don't like goodbyes," she said, trying to keep her tears in check.

Gabby made her way to Halima and held her tightly. "Halima," she whispered softly. Halima stayed back as Henry embraced the others but rushed to him just before he jumped in the taxi. "Halima," was all he said too. And then he and Gabby were gone.

It was an emotional end to an emotional day after an emotional week. Earlier that evening, Halima had written the last exam of her first year of university. She had slept little in the past two weeks of finals, and although she'd cooked some food, she found she couldn't eat. The bad news from home had been piling up. Her father had gone to a doctor in Nairobi for an operation on one eye and had been told that though the eye was dead, he needed an operation to save the other eye. But his blood sugar was too high for an operation of any kind. Then, just the night before, her brother-in-law had called her from Mogadishu. Halima's sister who was six months pregnant had gone into hospital for respiratory problems.

All Halima could do was send money and harden her resolve to find a way back home in the coming year. On the day she left Ifo, she'd tried to ignore the fearful voice in her head that said she would never see her father again. Now the voice was becoming more difficult to ignore. As a permanent resident of Canada, Halima had the right to apply for travel documents. But until she had a Canadian passport, she feared travelling to Kenya, where authorities treated Somalis harshly. In her latest plan, she'd decided she could go safely to Burundi on a travel document, and then, if she couldn't sneak into Kenya, she'd arrange for her family to visit her there.

In her room that evening, Somali music poured through her computer's speakers as she paced, one part nervous energy, one part pure exhaustion. She sat one moment to watch the singers on the computer screen, stood the next to walk to her table for a lotion to rub on her arms, which were always dry from washing them before each of her five daily prayers.

On the bulletin board in the lobby of the building, a sign was posted advising students they had to be out of residence by April 22, in four days' time. But Halima could stay in her room for the summer because Birch 5 would remain open for summer students. All the other Birch houses and the larger apartment residence would be emptied out and cleaned before opening again as bed-and-breakfast accommodations for summer travellers and conference participants. The next day Halima would begin training to become a part-time cleaner at those residences, and in May she would start summer courses in statistics at the university.

She had given up on the idea of switching to a nursing program and had decided to stick to the academic plan she had arrived with: a major in biology and a minor in chemistry at the Mount. Perhaps, if she kept up her grades, she could get a scholarship for graduate school. And she'd given up on the idea of moving to a university in the west. Her second year was too early to introduce more changes into her life so soon after she'd changed everything. Besides, she was learning her way around Halifax, had started to feel settled at the Mount and become comfortable with the people she had met. But now that she had decided to stay, she was alarmed that others— including Gabby, who had always been good to her, and Henry— were moving on.

More people in her life would be leaving soon, too. Sarah Chan, her WUSC friend, was moving to Ottawa in the summer for graduate school, and Mariam and her Somali family were considering moving back to Quebec, where tuition was cheaper. All the talk of departures unsettled Halima's sense that she was making a new home. At least she would have her resident assistant, Loyan, in Halifax a while longer. "Loyan is like my mother and my sister," Halima said. "Sometimes she cooks for both of us when I am not feeling well." Loyan would graduate that spring and was supposed to return to St. Lucia to work in hospitality, as expected by the government that had sponsored her, but she was now pregnant and staying in Canada until the following fall so she could have the baby in a Canadian hospital. If Halima was shocked by this, she didn't show it. Somehow, over the year— she couldn't understand the contradiction herself—she had learned to separate her feelings for her female friends from her disapproval of the choices women made in North America.

Halima often used the word "mother" to describe Paula Barry, too. Paula took her shopping, invited her to dinner and had included her in a family gathering at Christmas. Paula fussed over her first WUSC student and worried about her progress. She was concerned that Halima wasn't taking the need to save money for her second year seriously.enough: "I kind of expected that she may have stashed a little money away throughout the year, but I never asked her or prodded her to do that. But she hasn't. She called on Friday to say her cheque wasn't in her box. She had not a cent to her name. So she's living cheque to cheque."

Paula would still be there for Halima the next year, but in August their relationship would undergo a major change. Paula would have a second sponsored student to worry about, and Halima would be on her own financially. Paula felt less than confident that Halima was ready for the drastic alteration. She wanted to arrange for Halima to sit down with the university's financial aid adviser, who, she hoped, would make Halima focus on the paperwork for applying for a student loan and a bursary as well as help her plan her finances. "She could really save quite a bit of money," Paula said. "But I think we need to sit down and set up a budget, a goal, even a savings account."

Halima had talked to Paula about renting an apartment alone in the university neighbourhood of Clayton Park. Paula explained that if Halima had a roommate, not only would her rent costs be half but so would the extra costs such as the phone bill and electricity. If Halima really wanted to live alone, Paula told her, then perhaps they could find her a room or an apartment in a house owned by someone who worked on the campus, someone who might give her a break on rent.

Halima was trying to make some money. She had never heard back from the Canadian Tire gas bar where she had left her resumé in the winter, but she had found a part-time job at Dairy Queen in early spring and in the past month started a job changing beds at the Marriott Hotel downtown. Because of her exams, she hadn't worked enough shifts at either to really see how she liked the jobs, and now she realized she wouldn't be able to keep either of them once she started the summer classes and her cleaning job on campus. But just being able to get two jobs gave her some confidence that she could earn money to send to her father for his medical bills as well as save some for her second year.

Like many university students, Halima had trouble making wise decisions when it came to spending on food. Eating junk food was just quicker and easier than cooking meals in the residence. And she liked the taste of french fries, doughnuts and Tim Hortons snack wraps. In March, Halima had gone to Paula to ask for more money on her meal plan. "Why aren't you cooking? What's going on?'" Paula asked her. She said, "I don't know what to cook." So Paula made her a little recipe book of simple recipes that she thought she would like.

Halima did cook, but she often grew tired of eating the same thing over and over: spaghetti and rice dishes. For a while, she'd cooked eggs every day until she got sick of them. In the camp, meal variety had never been an option, but here, where there were all sorts of choices, Halima gravitated toward the tasty but nutritionally empty choices.

She was also trying to gain weight. Even by refugee-camp standards, Halima had always been thin. But in Ifo, where food was scarce, adding extra body fat had been low among her priorities. In Canada, she could easily accomplish her mission. By April she had gained five and a half kilograms. She was pleased with the weight gain, but not with the fact that many of her jeans no longer fit or that she could no longer zip up the favourite black skirt she liked to wear over them. That meant spending money on new clothes.

Halima had probably arrived in Canada with the iron and vitamin deficiencies her doctor discovered, but her new diet was not helping. Paula bought her multivitamins and iron pills. Halima didn't like the taste of the iron pills, and Paula suspected she wasn't taking them regularly. For a while, Halima had confused some painkillers for the iron pills and walked around in a daze, Paula said.

Halima was spending hours in her room online. "She's turned into a total computer addict," Paula said. When Halima complained of headaches, Paula took her to have her eyes checked. After the test they ushered her into their big gallery where they sold expensive glasses. Paula looked at Halima's prescription and saw it was for a minor correction. She said, "Halima, I've got to be honest. I think it's kind of silly to spend three or four hundred dollars on a pair of glasses. Why don't we go to the drugstore and get you some reading glasses? " So Paula bought Halima a $50 pair of glasses and told her to use them whenever she was on the computer or reading. In the upcoming year, Halima would have to make those kinds of decisions by herself.

Two days after her last exam, Halima started her first full day of work cleaning rooms on the campus. In the apartment residence, her supervisor pointed her to a suite at the end of the hallway. There, Halima found several young women working in the kitchen. Each room had to be thoroughly cleaned before the residence could open to summer guests.

Halima pulled on blue rubber gloves and began to scrub dried food from the refrigerator. Already she could tell she wasn't going to like this job. She saw a long spring and summer ahead of labour and studying, of worries about money and her father's health.

That evening, Halima wanted some fun. She wanted to get out of the city and mark the end of term. Outrunning the sun, we took the highway toward Peggy's Cove, the fishing village on St. Margaret's Bay that attracts tourists for its rocky shore and weathered wooden houses. Halima wanted me to drive to the lighthouse, where she had been on a previous visit. As I locked the car in the parking lot, she ran ahead, scampering across the broad rock face by the white and red lighthouse, the wind blowing her long black skirt. We were alone on the bare rock with the ocean before us. The clean air and the wide expanse of water invited calm, an emptying of worries, but

Halima's movements never stopped. She picked her way down to the shore and then quickly climbed back up, finally sitting a moment to look east. "I'd like to live by the sea," she said wistfully, as though it could never be.

Halima poses on the shoreline near Peggy's Cove.

She posed for a few pictures before suddenly pulling a peach-coloured hijab she'd carried with her over her jacket and headscarf and then directed me to take a series of pictures with the ocean behind her. Two sets of pictures of the same modest young woman.

Across the country the other Dadaab students were coming to their own decisions about the four months ahead when all their expenses would still be paid. They had to decide whether they would use that time to work and to build up funds for the coming year or push ahead with studies that would help them finish university in the shortest time possible. They were older, after all, than most first-year students, keen to get on with their lives and their responsibilities to their families.

In Toronto, not much was changing in the patterns of Abdirizak's Canadian life. The WUSC committee of University College would pay for his residence room until the end of August. He'd seen enough buildings in and around downtown Toronto to know that the residence building, Whitney Hall, with its mansard roof and solid wooden doors was architecturally beautiful. From its arched doorway, he could easily walk to the subway at Bloor Street or to Spadina Avenue for cheap clothes and haircuts. And he could be in his classes or at the college registrar's office in minutes. In his job at the registrar's, he filed papers and answered the questions of students who came in for course information. Over the year the job had helped him learn to talk to other students and had given him a better sense of all that his college offered. Despite his shyness and his knowledge that few shared his background, the job made him feel that he was part of the university.

During his first days on campus he had been baffled by everything he saw. There had been too many new buildings and new routes to absorb. But now, with the confidence gained at his job—and months of finding his own way—he enjoyed walking around the large U of T grounds. On a warm spring evening he could stop and admire buildings older than any he had seen before, like the splendidly gothic Hart House, taking pride in the university that had chosen him. He had registered again for the economics course he had dropped in the fall and felt back on track. He had learned one economic truth already: a Somali man he'd met who had come to Canada in the 1980s without an education was still driving a truck in Toronto.

At U of T's Scarborough campus, Mohamed had registered for summer courses. Over the winter he had beaten his nemesis, calculus—handily. He finished the term with an A+ in the course.

In Mississauga, Muno had chosen to fill her summer with courses in mathematics and sciences, courses that would allow her to move away from her English program. She was convinced—and friends like Halima had persuaded her—that a degree in English would not guarantee her a well-paying job after university. So she would spend the summer struggling through statistics and biology, subjects she had never enjoyed in the schools of Hagadera. But with sciences, she could get into nursing. If that didn't work out, she could still continue on in arts.

While Halima had decided against nursing, Muno now saw it as the sensible choice, one that would let her pay off her student loan and sponsor her family as soon as possible. Maybe when all that was taken care of, she could go to graduate school in social work. And that appealed to her more than nursing.

The career counsellor advising Muno didn't understand why she had also selected a course in children's literature, since she already had enough English credits for nursing. But Muno stuck to the course because she wanted to continue reading books and understanding them and, in her heart, was reluctant to let go of English literature. That spring she would leave behind Kafka and Woolf. *Alice in Wonderland* and the *Golden Compass* beckoned.

In Vancouver, Siyad was coming to the opposite conclusion from Muno. He had decided to put aside his first career choices—careers that could be practical and lucrative—to return to something he loved. He had arrived in Vancouver believing medicine would give him a way to help Africans, but he'd soon decided that becoming an engineer would be a more attainable goal. Through the year, he'd found the lab work in his first-year science courses demanding; he'd done well but had worked day and night to get the assignments done. He knew there would be even more lab work in the engineering program. "I don't want to stress myself anymore," he said. As he tried to decide on a new direction, he listened to advice from friends: "Do what you are happy with." In his room on the UBC campus, he mulled over that phrase for a long time and recalled how much he had loved learning mathematics as a boy—the pride he'd taken at winning competitions—and how much he had enjoyed teaching in the camp as a young man. And then he knew he could be happy as a mathematics teacher. "In the end, even if I go back to Somalia, there are so many people who are not studying." Somalia, he reasoned, would need teachers once there was peace, if there was ever peace. And if no peace came or he decided to stay in Canada, he could teach here. Over the summer he would take the courses that would allow him to switch his program.

In Brandon, Aden wouldn't let summer school interfere with his "awesome fun." He would take science courses to build up his credits for applying to medical school, but he planned to make sure he left enough time for his hobby of travelling. He had a friend's wedding in Ottawa to attend and new Somali families in Regina and Winnipeg to get to know. And there was new territory right around him to explore, now that "Manitoba was green everywhere."

While Aden was looking further down the road at a medical career, he was also strategizing how to cover his costs in the fall. With the cafeteria closed for the summer, he'd lost his cashier job. But word that he was a good worker got around and led him to a summer cleaning job in the Brandon residence. That had taught him a valuable foot-in-the-door lesson about experience and contacts. In the fall, he confidently believed, his reputation would lead to a higher-paying job on campus.

Some of the students weren't waiting for the fall to build up their funds. Both of the "Saskatoon boys" decided to work full-time over the summer. Dilalesa was able to expand his hours at his stockroom job. Regular work hours gave him some spare time to exercise in the warmer weather and the light-filled evenings. And it gave him the time to search for Oromos in the area and reconnect with his family in Ethiopia, two projects he had put on hold during the long, assignment-laden months of winter.

His friend Abdikadar decided he didn't want to work in Saskatoon or take courses at the university. All he'd done since arriving in late August was focus on schoolwork and his part-time job. He had confined himself to classrooms, residence, the stockroom where he worked and the routes in between. In that sense, his new life wasn't that much different from his old life in Dagahaley camp. He wanted to change it up, get out of the only city he'd known in Canada and travel. For the first time in his life he could move freely around a country, and he wanted to take advantage of that right. If he was going to become a doctor—and he still believed he would—he'd have to take a full slate of courses in the fall and start to study for the MCAT, the admission test for medical school. His first full summer in Canada might be his only free one. So he'd decided to visit another city in another province, and he'd bought himself a bus ticket—Saskatoon to Edmonton, Edmonton to Fort McMurray. He knew he wouldn't make big money in the northern city in a depressed economy and it would be hard to find work in the oil sands as other students had done in past years. But he'd find some kind of job, and he would enjoy the company of the Somalis who worked and lived there.

In Victoria, Marwo had taken on the task of earning money—with gusto, finding two jobs that left her little time for anything else. Although her WUSC committee would end its financial responsibility to her in August, it had helped her apply for a bursary at the university intended for international students but underused. Marwo could apply for the bursary only one time, but it would finance much of her second year, making the transition from full sponsorship to student living on a loan less of a shock.

Working and making money, however, helped Marwo regain that sense of adulthood she felt she'd lost in the strange new world she'd entered. So did navigating the city. She knew the bus routes around Victoria better than her Canadian friend Serina, a fact that she was proud of. And she knew which bank to go to in Victoria to send money to Vancouver and on to her aunt in Hagadera. Even though her aunt advised Marwo to concentrate on her studies, Marwo had taken it upon herself to send home about half of her money, knowing it would mean more daily luxuries like sugar, tea, new clothes and household items for her aunt's expanding compound.

Marwo worked as a cleaner seven days a week on two different shifts with two different employers. Every weeknight she worked in a Ministry of Health building downtown, on Blanshard Street, cleaning the empty offices. She worked alone and at her own pace, finishing for the night when the offices assigned to her were done. Five days a week, including weekends, she was training as a cleaner at the Queen Victoria Hotel and Suites at the foot of Douglas Street. She liked that job less. Some guests left the room a mess. Straightening up and making beds involved hard work. And none of her co-workers seemed able to get her name right. They often called her "Muro" or "Mawo."

Marwo's schedule was so tight she had little time for meals. She had never come to enjoy cooking during the year. She got used to buying prepared foods—vegetarian pizza was her favourite. She often went without lunch, but she was able to get a meal at the end of the day because she was living with a Somali family who prepared a supper for her.

By May, Marwo was living in her third dwelling in Victoria. Feeling settled was as important to her as feeling independent, but she hadn't had much luck with living arrangements. She had left the campus residence in January to save money by sharing an apartment with two other students, African women who had come to the University of Victoria on WUSC scholarships. But there had been frictions among the women, and after the university term ended, they had given up the apartment. Marwo had found a room she could rent for the summer in a house where several white Canadian young women lived, a room she'd have to leave in the fall once the room's original occupant returned. Now, while she waited for that room to become free for the summer, she was living temporarily in the subsidized townhouse of the Somali family she had spent Christmas break with. She couldn't stay there long, though. The family could only accommodate her for a short visit. In the meantime, she had packed most of her belongings away in boxes until the day she had a more permanent home.

She hoped to have that home by fall when she started back at the university. She had her study plan for her second year settled, at least. Her marks in her science courses had been disappointing, and, like Halima, she'd decided against applying for nursing. She had done well in her women's studies course, though—so well she'd decided she would major in the field. Often, in Hagadera, Marwo had wondered about the treatment of women in her culture. She had advocated openly for education for girls but had never felt comfortable enough to question female genital mutilation, forced marriages or domestic abuse outside her compound. In her women's studies course, she found that people wanted to hear about her experiences, wanted her to voice her viewpoints. That allowed her to reflect on what growing up female in Dadaab had meant to her.

The professor in the women's studies course had complimented Marwo's essays, especially when Marwo wrote about women in her own culture:

> The culture we are brought up in shapes our lives and how we understand the world. When I was a girl, I used to hear my Mum [her aunt] say "Hey, don't touch a ball. You are not a boy." Therefore, from a young age, I knew that it was boys who played football, not girls. I also used to hear Mum mention to my brother that he should not wash dishes or be around the kitchen to cook as those are women's duties. From childhood, I knew that my duties were cooking and washing dishes. These examples reflect how behaviors and world views are molded and shaped through certain roles and responsibilities assigned to different genders.

In another paper, she critiqued advertisers and the media for the negative effect they had on women in the West, whom she saw as pursuing beauty and thin bodies at all costs, adding that in her culture, women were not immune to the pressure to look beautiful:

> When I lived in Africa I used to see young girls use cosmetics to make themselves look brown because boys would not be attracted to black girls. Women struggled to change their skin colour to win the attention of men. I knew many young women who suffered skin problems relating to the chemicals they used to bring a physical appearance that attracts the desire of their boyfriends. What has

contributed to this is the media because young girls and boys see images of models with white or light skin on television and in advertisements. When young girls are asked why they use this chemical they say that they will be beautiful and men will be attracted to them.

Writing the essays crystallized Marwo's perceptions about girls in the camp. At seventeen, she'd felt too young for marriage but had watched as many of her female classmates dropped out of school because their families wanted them to marry. Marwo had no parents to arrange a marriage. She did have an aunt who saw that she was doing well in school and encouraged her to stay there. It was her aunt's presence in her life that made her want to take control of her own life now. She wrote:

The inequality of accessing education is a pressing issue as education empowers individuals. Empowering disadvantaged women from third-world countries where women have less economic power is an important strategy. However, the question remains: how to empower them. The cultural barriers such as FGM, early and forced marriages are hindering women from succeeding in participating in social roles. I believe education is an empowering tool. If women are educated they can understand their rights. They can have the choice of declining early marriages and FGM.

Without her aunt, Marwo might not have been saved from early marriage. Because of her aunt, Marwo believed that women could be leaders. She saw the possibilities in her aunt's actions: "She was a community leader and people liked her."

Marwo still accepted that she should cover herself in public because that was central to her beliefs as a Muslim. Sometimes in Victoria she'd catch people looking at her in a disapproving way: "Sometimes people don't sit close to me. They don't like the way I look. But I don't care. Some of them are nice and we talk. For the others, I don't care."

On campus, she had seen women—wives of international students, she believed—who completely covered their bodies, including their faces. Only a minority of women dressed that way in Dadaab. Marwo's aunt had never approved of women who wore burqas, which she said weren't a requirement in the Qu'ran. Her aunt thought those women were hiding something or using the cover to sneak off to see boyfriends so their parents wouldn't find out.

When Marwo first arrived in Canada, she had been shocked to learn that young female students sometimes lived with their boyfriends. But in her easygoing manner, she came to accept this as a cultural difference. And she didn't feel like censoring a Somali woman who had grown up in Canada and now wore trousers. It was a change that she noted, but did not condemn.

Marwo on the campus of the University of Victoria.

During the school year, Marwo had come to rely on the friendship of Serina Zapf. Serina had finished her degree that spring but was staying in Victoria for a year to work. She had been the coordinator of the volunteers for the WUSC local committee, a paid job that required a balancing act and a personal approach. "It would," she said, "have been easier for me to just sit in the office and say, 'You come in during my office hours and these are the kind of things we do. And it ends there.' But it's not like that at all. I have a friendship, I think, with everyone who's been involved in the program, whether they've been a volunteer or they're students who have come through."

Before Marwo arrived in Victoria, Serina and the committee knew only the basic facts about her past. They had made a choice not to read the personal stories of the students that WUSC included in the dossiers: "All we want to know is what they want to study and their grades to accept them. We're not saying, well, you know this person had more horrible things happen to them and is definitely worthy so that's the reason we made the decision."

Later, Serina learned Marwo's story as it came up naturally in conversations. Serina was finished with her WUSC duties, but she kept up with Marwo, whom she'd come to consider as one of her closest friends: "We hang out and we watch movies sometimes, and Saturday we're going out to Value Village, going shopping and stuff." Friend stuff. More important, she would be there to help Marwo find housing, advise her on her studies and help keep the loneliness Marwo felt for her family and her home at bay.

While Marwo worked night and day, Hussein was having no luck finding even a single job in Edmonton. A year earlier, the city had been on an economic high, but by the summer of 2008 the recession had lowered everyone's expectations. He knew that without any Canadian work experience, he was at a disadvantage. He had been a teacher in Ifo, but that didn't mean much to Canadian employers.

Hussein applied to various Tim Hortons locations around the city. In previous years the chain couldn't find enough employees for low-paying positions, but Hussein didn't get a single call back. He searched online and in the classifieds for "help wanted" advertisements, and he rode the bus around the city to drop his resumé off to potential employers. "I've tried everywhere. I tried malls. I tried factories." During the winter break he'd found work with a security firm that contacted him when they needed him. They had called him for three days' work in the winter but hadn't called him since. Hussein decided that if nothing turned up by June, he might as well take a summer course.

None of the jobs that other Somalis did in Edmonton were options for Hussein. Those who worked in the restaurants were usually relatives of the owners. Those who drove cabs had driver's licences. Other Somalis in the city travelled regularly to Fort McMurray, where they worked long stretches in the oil sands, but Hussein knew there weren't many jobs there this summer. "And it's hard working there," he said. "You work with dangerous gases." He still hoped he'd find something if he kept searching. "I'm not worried. The only thing is I don't like to be idle."

When I visited Hussein in the spring, his days were wide open and we had time to wander through his neighbourhood around the Grant MacEwan Residence and to talk at length. In the afternoon, we walked

Hussein in front of the tall residence building
at Grant MacEwan College in Edmonton.

233

down streets with newly planted trees and spring green leaves. Even with the trees in bloom, he was not convinced winter was over. He wore the same red jacket he'd worn in December and said there were three *w*'s you could not trust in life: women, wealth and weather. Hussein wanted to know the names of the trees we passed, and although I couldn't oblige him, I could reassure him that the fluff on the ground was pollen, not snow.

During our walk around the campus we ran into Irteza Omar, who had headed the Grant MacEwan committee in its first year. He was one of the students who'd met Hussein at the airport. "Technically, I was," he said somewhat sheepishly. "We're going to go [to the airport] two hours ahead from now on." As a Muslim, Omar had understood Hussein's dietary needs, but as someone who had grown up in Canada he admitted he hadn't understood how confounding everything around Hussein would be to him. As the two talked about finding Hussein a job, it was clear that through the year the relationship had not moved beyond discussions of Hussein's needs. Irteza reminded Hussein that although the college was sponsoring a second student that year from Dadaab, it had enough money to provide Hussein with some support.

When Hussein and I walked down an industrial-looking street to see the mosque he went to for Friday prayers, one of the leather sandals that he had brought from Africa fell apart. He felt certain he could never find a pair like them in Canada. We slowly headed back to his residence so he could put on shoes, and when he came out he had shed the coat, assuming, perhaps, that the worst of winter was over. We sat outside at the Tim Hortons across from his residence and talked for a couple of hours. He asked me about my work and my life and he told me that he got an 87 per cent average in the courses he'd taken but wanted to get 90 per cent in his courses the next year.

At one point, a young, skinny black man with a ponytail walked into the coffee shop. Hussein confirmed he was Somali but had grown up in Canada. Hussein knew it would be difficult to raise children in Canada and keep them in the Somali culture. That's why he wanted to take any children he had back to Africa from time to time so they could become immersed in their culture. It would be expensive, "but children are worth it," he said. If it was still too dangerous to take them back to Somalia, he could take them to Nairobi or somewhere in Ethiopia or Uganda where Somalis lived.

During that visit, I asked Hussein if he had become accustomed to the way women dressed and the way men and women interacted in Canada. "I think it is disgusting," he said. "The way they dress, the way they touch each other, kissing in class." He said it was nothing like how young women and men acted in his culture. But even before coming to Canada, he'd known that as long as he followed the Canadian laws, he could fulfill his Islamic laws. "I'm really tolerant of them and they're also tolerant," he said. "Basically, people here are polite, they are welcoming, they are good, but there is nothing I like about their cultures."

I had to ask him. I didn't wear the miniskirts or short tops of younger women whom he found disgusting, but I still was dressed like a Western woman, in jeans and a short-sleeved top. Yet, ever since that first evening I'd visited him in Edmonton, he'd seemed comfortable with me, as I had become with him. I asked why he was so friendly with me and whether it was because I was older.

"No," he said.

"What is the distinction?" I asked. He hesitated. "I assume you are not disgusted by me," I blurted. "Do you find me strange?"

"Not really strange," he said. "I actually don't know what the dressing code is. In the Somali community, a woman should wear hijab. I don't know how women should dress here. You know, you came to the camp. You saw where I lived. You came to my home. You know me better than most Canadians." It was the connection, the knowing, that had made the difference.

He was not connecting to many students in Edmonton other than those on his WUSC committee and some Somali and African students. He didn't know why. Perhaps he just wasn't interested. He still avoided the parties in the residence, even when there was no alcohol served, because he worried the strange foods might have alcohol mixed in them. He did know a few people from his classes and from the residence well enough to greet them, but, he said, "We don't talk about anything important."

As we sat sipping our tea at an outdoor table, Hussein told me his mother was doing well in the camp. He wasn't too worried about his family in Ifo. So far the overcrowding in the camps had not affected them. He had been hopeful for Somalia when Sheikh Sharif Ahmed, the leader of the Union of Islamic Courts, had become president in the winter. While he welcomed an Islamic leadership in the country and the basic principles of Sharia law, he felt the fighting between Islamists had "got out of hand," hampering the president's chance of creating any real government. "If they don't give him a chance, then this is the end of the country," he said. "And I don't know why they are fighting him. There is no reason because he says he is using the Islamic Sharia law. He's making a lot of changes. He says the government is going to use that law in their constitution. So I don't know why."

On May 15, 2009, Elizabeth A. Kennedy filed a report for the Associated Press, marking another turn of events in the disintegrating situation in Somalia:

> *After three months of hopeful glimmers in one of the most explosive countries in the world, violence again is roiling Somalia as mortar, machine-gun fire and rockets pound the bloodstained capital.*
>
> *More than 100 people, mostly civilians, have been slaughtered in a week and thousands are streaming out of Mogadishu as insurgents close in on the presidential palace. The Western-backed government is struggling to survive.*

Three days later, Doctors Without Borders/Médecins Sans Frontières issued a briefing paper on Dadaab, warning, "the situation for nutrition and for water and sanitation is alarming."

The Dadaab camps had grown to an estimated 270,000 people. Two-thirds of the population in Dagahaley had arrived from Somalia in the past year. Médicins Sans Frontières had stepped in to provide care at a clinic in Dagahaley camp. In health and nutrition surveys in the camp, it uncovered that the newcomers "had little access to food, shelter, health care services, and basic non-food items." Water scarcity, the organization reported, had "led to tensions and fighting among the refugees and host community."

For most of the Dadaab students in Canada, not a day went by when they didn't check what was happening in Somalia, when they didn't worry about their families in the camps. By May, Abdi had moved out of residence in London and was living in a basement room in a house near enough to the campus that he could quickly make it to his part-time job in the Huron library and to his summer classes. Taped to the wall of his room was a map of Greater Somalia that he had drawn on a lined piece of paper, showing the regions that made up the five points of the Somali flag, the regions in and around Somalia where Somalis lived. Across the top he had written the word *Dhulkayaga,* "homeland." Now that dreams of peace within Somalia itself looked more and more unattainable, even optimistic Abdi was sounding less hopeful. "I don't know," he said. "I don't understand the politics. I agreed when they were fighting with Ethiopian troops, but now they are fighting with themselves." He said that al-Shabab was in control of his home city of Kismayo and unless the militant group was willing to work with the government, it wouldn't be easy to get peace in Somalia in the near future. "If the country could only find peace," he said, a sliver of hope sliding into his words as he spoke, it could develop and build a new infrastructure quickly. He pointed to Rwanda, where systems in the country did come back after civil war.

Abdi still missed his friends in Dadaab, missed the life of Ifo, but he wasn't missing the restrictions or the police who abused their power. He had always taken care of himself in Dadaab, and he was learning to do that here without the feelings of hopelessness and fear he'd grown up with. The room he'd found for the summer was in a house on a quiet residential street. There were dogs at the house next door, but he had discovered that if he acknowledged them, they left him alone. In his basement kitchen he was learning to cook. He could now make spaghetti and rice and bought halal meat, chapatis and vegetables. But there were still traces of anxiety in Abdi that were understandable in someone who had lived for years in insecurity and whose strongest early memory was of armed men entering his home and killing his family. He was pleased that for the fall he had found an apartment, which he thought would be safer than a house. He didn't trust the security of houses, even in Canada. "Anything can happen," he said. "There is a control gate at the apartment. When you need your landlord, there is always someone available at the rental office."

His workload was heavy. The shorter summer courses were more intensely packed with assignments than the longer winter courses. He had five assignments to do each night. He was still trying to keep his options for graduate school in economics or pharmacology open. Mornings, he bought two Tim Hortons French vanilla cappuccinos to stay awake in class.

His workload meant he had to put the French immersion course he'd hoped to take in Quebec on hold. Of all the students, Abdi had the strongest interest in Canadian history and politics. He agonized over the country of his birth, but he wanted to feel he belonged to the country that had chosen him. He wanted to know as much about Canada as he could. In his spare time he'd been watching television, familiarizing himself with Canadian life and personalities through the medium. CBC Newsworld's *One on One* with Peter Mansbridge was his favourite television program because it introduced him to so many authors and public figures. That week in mid-May, he'd been intrigued by the televised coverage of Brian Mulroney at the public inquiry into the former prime minister's dealings with German-Canadian businessman Karlheinz Schreiber. The first thing that surprised him was that there could be political scandals and concerns about bribes in Canada just as there were in

Kenya. The second thing was how tough the inquiry lawyer was on a former prime minister. "Mulroney almost cried," he said.

One weekend in May, I drove Abdi to my favourite spot, Niagara Falls. I never ceased to be awed standing by the edge of the falls, and I hoped Abdi would find the experience equally thrilling. His curiosity about the world around him was evident throughout the drive. Looking out at the green fields east of London, he said he knew that farmers in Canada had electricity and even the Internet, but he wondered how they got their mail. When we drove by a nursery, he wanted to know why the plants were covered, and I told him about frost. Sometimes the things we passed sparked ideas he had about his future. When I told him that people spent holidays in the campers we drove past, he said that some day he would drive across the country—once he had a driver's licence and owned a car—just to see all of Canada, "just for a picnic." He had read that in some countries people had three months of vacation and wondered if Canadian holidays were that long. I said that most employees on salaries only got about three to four weeks off. He said even as a refugee with incentive pay in Kenya, he'd had a month off with pay, and the Kenyan nationals who worked in the camps had one month off for every four they worked.

At other times, sights along the way stirred nostalgia in him. The farms reminded him of the one his family had owned in Somalia outside of the city of Kismayo. I asked if he knew what had happened to the farm. He said he didn't. I asked if the stepfamily he had lost track of had been connected to the farm, and he said he didn't remember. And then, echoing a sentiment he often expressed, he ended the subject: "It is always good to forget about the past. Sometimes, when you remember, you can't keep yourself going."

When we drove past the city of Hamilton, Abdi, the numbers guy, wanted to know the population, and I, not a numbers person, could not tell him. I could, though, explain the plants and the smokestacks and the city's history as "Steel Town." And I was able to tell him that the Queen Elizabeth Way, the highway we were on, was the first divided highway between cities in Canada. He said he found it strange to compare this highway to Ifo Highway, which was just a small road, "and very dusty."

I pointed out the town of Grimsby, where I grew up, pointed out where my family's farm had been. Abdi suddenly became the interviewer and asked me what I felt when I saw the town. I admitted I felt some nostalgia of my own, that I'd had a pretty good childhood there and that much of my family's history was in that town. He asked if I had any brothers and sisters there, and I said they had all moved away. He asked about my parents, and I told him they were both dead.

In Niagara Falls, to my delight, he was agog. Even before we walked to the falls' edge, he was stunned by the rotating tower that looked like the CN Tower in Toronto, by the crowds and even by the cadets who were finishing a parade. He said "Wow" frequently or, sometimes, "Oh my God." I told him the story of the widow Annie Taylor, who in 1901 became the first person to go over the falls in a barrel just so she could make money from the publicity to support herself. When he asked what happened to her, he was outraged to hear that her manager had cheated her and she'd ended up in a pauper's grave. "The government should have helped that woman get the money the manager stole from her," he said. Injustices were something he understood.

At the edge of the falls, he stared at the rolling water the colour of old glass bottles. Within minutes, though, he wanted to know its speed. But I couldn't tell him. Instead, I pointed way down below to the river where the *Maid of the Mist* was making its way into the curve of the Horseshoe Falls and told him we could go on a boat just like that one. As we walked toward the ticket booth farther down the river, he said with some pride that the American falls were nothing in comparison to the Canadian falls. He could name falls in Africa— Victoria Falls, Gura Falls and the falls in Hell's Gate National Park— but he had never been able to visit any of them. He was torn about going on the boat ride. He didn't seem to want me to spend the money but did want the new experience. He thought he'd been on a boat before, a small fishing boat on the river near Garissa, but he was certain he'd never been on a boat as big as the *Maid of the Mist*. Finally he said, "I want to go."

Waiting for the boat to depart, he watched the cormorants dive, the gulls swoop overhead, stared at the nearby bridge with cars headed to the United States. "This is so close to America," he said. "Wow." As the horn blew and the boat pulled away from the dock, he looked solemn, almost sad. Once the mist hit us, he pulled his arms tight against his body beneath the thin plastic poncho all passengers wore. He listened to the tales of Niagara Falls over the boat's loudspeaker. "He's saying a boy in just a bathing suit went over the falls and survived!" he yelled to me when I couldn't hear.

The mist grew heavier as we approached the falls. We both had to close our eyes against its bite. Then the boat turned and the air cleared and the water's roar dropped to silence. As we slowed to dock, I reminded him of something he'd told me in the camp, that some had to get out and see the outside world so they could tell others what it was like. I asked if he would be able to describe what he had seen. "It will be hard to describe," he said, staring with a serious expression at the sharp cliffs on the side of the river. "But I will try."

On the way back to Toronto, he recognized the sign for Grimsby and asked me if I thought of my parents each time I drove by the town. I said I did. He asked if there was a place where they were. I said they were in a cemetery, and I could go and visit their graves. "You never forget your parents," he said.

He had made it clear soon after I met him that he didn't want to talk any more than he had to about his own parents' deaths. Now, as we drove by the town where my own parents were buried, I asked him if he remembered his parents well. He said simply, "Yah." Whenever he saw a child who didn't have parents in the camp he felt sad, he added. He searched for another word before settling on the word "sympathy." He said that sometimes Somali parents in the camp beat their children and he would rush into their compound and tell them that was no way to treat a child. He couldn't stand to hear children cry.

As quickly as the subject had come up, he pushed it aside and asked what the black mass was over the Niagara escarpment. I told him that it was a cloud. It looked like a storm up ahead.

Toward the end of spring, Halima walked through the Public Gardens in Halifax with her friend Sarah. Through the winter, when she'd gone by the gardens on the bus, she'd had no idea that they even existed. Now she liked to visit them whenever she could. She and Sarah walked past the bandshell, all white and red and fresh-looking, and along paths that meandered around garden beds, stopping to pose for photographs by statues and trees. Halima pulled out her cellphone to take pictures of the swans and ducks, asking what they were called. She loved the tranquility in the park, but in truth, it did little to sooth her. Within minutes she wanted to leave. Sarah obliged and they walked to the nearby Tim Hortons. Behind the counter, the staff was hanging blue and white streamers for Camp Day, a day each year when the chain raised money across Canada to send children to camp. Sarah had to explain the concept to her friend, who, for most of her life, had been confined in a very different kind of camp.

Back in her camp, the new arrivals were bringing Somali "methods of violence" with them. In her camp, her father's health was deteriorating. He could hardly walk now and appeared to be losing his memory. When Halima heard how sick he was, she'd cried for a week. She cried on the phone when she spoke with him, even though he told her funny stories to try to cheer her up. While she ate her chocolate-covered doughnut and laughed and argued with Sarah, she could forget about her worries, but the news about her father had rattled her, shaken her confidence in her plans. Pursuing a science degree seemed selfish to her now. But quitting school to make money at a minimum-wage job was not an option either. She had to find a middle way.

At no time in her secondary school years, at no time in her first university year, had she considered the career she now decided she would pursue. It was a career option that left Paula Barry bewildered, but it was one that would give Halima money in a few years so she could sponsor her parents and bring them to Canada. She blocked from her mind the thought that her father might not be alive to sponsor at all. She would do what she had to. Halima dropped her dream of becoming a biochemist. She would become an accountant instead.

CHAPTER NINE

It Never Feels Like Home

IN THE EARLY DAYS OF SUMMER, Siyad announced on his Facebook page that he was bored: "Life in Canada is boring. I feel like going back!!!!" He had successfully finished his summer courses and only had a few hours of work each week at the local Safeway.

He'd had no luck finding any other job. Often, he just stayed in his room at UBC and wrote messages online, his curtain separating him from the world outside.

Just below his window stood a carved wooden gate engraved with the words "Our future is rooted in our traditions." The gate had been a gift in 2001 from forestry students who had escaped the Soviet invasion in Hungary in 1957 and had been welcomed as refugees into the forestry program at UBC. The gate, the sculpted pine trees and the open green space offered Siyad an incredible view, although his Dadaab friends might have envied him more for the Tim Hortons that was inside the Forestry building just steps from his door.

There were those who didn't think Siyad appreciated how good he had it. Several responded to his Facebook message with comments on his page saying, "Going back to where?" or simply, "Irony." Aden from Brandon wrote, "Hahaha." One of the members from

Siyad's wusc committee advised him to get out of his room more.

In Dadaab, Siyad had seemed the best-equipped student to handle adjustments in the West. Before working as a teacher, he had been an interpreter for journalists and dignitaries who came to the camp— until CARE "sacked" him in budget cutbacks. As an interpreter he had come in contact with Westerners, both male and female, and had learned to accept the habits and the dress styles of North Americans as part of their tradition. The message that advisers delivered to the students before they left the camps resonated with him: "When we were going through orientation they said respect people's culture then you will be respected. And you have to accept that as part of your life."

On campus he had made friends with students in the Muslim Association and with two Somali students. He knew the international students in his house and the students on the wusc committee, but he hadn't made friends with any of the Canadian students in his classes. He'd made more friends at the Safeway in Point Grey, where a diverse group of people worked. They were all young and, no matter their background, talked to him easily and shared the kind of camaraderie common among junior employees in their first jobs.

Siyad liked his job at the Safeway. The people whose carts he pushed were friendly. It was easy to collect the grocery carts. The only thing that caused him problems was price checks. He had to find items by reading the cards beside unfamiliar produce and products.

I sat one day with Siyad at the beginning of summer outside the Tim Hortons beside his residence. He was going to get the steeped tea he always ordered, but perhaps because he was feeling in a bit of a rut he decided to try the French vanilla cappuccino that reminded the others of Somali tea. "Oh yes," he said, after his first sip. "I will take this from now on."

Despite his knowledge of Western ways, Siyad had always been rather shy around me. It wasn't that he was uncooperative or unwilling to answer my questions—he and Aden were the two students who responded quickest to emails I sent—but he hadn't wanted to go out to dinner with me or go on an excursion. I never knew how much of that was his nature and how much was caution. Because he had worked around journalists, he knew how they wrote things about people, maybe things they didn't want to share so widely.

When I'd asked if he had a girlfriend in the camp, he laughed and asked me, "Did the others talk to you about girlfriends?" When I replied that I hadn't asked them yet, he said, "They won't tell you. They wouldn't tell a journalist that; they wouldn't want it in a book." In fact, he was partially right. Later, several of the Somali students did tell me about their attachments in the camp but didn't want the relationships mentioned. Even from this distance, they didn't want their families to know, and they considered it unfair to involve another person's name in their story. They all qualified the terms "girlfriend," and "boyfriend," because of the North American connotations of physical contact. One of them even used air quotes when he described having someone "like a girlfriend" in the camp.

That day, Siyad showed me his route to work on the Number 19 bus, and walked me through the Safeway and introduced me to one of his friends there, an Asian woman who teased him about coming in on his day off. We went back together to the bus loop at UBC, where I could catch the bus downtown. After almost a year he still didn't know where all the buses parked there went. In the winter, he'd told me that the UBC campus was like a city itself and he felt no need to leave it. But now that he had time on his hands, he wanted to explore beyond the university enclave. He was even thinking of taking the ferry to Victoria, but he wasn't sure how to use the ferry or which buses would take him to the ferry station.

At the bus loop, Siyad asked me what I was going to do next and I said I didn't know exactly, that I had left the afternoon to visit him. He casually said he might come downtown with me. The crowded bus crawled over the Burrard Street Bridge in the late afternoon. I leaned forward in my seat to talk to Siyad, who sat nearby. "Where do you want to get off? Do you want to go by the water or on a street with stores?" I asked. "Anywhere," he said. I suggested we walk to the bottom of Burrard Street and along the harbour. When we got off the bus, he seemed surprised at all the tall buildings, the traffic, the fountain we passed. "But you've been here before," I said. He said he had, but only at night and only three times. He didn't remember seeing all those tall buildings on his previous visits.

At the harbour, I pointed toward Stanley Park. "It is one of the best parks," I told him. He had a free bus pass, one of the most beautiful cities in Canada and time on his hands, but clearly he had not felt comfortable enough or curious enough to visit much of the city yet. In the camps, the first time I met Siyad, he'd had on wire-framed glasses that he admitted he wore for appearance's sake only. They gave him a somewhat professorial look. The care he took with his clothing and the ease with which he spoke to Westerners in his clear English had led me to believe he was more urbane than some of the others. Even in Vancouver, he looked like a cool guy in a cool city, a tall, handsome man who blended in to the crowd on the city's multicultural streets. But I realized I might have been fooled about the ease he felt, and I was reminded of just how many differences the students were still coping with. If I, who had seen him both in his world in Dadaab and in his world here, could forget those challenges, how could strangers passing him on the streets of Vancouver possibly imagine them?

As we walked along the harbour, we heard the roar of a floatplane's engine. Siyad was amazed when he saw the plane skimming across the water. I explained how the pontoons kept the plane afloat as he craned his neck to watch it take off. We walked along the seaside path toward the park, stopping so Siyad could watch floatplanes take off or settle back on the water. With our meandering pace, we never made it as far as the park. Siyad had to get back to the campus for his sunset prayer. When we parted at the stop for his bus back to campus, he told me that now that he knew the way, he would come downtown again. He would explore Stanley Park on his own.

In Mississauga, the first warm days of summer were making Muno nostalgic for Hagadera. "I just realized I am even more homesick than when I first came," she said. "Perhaps it is because of the summer when there are a lot of people outside." When she arrived, there had been the excitement over her new life to counter her longing. Where would it take her? What would she become? Without the novelty of unfamiliar things to learn, she missed her family more intensely and came to realize hers was not an alienation that would slip away once she got used to her life.

Dressed in a brown one-piece hijab, Muno could have been on her way to Hagadera market—the market that she knew even before leaving would haunt her forever. Not much had changed in her appearance since the day she'd bartered for her prayer mat there. Some of the plumpness had gone from her face so that her high, sculpted cheekbones stood out more prominently. Her happy, curious expression had been replaced by a wiser, more wistful one, as if she had seen more sadness here than in all her years in the camp.

That summer day, instead of walking through the lanes between the *kamoor* fencing of the compounds, her feet sinking into the red sand of Hagadera, she walked on concrete sidewalks between the tall modern buildings of the UTM campus. After the winter term, she had taken her first summer courses at the downtown campus and stayed with Somalis. But now she had a course on the Mississauga campus, a part-time job working with an academic adviser at the registrar's office. So she'd taken advantage of her sponsorship money to live in residence again.

The residence was large, modern and closer to the cafeteria than the first apartment she'd had. She lived in a unit for four, but no one else was around now. She sat in one of the chairs in the sitting room beside the kitchenette. Perhaps if she had been here in the winter, living with more women, closer to the buildings of the university, she might not have felt as lonely. Perhaps.

It wasn't that she was sorry to be in Canada. It was just that she constantly felt conflict between her need to progress in life and her desperate wish to be back in her family compound again. In Dadaab, life was hard, especially for women and children. Here, food was plentiful and modern health care was available to everyone. Life was definitely easier. "It's beautiful and everyone is nice," Muno said of Canada. "I miss Hagadera. It's nothing like Hagadera. It never feels like family. It never feels as good. It never feels like home."

She had come to see, too, that people in the camps had "overestimated" Canada. "We didn't think that there were mosquitoes or cockroaches in Canada, but there are. There are places downtown that are dirtier than Nairobi." And violence. She had heard of killings in the city. "We thought it was some kind of heaven, with no crime." And she'd believed that with all the health care and medicine in Canada, everybody would be healthy. She was shocked that people here suffered from illnesses, particularly mental illnesses.

Still, she was proud to have this "lifetime opportunity." She wouldn't trade it for the chance to go back home. She'd been the youngest in the group—nineteen when she left home, twenty when she arrived in Canada—but she saw getting her education as a filial duty. Somali girls, she said, were no strangers to responsibility: "Girls get married at fifteen and they're responsible, although it's a little different when you are at home and you have the one family."

And that was the rub, the source of her conflicted feelings. She accepted her responsibility willingly even though it meant adjusting her personal desires. "I like English, but I cannot afford to feel, 'I like this. I don't like that.' I feel like I don't have the choice to do what I want." But she had to carry out her responsibility alone, in Canada, far from her family, far from a mother to console her. "They took me away at the wrong time." She laughed, a quiet, rueful laugh. "I am too young to be here. I should have stayed with my mom longer."

Her certainty that she would never be at home in Canada added to her homesickness for a place where she felt she did belong. She suspected that her Muslim beliefs, especially those relating to men and women, meant that she could never fully be part of mainstream Canadian life. Muno paid far less attention to the news than someone like Abdi did, but the criticisms of the Muslim faith and the public association of her faith with terrorists still got through. "We are the ones from the outside," she said.

As I sat with Muno that day, the voices of the previous sponsored students I'd spoken with echoed in my head. They had all—Muslims and Christians—gone through feelings of not belonging in Canada that had made them want to return to their homeland. When wars ended, when regimes changed, when it was safe to do so, many had gone back to visit. I didn't have the heart to tell Muno what I had learned from them: that after years away from their homeland, they didn't feel they belonged there anymore. Kakule Floribert Kamabu went back to the Democratic Republic of the Congo ten years after he first fled the country for his life. In those ten years, Floribert had become a nurse in Canada, fathered two children and brought two brothers and a sister to Canada. In 2007, when he returned to the DRC, he discovered he couldn't live there anymore, that Canada had become his home: "Everything was gone. The way of life was not the way of life that I was thinking it was. I was completely out of place."

Ambaye Kidane, now a senior civil servant in the Ontario Ministry of Finance, did find much of his old life and plenty of his old friends when he went back to Ethiopia. But while he was there, he longed to be at his Canadian job or the small Toronto coffee shops where he enjoyed drinking cappuccinos on Saturday mornings. He remains a news junkie who will forever follow the stories of Ethiopia and Africa, and he knows he will always feel torn between two continents. It is something he has come to accept: "The life of a refugee or immigrant is: You are here. You'll never fully adjust. A part of you is there— a good part is there. But you can't go back because you will be a refugee there. The first generation of refugees is in a perpetual state of being a refugee, a state of adjustment. You are condemned if you go back or if you stay here of feeling different."

With less than a year in Canada behind her, Muno's goal was to somehow mesh the two realms of her life. She believed she could take her Canadian education back to Africa, where she saw a real need for social work that would help women and children in their daily lives.

Women in Canada didn't need her help. From her perspective, they were doing fine. Maybe it was just the values she grew up with, she said, values that came from her religion, but she believed there needed to be some order in the family and that the wife should be obedient to the husband as the head of the household: "He doesn't have to force you or abuse your rights or anything, but in life we need some order. Even if I was earning more, I would owe obedience to my husband. It is part of my faith."

She resented the fact that people thought of an immigrant man working while the woman stayed at home to take care of the children as oppression of women: "If it's a Canadian woman, everybody knows that is her choice, but if it's an immigrant or a Muslim woman or an African woman, people think she was forced to do that. That may be true, but it's not always true." She didn't think that she could go along with the kind of decisions social workers in Canada made about domestic situations. She had heard that parents could lose their child for spanking that child, and she didn't think that was right.

It wasn't just her religion that made Muno feel like an outsider. The traditions, the institutions, the way people behaved in Canada— they all made sense to her intellectually. But there was always something that tripped her up, such as how to talk to professors: "Back home, it used to be very formal and you never called them by their names." She couldn't grasp the way Canadian students spoke to their professors. It wasn't quite the same informal tone used with friends, but it wasn't formal either: "I don't know if I have the right approach. I can talk to professors if I have a real question, but I cannot go up and talk to them and ask them general questions."

She had met other Somali students in her classes who had come to Canada when they were four or five or were born here, and they knew how to act like Canadians and even felt Canadian. "I don't know if I will ever feel like that," she said. "I know if I have kids, the kids will feel like that, but I don't know if I will ever feel like that."

She was grateful to those Somali friends who had helped her that year, but she always felt different from them: "The Somali girls are actually between two worlds and I am still in the old world." She now had a friend from her old world, a young woman whom she had once taught in Hagadera camp. The teenager's father lived in Toronto. He'd recently developed a disability and had sponsored his daughter so she could assist him in his downtown apartment. Muno often stayed at the apartment so the two friends could talk about their days back home.

"And I have Jane," she said to me that day. Through the year, my daughter, Jane, had become her Canadian friend. Muno was always interested in hearing about Jane's writing in her program at York University. The first time she met Jane, she'd asked to read one of her poems. It was a complicated, angry poem about the poet Ted Hughes and his dead wives. On first reading, Muno had trouble with its meaning, but she persisted, checking her perceptions with Jane until it made sense to her. Jane was impressed by the stories Muno had written in English back in the camp. Jane had studied French in school, but it hadn't come easily as a second language and she couldn't imagine how anyone could express themselves so clearly in a language not their own.

Jane would drive out to the Mississauga campus and the two would go out for tea. Jane lent Muno books, encouraged her to try J. K. Rowling's Harry Potter series. Muno recommended books from her class and from her knowledge of African literature. When I asked Muno if she found Western young women strange, she answered, "I find Somali-Canadian girls a little strange, different. But then for Jane, I thought she was going to be more different than that. I think what people see from outside, that's very different from when you get close. We all like the same things, we almost all have the same kind of values."

That day, as most days I met Muno, she talked about a book. This time it was a book she hadn't read but wanted to read. It was by Senegalese author Mariama Bâ, who was raised a Muslim and wrote about the injustices women suffered. The book was *The Scarlet Song*. "It's kind of a romantic book about a black guy who met a white woman and they fell in love and she decided to marry him against the wishes of her parents," Muno said. The author, she added, wrote the book when she had cancer and only one year to live. "It's very sad."

Later in the summer, Jane and I took Muno to Niagara Falls for her first boat ride. It was also her first trip out of the metropolitan Toronto area. Her WUSC committee had not sent anyone to the annual assembly in Ottawa, and even if it had, she admitted, she wouldn't have gone. She said she had been feeling like a coward in the autumn. Now, she said, she wanted to see places. She said it with the same determination she'd shown about meeting a dog for the first time.

Unlike Abdi, she did not look out the window during the drive or ask a lot of questions about the sights we were passing. In fact, she seemed unaware of the world outside the car. She talked to Jane about cellphone plans and books. Jane handed her a copy of *Alice in Wonderland,* but Muno said it was too late—she'd already bought the book. But it didn't matter. She'd dropped the course in children's literature because she was finding the biology course so hard. She hoped to take a course in detective fiction in September. "But I am reading again," she said. She pulled a thin book out of her black handbag. It was a novel by the Somali writer Nuruddin Farah, *From a Crooked Rib,* another book about the hard lives of women. She said it was not great. Muno found the portrayal of women's lives fairly accurate but somewhat exaggerated. When her friend Abdinoor saw her reading it, he warned her she would turn into a feminist.

Jane showed Muno her blue nail polish and said she could paint Muno's nails sometime. Muno laughed. She described how girls who used henna in the camps applied it all around the top of the finger, not just on the nail. Jane said she tried to get the polish on the nail but usually got it on her finger as well, and described the small brush she had to use. I said I thought I'd seen nail polish on some of the girls' toenails in the camps. Muno said it was not polish but something else. Her father let her use the henna but not the darker dye.

By the falls, I pointed out the *Maid of the Mist.* "Will I fall out?" Muno asked. Jane assured her she wouldn't and pointed at the people on board in their blue plastic ponchos. The ponchos reminded Muno of the uniforms the students in her school had worn. She seemed hesitant to go on the boat now that she had the chance. But she found her courage, and once we started down the spiral stairs toward the dock, she got ahead of us in the crowd. She had a quiet way of moving past people, a skill I suggested to her she'd learned in the food lines at Hagadera. We laughed but then she grew serious when I asked her about a video I'd seen online of people pushing in the Hagadera food line and someone hitting them with a stick to try to keep them back. The lines were like that, she said. She'd seen the video too and thought she recognized the young man using the stick. She wondered what he felt being on YouTube, hitting people for the whole world to see.

We were the last three on the boat and stood on the lower deck. The wind was strong that day and the mist heavy. We got soaked. I couldn't tell if the expression on Muno's face was awe or fear, but I

Friends Jane and Muno on a summer trip
on the *Maid of the Mist* at Niagara Falls.

told her I could walk her to the stairs in the middle of the boat if she wanted to get away from the edge. She dismissed my suggestion with a tightening around her lips that hinted at both determination and annoyance, and held onto the railing. If it was awe she was feeling, she wouldn't want to miss out on the moment. If it was fear, she would conquer it.

After the ride, Muno pointed to a frozen yogourt stand and suggested we get cones. I had made a picnic lunch for us, which we'd eaten earlier. She said she wanted to pay for the cones because I had already done so much. I was touched by her gratitude but knew the cones would be expensive so close to the falls. Jane protested openly. She had heard all the stories of the students by now, knew they had had none of her economic advantages in life and didn't want Muno to spend her money. Muno glared at an oblivious Jane and I shushed my daughter, warning her to let it go. When it came time to pay, Muno pulled a debit card out of her purse. The vendor told her he couldn't take debit. "Cash only," he said dismissively, impatiently waiting for payment so he could serve the next person in line. Muno pulled a $5 bill from her purse, all the cash she had with her but not enough, and I handed the vendor another bill to cover the rest of the cost.

We took our cones, which were melting rapidly in the heat, and sat on the grass nearby, trying to eat them quickly before they dripped all over our clothes. "Thank you, Muno," Jane said. "I don't know what for," Muno answered sharply. Jane didn't seem to notice the tone or the frustration in Muno's voice. And I didn't know what to say at that moment that wouldn't embarrass her further.

By mid-July the Islamist militia, al-Shabab, controlled much of south and central Somali and all but a few blocks in Mogadishu. In the capital they fought alongside another Islamic group, called Hizbul Islam, against national security forces and African Union soldiers who were protecting the government of Somali president Sheikh Sharif Ahmed. From Geneva, Navi Pillay, the UN human rights chief, charged that both insurgents and government troops were committing war crimes. Both sides were firing mortars into populated civilian areas. And, he said, the insurgents were using civilians as human shields and setting up tribunals ordering people to be stoned or decapitated.

Earlier in the month, Somalia's Prime Minister Omar Abdirashid Ali Sharmarke had warned, in an interview with ABC News, that foreigners backed by al-Qaeda were fighting alongside al-Shabab, making the country "uncontrollable." He appealed to the international community for help, hoping to reignite American involvement in the country, involvement that had remained low-key since the disaster of Black Hawk Down.

ABC News also reported on the contents of a memo in which U.S. officials had requested an exemption to an arms embargo for Somalia that had been in place for seventeen years. ABC said that the memo requested "permission to ship 19 tons of ammunition including small arms, RPGs and mortars directly to Somalia's Transitional Federal Government forces."

In July, the United Nations reported that more than 200,000 had fled the capital since the fighting intensified there in the spring. Asha Sha'ur, a member of Somalia's beleaguered civil society—a segment of the population that had worked through years of warfare to keep institutions running—told the UN's news service, IRIN, that the situation in Mogadishu "was worse than at any time in the past. I know we have said so many times that the situation is bad, but I honestly cannot remember when the suffering was this bad."

Most of those fleeing would get only as far as camps for the internally displaced within Somalia, but some escaped on boats to Yemen and some were still able to get through the closed border into Kenya and find their way to Dadaab. By late July, the biggest refugee camp in the world had swelled to more than 286,000 people. In June, UNHCR registered 7,000 new arrivals, up from 5,000 in May. UNHCR was still trying to get agreement for another section of land, calling the need for a fourth camp "urgent."

———

Mohamed was taking four half-courses that summer, trying to get a total of four credits before his scholarship ended and he became a full-time, self-supporting student the next year. But even when he had exams to study for and difficult assignments to finish, Mohamed always found time to pay attention to Somalia. The events of the spring, and the failure of the expanded Somali government to take hold, had left him depressed. "I'm giving up hope now," he said. "I'm very pessimistic about what is happening. I was hoping the new government would bring something out of nothing and they would create some peace. But out of the blue, we have this fighting. I think the last fifteen, sixteen years was a different war altogether. Now we are beginning a new phase. It might take another fifteen, sixteen years."

Other than dealing with questions surrounding his transition, Mohamed didn't see much of his WUSC committee at the Scarborough campus anymore. Everyone, including Mohamed, was busy, and Mohamed also wanted to "break" his dependence. Jennifer Cabell, who had helped him so much in the first weeks by getting him a computer and a radio and making sure he understood the financial arrangements, wasn't often at the Scarborough campus during the summer. She said that the group wanted to take Mohamed to celebrate the end of his term but that he had said he was too tired and had a schedule so busy it was hard to find another free evening.

Jennifer says her goal on the WUSC committee was to become a friend as well as an adviser. She believes that sponsored students would come to trust her more that way. But at the same time she didn't want to push herself on Mohamed, especially since she would be leaving the university. She also found that Mohamed began to feel more comfortable with the young men in the Muslim Student Association than with her.

Jennifer hopes to become an immigrant practitioner and is interested in the issues of separate societies in Toronto. She'd written a paper exploring the idea of whether encouraging newcomers to keep their cultural identity harmed them in the end. "You have these split identities within Toronto," she told me. "You have all these people who do not identify with being Canadian. But the minute you move into a society and leave [your homeland] it's never the same. I believe it's a huge issue for people after they immigrate. Down the road, are they going to feel like they are lost, or are they going to mix with all those other individuals who are lost and have a bitter feeling towards the society?"

One of the reasons Jennifer believes in the WUSC program is the Canadian experience it offers students in their first year, something most refugees and immigrants don't get when they first arrive. She knows of students who felt abandoned in their second year, after the scholarship ended, but she saw no signs that that would happen in Mohamed's case: "He's joined the soccer club, which is really good for him, made new friends, joined the Muslim Society so he has that support."

With all the expenses ahead in his second year, Mohamed wasn't certain he would be able to send much money home to his mother in Dagahaley. The last time he had spoken to his family, everyone was doing fine, he said. His brother had been promoted from a lower primary teacher to an upper primary teacher, which meant he brought home about $15 more a month. Mohamed's brother didn't have the grades to apply for a WUSC scholarship, but he was among the few teachers receiving training for the job. "That's the good thing," Mohamed said. "He's going to be a professional teacher."

But Mohamed knew things were getting bad in the camp. With all the newcomers, his mother and brother often didn't recognize any of the people they passed in the laneways of Dagahaley. Prices were rising and resources were getting scarce. There wasn't enough water to go around anymore; the same water-pumping stations had to serve so many more. People had to "line up for hours just to get twenty litres," Mohamed said. Even so, he took a philosophical approach to it all. Things were how they were and he couldn't change them. All he could do was concentrate on the reasons he was here and put studying before anything else. He knew he would never be like other students on campus who socialized as much as they studied.

The pressure he felt emanated from Mohamed whenever I saw him in Canada. I could see it in the far-off look in his eyes and the worry and impatience he showed when waiters were slow or traffic was congested. He still smiled, but not the gentle smile of his days in the camp. There was a new tightness at the corners of his mouth, a sadness in the clamped lips. He seemed as overwhelmed as he was determined. But he was always courteous and engaging. It was easy to see why Jennifer said, "He's such a nice guy."

During my summer visit I asked if he would like to go out to supper. He suggested we go to "our place," which caused us both to laugh. "Our place" was Cafe Sinai, a small Somali restaurant in a strip mall on Lawrence Avenue East where Mohamed had eaten his first Canadian *anjera*. That evening he was feeling good about his own independence: "I can go downtown. I can go places. I know how to use the subway. I know how to use the buses." He could laugh now recalling one evening soon after he arrived when he'd been lost on the Scarborough transit system. He had been to a mosque with a student who was showing him around. They had become separated when the student left Mohamed on a bus while he got a transfer and the bus took off before he got back. Mohamed had no idea where he was going. "It was during the first few days," he said, "and I don't know where to alight. If it had been daytime I could have seen the signs, but it was night and once more it was raining, and I was like, how is this going to end?" He got off at the first stop and the friend found him there without understanding his alarm.

On that warm summer evening, Somali men stood outside Cafe Sinai talking. Inside, there were only a few diners, all male. But Mohamed didn't seem at all bothered to be the only Somali man sitting with a white woman. He ordered goat stew. The waiter asked me if I wanted a banana with my chicken. When I said yes, he nodded. "The Somali way." Over glasses of pink guava juice, Mohamed told me about his university soccer league. There were girls on his team, which he found strange at first, not only because girls don't play with boys in the camps, but because women don't play on the same teams as men in professional soccer. He said the girls played well, though, and his team won, receiving T-shirts that read "Champions."

Now that he had made so many adjustments, he wanted to help the next sponsored student, a Sudanese refugee who was coming from Kakuma. "I'll probably be his mentor, taking him around," he said. He laughed at the idea that he would be the one telling the new student, "It's going to be okay," just as people had told him. "People tell you it's going to be fine, but you never know if it is going to be fine. You say, 'When am I going to be fine?'"

In his process of becoming self-sufficient on the downtown U of T campus, Abdirizak had lost some of his reserve. "You have to get used to new people," he said. "You can't live on an island. You can't be all by yourself. But it's good to be careful not to make too many friends because you have to stay focused."

As Abdirizak spoke to me in the lobby of the university's main library, it was easy to see the change in him. There was a confidence that came from conquering the first year and being accepted into the commerce program he wanted. But he was also more affable, more expansive in expressing his ideas. It was true that he had come to know me better, and he had always said he was a man who took a while with people before he opened up. But there was something more to it. He seemed looser, less wary of the students who walked past us.

Abdirizak had had to learn tolerance to make new friends. "What can you do? You can't complain all the time. You have to look for ways of marrying your values and attitudes with your new way of life. You'll see that the way people dress here is different from the way people dress there. The way people behave here generally is different from the way people behave there. So there is always culture shock. I'm not denying that, but then you get used to it. You have to get acclimatized. That is the most important thing and of course not to lose the sense of yourself, your religion and identity, your values."

But there were things that still surprised him. He had never heard about homosexuality before he came to Canada. He didn't understand why men in his residence laughed at him in his *ma'awis,* the traditional wrap-skirt, and he didn't understand why his Somali friend shook his hand away when he tried to hold it until the friend explained that two men holding hands was seen differently in North America. "It's their way of life," Abdirizak said, "and when I'm here I will be forced to get used to everything whether I want it or not, whether I do it or not. You just have to develop a mechanism of being yourself and also living among the people you are living with."

If he had come to Canada thinking life would be easy, he knew better now: "Life here is not always a bed of roses. You have to work, and that calls for struggle. You have to grow up with life here, the social sense, the economic sense, and that calls for struggle. You'll see people who are white Canadians and they are suffering. They're very poor. You'll see somebody asking for change. You'll see somebody who does not have a home. You'll see somebody who has been evicted out of his home because he has failed to pay the mortgage."

As well as he was adapting, Abdirizak felt the same pressure as Mohamed did to use this opportunity both to help others in practical terms and to remain an example of hope for those left behind. He believed that it would be up to people like him, the lucky few who had escaped what happened to his generation in Somalia, to help rebuild the country someday: "Those people who are inside Somalia, all they think about is the short term because they have not been exposed to the real world. They do not know how stable and peaceful the world is. All they know is, okay, today you have someone who was killed by this person. Tomorrow you have to get revenge. All they know is, how do you get food tomorrow. So most of their thinking is preoccupied with really short, targeted thoughts and most ominous, really bad ones. And such people cannot think about the future. They can't be expected to be good patriots. Those people who are outside Somalia, whether in Kenya, whether in Africa, whether in Europe or America, if anybody can help, they are the ones who can help and will. If anybody wants good things for Africa, those are the ones."

He still couldn't see far enough into the future to decide if he would move back to Somalia someday or help from afar, but he knew his ties to the country would never dissolve. How could he turn his back on it, especially when he still didn't know if his father was dead or alive there? How could he turn his back on a homeland when he had followed each agonizing and violent new twist? "When we left our country we were small," he recalled. "In Kenya we were pretty much in touch with what was going on in Somalia. If we had come to Canada when we were young, that would be a different story. I talked to people who came here when they were young. They have no sense of what I am talking about. They think that the clash is not as bad as it is or life is just as good as it is here. So that helps, the fact that when we came here we were older and more mature intellectually."

Abdi felt the same pull toward the sorrows of his homeland: "As a human being, not even as a Somalia citizen, we can't stop and look away from what is happening. There are innocent people killed there. There's chaos there. There's hunger. There's disease. There are floods there and other natural disasters. A lot of people are dying. I'm related to those people by blood."

The killings in Somalia took Abdi back to a time he wanted to forget: "It's almost common to Somali people. Killing is common. You'll hear someone is killed somewhere and they'll say let's go and bury him because it's common. Millions are being killed. Thinking back on my family, I cope with living without them, but those other people who are in Somalia are now dying because of the fighting of al-Shabab. Al-Shabab is another disease now. That's what I call them."

There was no support among Somalis for the insurgents, Abdi said. Al-Shabab's links to al-Qaeda and its call to wage war on neighbouring countries, such as Ethiopia and Kenya, could only make matters worse. "They don't even understand that Kenya has been holding these refugees from Somalia for so long," he said. Regardless of how restricted his life had been in Kenya, Abdi felt gratitude for the peace he had been able to find there. And if Somalia threatened Kenya, the refugees in Dadaab could become the victims of harsher treatment at the hands of their hosts, who were already suspicious that terrorists lived among them.

Abdi had no wish to go back to his restricted life in "dusty Ifo," as he so often referred to it, but he longed to see his friends. He agonized at how stuck they were in their lives there. Throughout the year, he'd been sending about $200 a month back to his uncle, sister and friends and was often besieged by email requests for more help from others. "Some of them will tell you their health is not good. They are going to go for some testing in Nairobi. Some other friends will tell you they are going to wed, that's expensive."

He couldn't help all of them, and couldn't help any of them find a solution to their status as refugees in a situation that seemed to have no end in sight. "There's no peaceful environment in Somalia, so repatriation is failing. And there's no local integration happening. People are closed in that Dadaab camp. So the only way out of the camp is resettlement." He was always willing to talk about Dadaab in any forum if it brought attention to the problems and helped find solutions. "I believe I am part of the change. My ambition is to make sure that there are no refugees in Dadaab. That's what I want to see."

But Abdi also felt the responsibility that went hand in hand with his new status as permanent resident and eventual citizen of Canada. He had little time for refugees and immigrants who lingered in public housing when they were capable of working: "If I have the opportunity to work, the opportunity to make money and help myself, then I have to take advantage of that and become a loyal Canadian taxpayer. Why should I be receiving tax from other people?"

He had done well through the year and during the summer, averaging 85 per cent, in courses that could lead to graduate work in either economics or pharmacology. But he had now decided he would choose economics and would narrow his studies down further to business and accounting. That way, he reasoned, "just in case" he didn't go to graduate school, he could get a job as an accountant or a financial assistant.

One incident that helped him make up his mind was a visit to a restaurant in London. He went there one day to buy a shawarma wrap and ended up talking to a young man who had studied biology at Western several years earlier—"and now he's selling shawarmas." Then Abdi's academic counsellor confirmed that someone who had come from a refugee camp and wanted to earn money to help others there needed to be in a field that could pay him back immediately.

When I talked to Abdi in August, it was one year after I'd first met him in the CARE compound in Dadaab. As soon as I saw him that day, I could tell something was bothering him. His face had the same anxious expression I'd observed in the camp. As we talked, I missed the sudden bursts of laughter that often emitted from him, the kind of laughter that made me want to say something funny just so I could hear it.

I had driven to Waterloo, Ontario, to connect with him before he went off to a WUSC leadership meeting—putting the inspiration he'd felt at the annual meeting into practice. Before travelling to that meeting, he had come to visit students from Dadaab who were working and studying in Waterloo. It was a hot, overcast day that reminded me of the weather in Dadaab when I'd first met him. But there was nothing about the street he had directed me to that looked like Dadaab. He was staying in an old yellow-brick house, the kind of house that was typical in southwestern Ontario a century ago but was now a residence.

There was a picnic table without benches on the side lawn. Abdi brought out two kitchen chairs so we could sit at it for our conversation. Pine trees and large maples shaded us. I reminded Abdi of the round picnic table we'd sat at a year earlier and was rewarded with a smile, not a laugh.

It didn't take long to discover what was bothering him. He asked if I remembered our first meeting and how I had asked him about his clan. I said I did. I also remembered the email I had received from Ibrahim soon after, warning me away from the subject. "I request something when you are writing the book," he said. He requested that I not mention the clan he was from or what clan had been responsible for his family's death. "That's the thing I'm most worried about, the clans. I mean, a lot of Somalis will read this book," he said. He explained that he didn't want to stir up the issue of tribalism. "The issue is," he said, "people have a lot of expectations from us. We are people who are studying. We are learning. We are the people who are supposed to help the Somalis regardless of what happened. Any Somali is my brother or my sister, and one of my ambitions is to eliminate this clan issue. When people ask me if I am Somali, some people try to ask me from which clan, and I am not going to answer it."

Other students had shared their family history with me, often advising me on the sensitivity of the subject. But with Abdi, who had lost both of his parents and his brothers, the issue was particularly raw. "When I associate myself with a clan," he said, "I blame another clan for the tragedy of my family. That would be something I don't like. It would be against my principles." I acquiesced to his request.

By late August, Siyad was feeling more optimistic about both his summer and about life in Canada. He hadn't found another job, but he was now getting close to full-time hours at Safeway. And he was realizing how lucky he was. "Sometimes I go to YouTube and look at the news in Somalia. When I find people being shot, small kids lying dead, I feel very disappointed. I say, 'What is wrong with these guys? What happened?' So when I compare my life with theirs, I say *Alhamdulilah,* which means 'praise be to Allah.' I thank God for giving me this chance to live in freedom, with this security. That's how I feel about it."

He was exploring more of his new world now. He'd found someone to help him with the ferry ride to Victoria. "The ferry is wonderful," he said. But the small city of Victoria made him appreciate all that Vancouver had to offer. He was going on the bus more now, visiting downtown, taking the SkyTrain to visit friends in different suburbs of the city. "And I have been to Stanley Park. English Bay. I have been there." And he was drinking French vanilla cappuccinos like the others. "Not only French vanilla, but I tried the iced cap," he said.

PART FIVE

A Year of Freedom

CHAPTER TEN

I Can Do Whatever I Want To

FORT MCMURRAY HAD NONE of the feel of a boomtown by mid-August 2009. Low oil prices and the global recession that year had deflated the boom. There was little traffic on the highway from the airport, and there were few guests in the hotels. Competing signs on the highway duelled for customers. On one side, the Lion's Den Pub claimed, "Our draft pours at –2 Celsius." On the other, McRay's Roadhouse Grill advertised "the coldest beer in Canada."

Booze, drugs and sex had come to Fort McMurray with the boom and hadn't left with the recession, but if Abdikadar, who'd come for the summer, knew about the city's sleazier side, he wasn't having anything to do with it. "I don't go outside mostly," he said, "and I don't go to the hotels. I don't go to bars. I just go to work and I come back and I stay home." He didn't explore the city or the wilderness beyond the city's limits at all and spent most of his time in his apartment with his friends.

It was a good thing Abdikadar hadn't come to Fort McMurray to get rich. He wouldn't, not with the job he'd found as a cashier at Walmart. "I met with some friends. I met new people. I learned about new people in Canada who, if I need help, I can contact anytime.

So in fact that's why I came. I did not come here to make money."

In sixteen years in Dadaab, Abdikadar had left the camps once. The trip to Fort McMurray was his first chance in Canada to exercise his right to move around in a country: "I can move from place to place. I can take an airplane. Nobody's going to stop me and ask for a passport. I can just use my landed immigrant card. So, in fact, I feel, inside, I have a lot of freedom. Now, I have the same right as any Canadian. I can move. I can live wherever I like." After twelve hours of riding on buses to get to Fort McMurray, he'd made the choice of flying back to Saskatoon.

Living in one place for sixteen crucial years of his life meant that his attachment to Dadaab remained strong, in spite of the restrictions. "That's where I grew up. That's where I studied. That's where I changed my life." Abdikadar was the only person from his family who was outside of the camps. His younger brother still had a year to go in school. His father did make some money in the market with his cart, but not a lot. When Abdikadar couldn't send money, they didn't complain. "I came to the new world with a lot of expectations. Then I came to know that my expectations cannot be reached in one day or in one year. I came to know that what I can achieve only is my studies and any expectation I have in my future to change the life of people shall come after my studies."

My cab driver, Ali, drove me through streets of bungalows in the bright evening light of a northern summer to find the address Abdikadar had given me. It was my first time in Fort McMurray, and I asked Ali where downtown was. "This is it," he said. When I expressed surprise, he said he'd had the same reaction when he came to work there for the summer. Everyone I met that evening was someone who had come from somewhere else via somewhere else. The East Indian clerk at the hotel had come from Brampton, Ontario. The Lebanese-born woman who drove the airport shuttle to the hotel had come from Edmonton. In that sense Abdikadar fit right in.

Ali finally found the building, the only apartment building at the end of a residential street. Covered Somali women walked through the parking lot and in the front door. Abdikadar was waiting for me on the steps. He was dressed in brand-new blue jeans with the sticky tape indicating their size running down one leg, and a grey button-down shirt with the folds from the packaging still criss-crossing it. At Walmart, he explained, he got 10 per cent off his purchases.

He led me downstairs to the basement apartment, through a hallway where several pairs of shoes and sandals were neatly lined up and into a living room with little furniture. I had been extremely curious about something in my days leading up to my visit. On his Facebook page Abdikadar had changed his status to "married." I knew that some of the young men joked about relationships and hinted at girlfriends, but Abdikadar seldom joked on Facebook at all. When I asked the others whether Abdikadar was really married, they said they hadn't heard any news. And as one young Somali woman told me about keeping track of each other, "The walls have ears."

In the camps, a young man wanting to marry had to offer a dowry to the bride's family, pay for the wedding feast and furnish the new home. It took an income or assistance from relatives abroad to come up with that kind of money. By those rules, a student in Canada would be hard pressed to afford marriage. But marriage in Canada without a good income wasn't an impossibility. A couple of the young men had told me the rules were different here. And two of the WUSC students from Dadaab from previous years, one of them a young man, had married in Canada before finishing school.

Abdikadar laughed when I asked him about the Facebook entry. "Oh, it was just for fun," he said. "Some people said, 'You got married?' and I told them I was married forever, even when I was in Kenya. I told them I was married to education and I don't have time for anything else." He smiled at his own joke and I had to admit that Somali humour might be another part of the culture I would never completely understand.

In Saskatoon, Dilalesa had the evening off from his job. There was a soccer game scheduled in the field near his residence. In Dadaab, he had played on the "minority" team against a team of Somalis. Here, the game was open for anyone registered at the university. By seven, students dressed in sports jerseys and T-shirts of every colour began turning up. In the soft light, they kicked balls around the field in twos and threes. Among the women, one wore a hijab. Dilalesa ran on to the field in his red Manchester United jersey, the jersey he'd had in his house in Dagahaley: "Number 7, Dilalesa." With his long

blue knee socks and brown sports shorts, he looked ready to join an organized team. A Spanish team in the city had asked him to play, but he didn't have time for a league with his work and with the school term starting soon. He kicked a ball high and far and then practised bouncing it on his knee. When the game finally started, it was clear the students had come out to have fun. They ran hard and kicked hard, but they played with a good humour. Dilalesa smiled as he ran toward the ball on the spacious green lawn.

Dilalesa takes part in a friendly soccer game at University of Saskatchewan.

The feeling of space was one of the things Dilalesa had come to love about Canada. Not just the physical space, but the mental space that allowed him finally to move ahead with legally changing his name back to Dilalesa, his name by birth. "One thing I came to understand is that Canada is a country where I can do whatever I want to do, if I really do it in the right manner." He had applied to the Province of Saskatchewan and received a certificate legally changing his name to Dilalesa Guta Dilalesa, officially leaving behind Dereje, the name he had grown to hate and to see as a symbol of the oppression of the Oromos in Ethiopia. The name change also became a symbol of the huge transformation he had gone through, and would continue to go through in his life once he became a citizen of Canada.

He still had not worked his way through Canadian bureaucracy, however, and seemed surprised that it could be so complicated. Although his new name was registered in Saskatchewan, he couldn't find a way to get it changed on his permanent residence card and couldn't understand the information he'd received on the matter from Citizenship and Immigration Canada: "Whenever you call Canada Immigration, you can't easily get hold of them. All you hear is a voice message." He was growing worried about walking around with two different identifications. "My health card shows Dilalesa, which is the right name, but when it comes to the permanent resident card, I still use the name that I don't want anymore. I'm creating confusion here." The story in the newspapers that week about Suaad Hagi Mohamud, the Somali-Canadian woman who had been prevented from leaving Nairobi because both Kenyan and Canadian officials questioned her picture, had intensified his concern about getting his identity in order.

Over the spring and summer, Dilalesa had begun another process from the safety of Canada: reconnecting with his friends and family. In his years in Kenya, his years in exile from Ethiopia, he had avoided contacting his father, worried—rightly or wrongly—that it might put his family in danger. During his first winter in Canada, there had been no time to search for his father's telephone number or address in Ethiopia. A friend had somehow got word to his father that he was safe in Canada and had given him a number. In the spring, Dilalesa had spoken to him for the first time in fifteen years. His father was prospering. But Dilalesa discovered that a sister and brother needed financial help and started sending money through the Western Union office in a Safeway in Saskatoon. Being able to send that money represented another significant change in his life. "In Dadaab, I felt like a beggar because I always got help from other people," he said. "What made me feel like a beggar? I had to carry a sack to the distribution centre and line up and wait for maybe one scoop of porridge and one scoop of maize, and the Somali people, they despise you. They just spit in front of you and you lose your dignity. Psychologically, you get intimidated. And you expect everything from an organization like UNHCR. But now I sleep on a nice bed. I eat well. I go to a nice school. I have a job. I don't feel like a beggar. I feel like someone who can help other people. Before I was getting help. I have now started helping people, all in one year."

In the camps, Dilalesa had expressed his fondness to a young Somali woman, but when she told him her strict Muslim father would never permit a marriage, he'd given up pursuing her. In the spring, while he was making connections back home, he had learned about the whereabouts of his former Oromo girlfriend from Ethiopia. He hadn't seen Sarah since 2002, two years before he fled as a refugee. She had disappeared and he'd never known exactly what had become of her. Now he discovered she had ended up in Dubai running a hotel and helping her family back home. The two had been communicating online through the spring, and she had sent him pictures that looked as though they'd been taken in a studio. He was surprised how she had changed. In some of the pictures she wore modern, almost provocative clothing. He preferred the picture of her in a simple dress with her hair combed straight. Sarah was prepared to move to Canada and eager to start a family. Dilalesa knew they would have to meet in person and see if they still got along before making any decisions about something as important as marriage. That was one reason he wanted to get his identification in order, so he could get a travel document and visit Sarah in Dubai the following year.

Dilalesa was also sending money to some of the Oromo teachers he'd had to leave behind. He sent the money through a friend in Nairobi, who sent it on to the camps. "I'm here today while my fellow

Oromo are still suffering in Dadaab, where life is in the morsel of bread, maybe a bowl of porridge."

Dilalesa's room in residence had none of the chaotic mess usual to a university student. It was clean, with the same sense of order and purpose as his house in Dagahaley. Two barbells—manufactured ones, not ones he'd constructed out of cans and concrete—lay on the floor by his closet. He didn't use the new ones as much as he'd used his prized set in Dadaab. There, exercise had been essential to his sanity. Here, he fit it in when he could.

Textbooks were arranged on the shelves above his desk. In the middle of the room he had placed a small table, making the narrow room double as a sitting room, the bed as a sofa. For my visit he set out four cans of apple juice, a plate of bananas and a bowl of grapes. Each grape had been carefully removed from the stem.

In Canada, Dilalesa had hoped to pick up his studies in philosophy again, a subject he had loved in Ethiopia, but of all the courses he'd taken that first year, he'd received his worst grade in philosophy. He turned to anthropology. "It's really cool, really interesting," he said. "It teaches you how you should not demonize or degrade someone's culture or identity, try to live with tolerance. It teaches you everything about how societies live."

After his first year, though, he had decided to major in international studies and conflict resolution. In his dreams, he hoped his studies could help him become a leader among the Oromo people. In practical terms, he hoped to one day have a career in humanitarian work: "In five years, I might be one of the UNHCR officers travelling across the world to help fellow refugees like me. I want to work with humanitarian organizations because, during my work time as an interpreter, I have seen some merits and demerits of UNHCR officers, the way they treat refugees, and if I happen to be one of those officers, I believe I will do better for the refugees without being biased toward them."

Dilalesa showed me one of his prized possessions, a keychain made of green stone cut in the shape of an *odaa* tree, an evergreen tree considered sacred by the Oromo. "We believe in nature and what nature produces, so whenever there is a dispute and reconciliation process, we sit under this tree to resolve disputes among tribes and individuals and say, 'God who created this evergreen tree make our children as green as this tree.'" Someday, Dilalesa hoped, he could do reconciliation work under a real *odaa* tree.

In Victoria, Marwo was still feeling like a nomad. She had come to terms with many aspects of her new life in Canada, but she felt desperately unsettled. The room she was temporarily occupying in a house in Victoria had none of the order of Dilalesa's. It was the room of someone who was just passing through. Most of her belongings filled cardboard boxes and plastic milk crates shoved in the floor space of the open closet and under the bed. It was her fourth room in Canada, and she was getting tired of moving. "That is still stressing me," she said. "I have to move from one place to another. I've never been settled."

The house was on a quiet street in Victoria with easy bus connections to downtown and not too far from the university. Marwo would have been happy to stay put if she could. She'd known in the spring that she would have to find somewhere else when the room's occupant returned, but she'd had little time to look for anything else because of her job. Any apartment with a reasonable rent was snatched up quickly in Victoria's tight housing market before she and her friend Serina even had a chance to look at it. She thought she would be okay when she learned the room's occupant was not returning, but the other women in the house told her they were giving the room to someone else, a friend, and Marwo would have to move out as planned. Marwo said the women were "nice," but the incident irked her. "It's human to help your friends," she said, but she sounded hurt.

Marwo was getting more comfortable with Canadian food. Most of the vegetables in the grocery store were still unfamiliar, but she bought salad now and had tried broccoli. She still didn't like cooking and often grabbed packaged food. Her first Canadian food had been pizza, but she'd eaten it so often she was now sick of it and had moved on to sushi. "Sushi is the new pizza," she said. But I discovered she didn't fully understand what sushi was when we went to a Japanese restaurant on Fort Street in downtown Victoria. I have never been a sushi fan so I asked what kind of sushi she wanted to order. When I read her the names of the fish from the menu, she recognized crab, salmon, tuna and shrimp, so we ordered a combination of those for her. But she looked horrified when the waitress set a long platter of the individual sushi on the table in front of her. Pulling off the tail she ate the shrimp and then worked her way through the others. When she got to her tuna sushi, she said she didn't think it was cooked, that it tasted raw. I told her sushi was raw fish, which surprised her. The sushi she'd had before had been cut from rolls and hadn't tasted that way. She decided to try an order of California rolls instead, but they still didn't taste quite like the sushi she bought at Sushi2GO.

Marwo easily shrugged off those missteps of adaptation, but some incidents churned up feelings of vulnerability and longing for the comfort of family and a larger Somali community. "I want to be where there are more Somalis around," she said. "I am really missing Somali company." All the moves and the struggle to find a suitable apartment, a place where she could finally feel at home, took their toll. On Facebook late one night, she wrote asking for God's help. When a friend wrote back and asked her what was wrong, she replied simply, "Something is not going well for me."

Work, which for the most part boosted her confidence, had also contributed to her feelings of vulnerability. She now worked full-time at the Queen Victoria Hotel and Suites and had come to like the job. Cleaning hotel rooms all day long, six days a week, was tiring work, but she'd made friends with some other workers there—two young women who were born in Sierra Leone—and the job paid $12 an hour, which was more than she'd received cleaning offices at night. Over dinner she told me she had quit the job with the office-cleaning service, claiming her knees were bothering her. But that hadn't been the real reason. She'd become uncomfortable with the unwelcome remarks and advances from a man on the night shift. "He was saying inappropriate things to me, things I didn't like. I told him to stop and then he started criticizing my work, saying bad things about my work to others."

I told Marwo that kind of harassment was not legal and she could have complained. She knew all about the harassment of women, not just through her job in the camp with FilmAid International and her women's studies course, but from personal experience. One time, on her way to a conference in Nairobi, a Kenyan policeman had taken her off the bus and put her in a cell at the Tana River checkpoint. She knew there was the possibility he would rape her and that there was nothing she'd be able to do. She had tried to stay calm, and waited in the cell until she was released unharmed.

I asked Marwo if she had told Serina, who I knew would defend her, about the incident. She hadn't. She said she didn't want to get the man in trouble. "He has children to support." Instead, she had quietly left the job.

Even though times like that made Marwo miss the nurturing of Somali friends and family, she did not miss hearing what Somalis were doing to each other in their homeland. In fact, she avoided the news. "I'm just kind of tired of Somali issues," she told me. "I was paying attention to Somalia before, when I was in Dadaab, and I still love my country. But I just almost lost hope."

Marwo felt the growing conservatism in Somalia harmed women and affected the political situation negatively. Before U.S. secretary of state Hillary Clinton held talks with Somali president Sheikh Sharif Ahmed in Nairobi in early August over what kind of support Americans could offer the failing Somali government, there had been as much attention paid to whether the two would shake hands as to the contents of their discussion. Since handshaking between an unrelated male and female is seen as a taboo in Islam, al-Shabab and other conservatives said that a diplomatic handshake would prove President Ahmed was an impure Muslim and a puppet to the West. When the president accepted Mrs. Clinton's hand, the controversy continued on websites and YouTube. "That's why Somalis will never have peace," Marwo said. "That's why I feel so disconnected from them."

Removed from the constant flow of bad news about the fighting, the memories of childhood and the years in Dadaab were flooding back to her: "They just come into my head. I'm kind of reflecting back to whatever life I passed through, the way things were in the Dadaab refugee life, when I went to school, when my parents died, when I lived with my aunt. I still remember them. Even when I am working, I remember them."

Marwo thought she could forget about Dadaab and move on if only her aunt, her siblings and her cousins were out of the place, back in a peaceful Somalia or in a third country like she was. Her aunt had disapproved of those with *buufis* who did anything to get out of the camp. She wanted nothing to do with the cheating people did to get resettlement. "She was once called by UNHCR," Marwo said, "and they asked her what kind of problems she had, and my aunt, even if she had problems, said, 'No. I'm okay. I work and eat and I sleep and I'm healthy.' She's so proud. Some people lie because they want the chance to resettle. My aunt is kind of unique that way."

Of the three young Somali women who had come from Dadaab a year earlier, Marwo had left the camps with the most liberal attitude and had shown the greatest openness in Canada. She talked of a time when her grandmother had lived in Somalia and had not covered her head in public. Although she never wore the one-piece hijab that fell from the top of the head to the waist, she wanted to make sure people understood that she had not given up on the principle of hijab. By covering her head with a scarf, she was carrying out the requirement of her religion, but in a way *she* chose to do.

Talking about FGM remains difficult for Somali women even years after they have come to Canada. It is the most private of topics, the most awful matter to explain to the Canadian women they know. In order to protect the women who did talk to me about it, I have chosen to describe this scene anonymously.

In a coffee shop in Canada, a Somali-born woman sat with three Canadian women. They talked that day about the Somali practice of female genital mutilation. The Somali woman had grown up believing that the custom was necessary to control women's sexual urges, accepting that uncircumcised women would have such strong sexual urges they might try to rape men. The Canadian women were horrified at the very thought of the practice. It was difficult for them to keep their faces from showing the abhorrence they felt.

The Somali woman knew the physical cost of FGM all too well— the pain she experienced each month during menstruation when the blood could not flow freely as it did for other women because of the small hole left after her vaginal area had been stitched nearly shut when she was a child. A Canadian gynecologist had told her there were operations that could help her, operations to make the opening wider, but she was not ready to consider them.

In Somaliland that summer, organizations were working on a declaration to abandon FGM. By fall, twenty communities would publicly support the declaration. But agencies had been fighting against the practice for years with little effect. Virtually all Somali women were circumcised, and they and their husbands would have to decide whether their daughters would be treated differently.

The Somali woman in Canada had once assumed that when she had daughters of her own, they would be circumcised in the customary pharaonic manner, the clitoris and part of the labia cut away and the vaginal area stitched nearly shut. Like her parents' generation, she'd always believed that no Somali man would marry her daughters otherwise. But now, after living in Canada, she didn't know what to think anymore. Sometimes she defended the practice; sometimes she called it torture. It was hard to change a view that was so engrained. Perhaps she would subject her daughters only to the less severe *sunna* circumcision, snipping off the hood of the clitoris, a practice that did not cause the same medical problems for women, that did not cause women pain in menstruation and during sexual intercourse, that could save them from dying in childbirth. Perhaps she wouldn't circumcise her daughters at all.

Later, out on the street, one of the Canadian women berated another for bringing up the subject, for being so insensitive. The three Canadian women could talk about FGM all they wanted. It was theoretical. It hadn't been done to them. What could the Somali woman do? There was no way she could change what had been done to her. She had little choice but to believe there was some reason for the practice, or accept that she had been mutilated.

My last talk with Hussein was to take place at three-thirty in the morning at the Grant MacEwan residence in Edmonton. In the middle of the night, the residence was a quiet place. There was no one in the lobby playing video games, just a young woman at the desk behind the locked glass doors. Outside, where I waited for Hussein, the only sound came from sprinklers watering the young poplars on each side of the path to the door. No one walked on the sidewalks, and only a few cars and taxis drove by, some turning in to the all-night Tim Hortons across the way.

It was a strange time for a meeting, but in some way fitting for the odd relationship I had developed with Hussein over the year. He and I would never see women in the same light. I would never be able to accept the limitations he did for women; he would never be able to accept the freedoms I assumed were a woman's right. But we had always been able to see the humanity in each other.

I had set up our meeting for a more reasonable time, but the day before I arrived he emailed me to say he didn't think he would be able to see me. After months without work, Hussein was finally getting some shifts with a security company watching over businesses, and when work had come up that week, he couldn't refuse it. Since I couldn't change my plans, I went to Edmonton anyway, prepared to meet him whenever it was possible. I finally reached him on the phone in his evening break and we tried to find a time that matched our conflicting schedules. "I know it is important that you talk to me at the end of the year," he said. He agreed to meet me after his shift before he crashed for the night.

A small car pulled up and Hussein jumped out, saying goodbye to the man who had driven him home from his shift inside a bank. The shifts he had been on were taking him into the heart of Western commercial enterprises, like the Apple Store and La Senza, the lingerie store, watching painters and renovators to make sure they didn't take any merchandise. He was not armed and could not confront anyone. "You don't need to use force," he said.

As we sat in the still lobby, he told me he had decided to leave Grant MacEwan College despite the offer of some support in his second year. The college would become Grant MacEwan University in the fall, but it still didn't have the program he wanted. In September, he would begin studying at the University of Alberta for his bachelor of commerce, majoring in accounting. "All this leads to building a very good future if everything goes as planned."

Just being able to make those kinds of decisions was a measure of how much his life had changed in a year. "There you didn't have any hope. You just finish school. And then you go and teach," he said. "There was no future, there was no target." He felt relieved to be free of Dadaab's restrictions. "It was like living in a prison. No movement." But he'd been at home with the culture there, and he missed his mother, brothers and sisters. "I worry about them every minute."

The students who had come to Edmonton the summer before were back, and they took him around, showing Hussein for the first time what foods he could eat in non-Somali restaurants. "I didn't know what was halal and what was *haram*," he said. "But they have been here for so long they actually know what Canadian foods are halal, like pizza, fruits, salad. There's tuna, which I never ate. The only thing we avoid is the pork, and they told me the pork has got many names, like pepperoni, ham, bacon. They gave me a list."

As his first year in Canada ended, Hussein still longed for the physical environment of Africa, the equatorial evenness of the days with their clear divide between light and darkness. In Edmonton, the long summer days and the bright city lights brought no real night. Hussein couldn't imagine lying outside on his back at night, as he'd done in Ifo, staring up at the natural beauty of the passing clouds, the stars and the moon. "The moon there, it's bright," he said smiling at a happy memory.

Sometimes, in Edmonton in the summer, he could feel his old world in the new world. "I can go and sit under a tree and talk with friends and say, this tree resembles a tree we saw in Dadaab, or this ground looks like that. I actually miss that place, but I see things that look like it here. I also saw people selling food on the road like what's happening in Nairobi. So, whenever I see something that looks familiar, I feel at home. But in winter it is really hard." He still missed washing on the ground and watching the water soak into the soil and clipping his nails and leaving them in the earth. He had decided that even in summer, it was wiser to throw the clippings in the garbage rather than burying them. "If I go down and dig a hole, they may think I am putting a bomb or something, that I was a terrorist."

Before leaving, I wanted to find out if he had changed his views on Western culture since I'd last seen him. He said he had not. He knew he had to accept the way women behaved here, but he still found it shocking. Somali women wearing jeans and other Western clothing upset him the most. But when we spoke of other matters, I noticed some nuances in his thinking that may or may not have been there before. When he talked about the handshake between the Somali president and Mrs. Clinton, for instance, he said he accepted that it was prohibited in Islam, but it disturbed him that the fuss over the handshake took the emphasis away from the hope of the meeting, a hope that Somalia, where civilians were dying daily, would finally get some help. "Shaking hands is just a small part of the religion," he said. "For me, I see no purpose in having two groups, one saying it's right shaking hands and another group saying it's wrong. Then there's another conflict. I don't like that."

When the taxi I'd called pulled up in front of the residence, we both rose. Hussein walked me to the door and we nodded goodbye to each other.

CHAPTER ELEVEN

A Sense of Belonging

ADEN LEANED BACK in a chair in his summer home in the women's residence at Brandon University. He put his feet up on his desk and watched a tennis match on the television while scrolling through online messages and sending responses. He was waiting for his computer to call him to the *dhuhr,* the second prayer of the day. He missed hearing the *athan,* the call to prayer spoken before prayer times at the mosques in the Hagadera, but he'd downloaded a program he'd found on IslamicFinder.org that played the *athan* at the correct time for his location.

He wore one of the T-shirts he'd bought when he first came, the ones he'd picked out at Zeller's because they had sayings on them. This one read, "I'm Not Bossy. I Just Have Better Ideas." A gauze bandage encircled his bare right arm. He'd cut his arm riding his bicycle. In Hagadera, he had never learned to ride a bicycle. No one had bicycles there because it was impossible to ride in the loose sand. Here, he had two. They stood in one corner, the bike the WUSC committee had given him and the one he'd bought for a couple of bucks at a garage sale. He enjoyed the speeds he could reach on the hard asphalt roads, although he still couldn't assess whether he was going too fast for the situation. "I was chasing a car trying to see if I could keep up with the car and I finally tried to make a curve when I was on the high speed and the bike slid. It was not wet. It was dry but I lost control and I found myself on the ground."

Two aspects of the accident's aftermath reminded him of how his life had improved in Canada. In Kenya, he had viewed the police as corrupt and cruel to refugees. In Brandon, he found the police friendly and polite. "There was a police car following me and they didn't shout at me. They were sympathetic. They said, 'How are you doing? Are you okay?' And when I said, 'Fine, thanks,' they just left me, not blaming me for playing on the road." And after the accident he was able to go to his own doctor across from the university and get the dressing on his arm without paying for the service.

"There are so many good things about Canada," he said. "And the first thing is about the people. They all seem to be kind and good. Here we have freedom, and there's also a sense of belonging, a sense of socialization. You can do whatever you want and people are kind to you, from what I have experienced."

It was like Aden to dwell on the positive. Sometimes Brandy Robertson, from the local WUSC committee, wondered how he was really doing. She knew he was adjusting. He'd done well in his studies and took part in all sorts of activities. "I think he's happy," she said, her expression more of a grimace than a smile, her words more of a question than a statement.

"Sometimes when I am with my friends," Aden said, "they feel like I am not doing good some days. They ask me, 'What is wrong with you?' And I will say, 'I'm good.' I don't want to let them know that I am having some sadness in my heart, missing my family. I don't want to worry them. They are already helping me."

One of his worries that summer had been where he would live in September. "When I looked for a room, it always seemed to be girls wanting girl roommates. One time I talked to a girl, and said I needed to be a roommate. 'Why are you looking for a girl?' I said I was a good roommate and they wanted me to move in with them." But then a better place came up, a room in a house five minutes from campus. A music professor owned the small white house with deep blue trim, and Aden would share the house with him and be able to cook for himself.

Aden's new cellphone rang with a loud bit of Somali music. He spoke in Somali and then said briefly in English, "Visitor, guest from Toronto," before winding up the call. After educating himself on the best plans, he'd ventured back into the expensive world of Canadian cellphones. The phone he'd picked came with earphones and a volume control that he wore pinned to his T-shirt and constantly adjusted while he was in a conversation. To keep his monthly statements low and avoid endless calls from home, he'd given his number only to his family and closest friends in the camp and he'd signed up for call display so he could refuse calls.

The person calling was a new friend, a Somali woman about his age who had resettled in Winnipeg with her family. He had many new friends now, he said. He'd been to Regina several times to visit the Somali family who had resettled there. But not all his new friends were Somali. He worked with a Latino student who had a band. Aden had gone to their concert in Winnipeg and become such a big fan of the Son Latino Band that he had chosen to study Spanish in his second year instead of French.

He had ten courses under his belt now and in the fall he'd continue on with other courses that could lead to medical school. He had a good job lined up in the cafeteria, and a position with the student union that gave him rebates, which cut his tuition in half. He would have the title and income of science commissioner until the following spring. He could run again but didn't think he would. One year, he'd decided, would be enough experience for his resumé for medical school.

He saw himself living in Brandon until he had to go to elsewhere for medical school. "Your first place in Canada, you love it," he said, echoing the words I had heard from other WUSC students who had come over the years. "I tell my friends Brandon is the best place to be. They say, 'Is it better than Toronto?' I say, 'Yah.'" His envy of the guys in their big cities with their large Somali communities was over. When he was finished his studies, maybe then he would move to a city where there were Somalis. "Winnipeg, Regina. There are more Somalis. I don't care [about having] many Somalis, but some Somalis."

At 1:45 p.m., the call to prayer sounded from Aden's computer. Without turning off his television he stood with his arms crossed and faced the door. He looked up to the ceiling, bowed, knelt and repeated the motions of his *dhuhr* prayer to the sound of lobbing balls and the hushed tones of the tennis match announcer.

After my first visit to Brandon, Aden had kept in touch by email, asking me when I might come again. When I returned to Brandon late one night, as he finished his first year in Canada, I turned on my computer in my hotel room. I laughed—lol—when I opened my Facebook account and discovered he had posted news of my arrival on his page.

Throughout that last trip, he was as considerate and firm a host as he had been before. Since the cafeteria was closed, he had prepared lunch for us, which we would eat in his room. His dresser had become his kitchen cupboards. The plug on the wall beside it powered a toaster, a microwave, his compact refrigerator and a kettle.

I watched as he pulled a pot of rice and beans from the fridge. He had cooked the dish in the residence's kitchen. Next, he pulled out a large bowl filled with the "soup" he had made without a recipe or guidance. From the drawer he took two plates and cutlery. His committee had given him the dishes when he'd arrived, but he hadn't cooked at all during the year. Now that he had to economize, he was taking on the task the same way he did everything—with all he had. He pulled a sticker from a new spoon and washed everything in a small porcelain sink. Juggling plates and bowls, he heated two plate-fuls of rice and beans and topped them with the soup. As the food was heating up, a sweet, spicy smell filled the room. And when I tasted it, I was surprised how good it was. The "soup" was full of yellow peppers, onions, potatoes and carrots in a curried broth. When I complimented him on the meal, he said he remembered watching his mother and sister cook and had figured out how to make the dishes from those memories.

After his early afternoon prayer we decided to go on another tour. This time we would go farther than the two ends of the city as we had done on our winter drive. We both wanted to get out into the prairie. We got as far as the sign for the town of Carberry, which Aden thought would be a good spot to explore. He had started taking driving lessons and had driven one time to Carberry. We wandered by rows of flowers and admired the fields of grain. It was the kind of clear-skies day that made it easy to enjoy the moment, and Aden was good at that. But he was looking around with different eyes that day. He was imagining where he could bring someone else, how he would introduce the city of Brandon and the prairie around it to the second Somali in Brandon, the new WUSC student arriving in just one week.

Throughout our excursion, Aden kept his earphones on. In the middle of our walk, he received a call and, fidgeting with the volume, spoke in English. Carol McRae, his supervisor for his summer job, was calling to invite him to a steak dinner. He wanted to go but seemed reluctant to abandon me. I encouraged him to go and said we could meet after dinner.

As we drove back to Brandon, Aden told me how kind Carol and her family had been to him. They had a big HD television, he said, and invited him over to watch TV whenever there was something special on, such as *So You Think You Can Dance*.

One year after arriving, Aden stands by train tracks in the prairies near his Brandon home.

Later that evening, as we met over coffee, Aden received another call from his female Somali friend in Winnipeg. He leaned back in his chair and spoke to her, one hand behind his head, the other wrapped around his paper cup, a broad smile on his face.

The next morning I met Aden one last time in the common room where the staff gathered for their break. There were three middle-aged women sitting on a couch, including Carol McRae, who had invited him to dinner, as well as the Latino friend who had introduced him to Latin music and taught him how to ride a bike. It was clear the older women were fond of Aden. "You never make us tea," they said, pointing to the cup of tea Aden had given me. "We like to tease him," Carol said. "He's easy to tease," she added, passing out cookies she had made and leaving those remaining in the bag with Aden. Carol told me Aden was doing really well, that he was a good boy and worked hard. In the fall, she'd noticed, he'd had the two Iraqi friends in residence but by spring he had lots of other friends. The women had taught Aden how to use the toaster, and one of them had taken him shopping and demonstrated the economical advantage of buying a bag of cooking onions instead of one big red onion. They joked about his "friend" in Winnipeg, and Carol said proudly that he had learned to ride a bike. When I said he had also learned to drive, Carol corrected me. "Learning," she said firmly.

Aden seemed to take the teasing and the comments in stride, but he did look a little embarrassed when Carol told the story of how he had lasted a day at the Wok Box restaurant in town, when he'd cut himself badly. He'd grown tired of chopping vegetables with his right hand, she said, and had switched to his less agile left hand.

Carol asked if I knew that Aden's father had come back to the camp. I hadn't thought to ask Aden about his father, who had lived separately from the family before the war and had disappeared during it. And Aden hadn't mentioned his father's return. Before going back to work, Aden walked outside to see me off and I asked him about his father. He told me his father had been living near the Ethiopian border and had recently made his way to Dadaab. He was now living in Hagadera near Aden's mother and sister. Aden had spoken to his father and would soon get pictures of him from the family. "Now, everyone is in the camp—my sister, Mother, Father," he said. While there was relief in his words, there was also a sense that his burden had become a little bit heavier. He was building a new life in Brandon; in a week he'd be one of two Somalis in the city. But he could never stop worrying about those left behind. They were the ballast to his soaring dreams.

For a young woman who didn't believe women could be leaders, Halima had a natural instinct for creating a collective. She had turned her room in Birch 5 at Mount Saint Vincent into a meeting room for young Somali women. Farhiyo Barkedle, the Somali student from the Kakuma refugee camp who had gone to Acadia University on a WUSC scholarship the year before Halima arrived, had come to Halifax in the summer to work alongside Halima as a cleaner. On breaks they both came to Halima's room to eat their meals, to pray and to watch the discs from Season One of *Grey's Anatomy* that Halima had borrowed from the library. Farhiyo sat on Halima's desk chair, staring at the American nurses and doctors on her laptop computer screen, and Halima sat on the floor while they ate their lunch of rice and turkey stew. Farhiyo's presence had erased much of the loneliness Halima had felt during the year. "She's just like a sister to me," Halima said. "When I first came here in the fall, it was really terrible for me adjusting, and then the winter came and I felt like, you know what, this loneliness will end someday so never mind. So I got kind of settled. And then all of a sudden Farhiyo came and we were like squabbling with each other, shouting at each other, doing things at the same time. I felt very comfortable with her."

While the two young women were eating, Mariam, the Somali-Canadian student who had taken classes with Halima, came into the room with her younger sister. They were both cleaning in the residence too and had brought couscous that their mother had made, enough for all four women. When they saw that Halima and Farhiyo were already eating, they went back into the kitchen. Mariam was transferring to Concordia University in Montreal in the fall but her family was staying in Halifax, so Halima would still have a Somali family to rely on.

Farhiyo would soon be going back to Wolfville for her classes, but she would visit during the year. When she left, though, Halima would have another sister to fill the void. A young Somali woman also named Farhiyo—Farhiyo Ahmed—was coming to Mount Saint Vincent University from Kakuma refugee camp. "Farhiyo will come, so I feel like, wow, it's a family I have now—and another sister," Halima said. "Having her around will make such a difference to me in case I fall sick or whatever. She'll be there for me, just as I am for her."

As a member of the WUSC committee, Halima had chosen Farhiyo Ahmed from the list WUSC Ottawa had sent to the university. It was a choice Paula Barry supported: "I said to Halima, 'Can you imagine how it would have been if [someone like] you were here when you arrived, how much easier things would have been.' Because it's hard for me to know everything pre-emptively." Paula described Farhiyo as "a bit like the second baby." Before welcoming their first WUSC student, Paula and the committee had made "all sorts of plans for Halima, had a detailed itinerary and all sorts of activities." They'd left Halima to make many of the arrangements for Farhiyo. Although most of her own first days in Halifax were a blur, Halima was taking the job of entertaining Farhiyo very seriously. Down at the harbour, she compared the cost of cruises. Earlier in the summer she had watched the arrival of the tall ships and been amazed at the beautiful sailing ships that had come from as far away as Russia. Her only journey on water had been on the ferry to Dartmouth. She wanted to include an outing on a tall ship in Farhiyo's orientation and was heartened to learn that the ship sailing out from the dock with a load of tourists cost only $12 an hour. On her first visit to Point Pleasant Park, she wanted to find out the bus routes to the park as soon as possible so she could bring Farhiyo there.

Halima was organizing Farhiyo's life to such a degree that Paula felt she had to remind her to let the new student adjust in her own way. When Halima started talking about how the two would share an apartment the following year, Paula cautioned her that she didn't even know this person yet and to consider that they might not get along.

Halima still thought of Paula as a mother and of Loyan, who would be in Halifax a few months longer until she delivered her baby, as a sister. She and Sarah had promised to stay in touch. Halima had also become friends over the summer with a young man from Turks and Caicos and a young woman from Trinidad. But for Halima none of those relationships could offer her the comfort and understanding a Somali "sister" could. "I can't really talk to a Canadian girl the same way I talk to my sister, my friend who's coming. So to me it really means a lot."

The WUSC committee had decided to subsidize Halima in her second year so she could stay in residence with Farhiyo Ahmed. Residence cost $4,800, and the committee would give her $1,700 toward that. But Paula still worried that Halima didn't understand how much money she needed to save. Halima had asked the committee for money for a video camera for her brother and for a new computer. And Paula had had to tell her the committee didn't have that kind of money.

Halima admitted she hadn't saved much money from her summer job. Her father had been sick again and she'd helped finance his month-long stay in Nairobi. Her sister in Mogadishu, who had safely given birth to her baby, had her own family to think about. Her other sister, who worked in Nairobi, and her brother, who taught in Dadaab, helped, but Halima, as the only family member in the West, felt she had to do her share. She hoped she could get by in her second year on her student loan, but the maximum she could receive was $12,000 to cover $9,000 to $10,000 in expenses.

She didn't know how she could send money home or respond to other requests for help in the fall without a part-time job. "People think when you go to the West, you get money like this," she said, snapping her fingers. "They think money's everywhere. But that's not the reality, right? You come here. You have to work hard. You have all this schoolwork you have to do and then you have family back home. There is no one time you will be 100 per cent settled. The hell you undergo."

Throughout the year Halima had tried to figure out a way to go back home to see her family, especially her ailing father, but her plans were still uncertain, shifting even as she spoke about them. "I'm thinking of going back or taking him to Mecca in Saudi Arabia. That's a really big thing in his faith. Instead of me going back home, I will send him the means to go to Mecca and that will really mean something to him. I don't know how it will happen, but we'll see. I could afford to send him to Mecca this year with the money I made, but then half of my money went to him for medication and stuff. I sent like $1,000."

She was staying firm on her decision to study accounting even though it tore at her: "When I go out and see a doctor or a nurse I feel just like I betrayed myself for going from science to business." She hoped that she could somehow keep her dream of working in medicine alive by taking more science courses as electives, so that if somehow her life became easier or her family was given resettlement to the United States, she could do the MCATs in the future.

On August 19, one day before Farhiyo Ahmed's arrival in Halifax, Halima started packing up her belongings. She would be moving up to the second floor of the residence, which she thought would be quieter for studying. She pulled the suitcases that had come with her from Africa out of the cupboard and began folding skirts and scarves. As she packed, she ran videos on her computer of Somalia in the '70s. There were scenes of soldiers marching and camels crossing the desert. She liked watching images of "when Somalia was still Somalia."

She had lived a year in that room, and she knew she was a different person in many ways from the person who had slept there alone for the first time. She felt more mature after making it through that year. She had come fearing that in a Christian country, a country of white people, she would not know how to interact with others, but she had found people who were kind and friendly. She had come fearing that she might be forced to change her beliefs, the person she had become: "Back home people have this thing like you go there and you can't practise your religion the way you want, but then I came here and found nobody cares. Nobody bothers. You just pray wherever you want. You can wear whatever you want."

"From my experience I really think this is a good place," she said of Canada. She had talked to people online who lived in Minneapolis, Minnesota. "It has the highest [Somali] population in the West and Toronto has the second highest," she told me. She had decided that assimilation was more of a requirement in the United States than it was in Canada, where there was more active interaction between cultures than her friends in the United States described. "You bring your culture to this country. You have the right to practise your own culture and nobody will stop that. It's you who can change yourself."

And Halima had changed herself by becoming more accepting of the habits of young people in Canada. She was no longer as horrified as she had been during her first summer to see men and women being affectionate in public. "The big thing was to adapt to the culture of these people, the way they behave, and it really took a while to get used to that because I came from this conservative society where you are taught differently. So when you come you go, whoa. But that's human nature. Your mind, your body will get used to whatever it sees. In class, people do some nasty stuff and when I first came here I was like, oh my God, this is crazy. But now I feel like, oh my God, let them do whatever they want."

But a change in attitude toward others did not mean she was ready to change herself. She could not imagine wearing pants or going without a headscarf. "Life may totally change, but not the way you feel about yourself," she said. "If you are thought of as a good child and, when you grow up, you are very religious, you will still have those things as part of your life. And really you can't change so drastically, so abruptly."

During the school year she had felt self-conscious in classes where she and Mariam were the only two women wearing hijabs. But she felt better once she started venturing out in the wider community of Halifax and saw other women, mainly Arab women, wearing hijabs. "I'm just normal. I will go to the mall and I will see many women wearing hijab, so I don't think I feel any different."

Halima looked at each scarf and hijab as she folded them for packing. There were scarves she had brought from Africa, ones her sister or Muno had sent her and others she'd bought herself. She turned to her desk for a moment to find some Somali music on her computer but then searched instead for a video on YouTube of the Somali-Canadian rapper and musician K'naan. K'naan was a role model to a generation of displaced Somalis. He had successfully integrated his life here with his Somali family heritage as poets. He had used his fame to write articles trying to explain to the West why pirates hijacked ships off the coast of Somalia. The video was a performance of one of his songs on Parliament Hill on Canada Day. The song was "Wavin' Flag," a favourite of Halima's. It suggested the struggles of Somalia, but the young crowd on the Hill held up small Canadian flags as they joined in his refrain about freedom and getting older and stronger.

After one year, Halima was content to stay put. She had found friends in Halifax, Somali refugees like her, international students who were also far away from home and Canadians who had been good to her. And Halifax was growing on her now that she was learning its "every nook and corner."

CHAPTER TWELVE

Almost Used to Life Here

THE AIRLINE WAS DIFFERENT, the terminal was different, but for those waiting in Terminal 1 of Pearson International Airport in Toronto for Air Canada Flight 857 from London, the anticipation was the same. It was August 20, 2009, exactly one year after the eleven students from Dadaab had landed in Canada. Two of the students who had arrived a year earlier were among the group gathering to welcome the newly sponsored students. In one short year, the greeted had become the greeters. They stood among the larger crowd in the sunlit hall, among people waiting for flights from Madrid, Istanbul and Warsaw. They stood holding the kind of "Welcome to Canada" signs that they had searched the crowd for one year before.

Abdirizak chatted with his group from University College as he waited for the Sudanese student who would replace him, a student he hoped to mentor. "Eighty per cent of what a new student has to know will be delivered by a previous WUSC student," he said. Each time the doors opened, he held his sign high above his head with a Norma Rae determination. Being at the airport reminded him of how far he had come: "You see how naive you were when you first came about life here, about school, about people and acquaintances and everything. When you are at the airport, welcoming a new student, you feel like you know what he doesn't know and you feel the urge of telling him everything."

Abdirizak had everything in place for his second year. He would share an apartment at Dundas Street West and Spadina Avenue with Ibrahim and Abdinoor, who had come from Dadaab the year before him. Soon he would pack the picture frames that his WUSC committee had left in his room for his arrival. He would carry them to his new place. The frames still held the original manufacturers' artwork, but perhaps in his new place he would slide some photographs from his life in Canada under the glass.

At Pearson International Airport, Abdirizak holds a sign welcoming a new WUSC student to his college, exactly one year after he arrived at the same airport himself.

After a year in Canada, Abdirizak said he had "almost got used to life here. You can be a Canadian citizen but you can't be originally from Canada. You are always going to be something different. Thank goodness Canada has really welcomed us and we are really grateful, but nonetheless I am afraid that nobody can forget home. There's always something you are missing, your family, your country."

Muno was in the crowd with her committee from the Mississauga campus of the University of Toronto. Her group was waiting for a male student from Dagahaley camp. Muno had been hoping that, like Halima, she would have another Somali female to share her university experiences with. But as a kind friend, she was happy for Halima. Muno already had Somali friends and would soon be living near them on Parliament

Street in downtown Toronto with a family who were distant cousins.

While she waited for the newcomers to exit, Muno held onto the end of a long welcome sign and spoke to Halima in Halifax on her cellphone, thanking her for the presents she had sent. Halima had remembered it was Muno's twenty-first birthday and, adopting the Canadian tradition, had marked the day with gifts of a hijab, jewellery and candy.

Muno was oblivious to her surroundings, unaware she was standing in a different terminal than the one she'd arrived at a year earlier. She had very few memories of her first moments in that airport. "I was so unsettled when I came. A whole new world. I was just wondering what it was going to be like." A year later, even though she was "still not half as comfortable" as she'd been back home, she felt stronger and more independent than she had on her twentieth birthday. "I can go anywhere in the world, talk to people, take care of myself." She still didn't know if she would ever belong to this new world, but she was starting to feel like a citizen who could make a life in Canada, find a good job and raise a family.

Eighteen students from Dadaab would be landing in Canada that day, seven more than the previous year. Twenty-nine students had already been selected to come the following year. Muno and the others took heart in the fact that more and more of the refugee students were getting out. It was the only bit of good news about the Dadaab camps in an otherwise distressing year. On MSN messaging, Muno heard from young people who remained in the camp. The word "still" occurred over and over in their messages: "still here," "still pushing," "still struggling." On August 18, 2009, UNHCR had reported there was a record 289,500 people in the camps, 80,000 more refugees than the year before. Negotiations for more land near Dadaab to build a fourth camp were nearing completion. But desperate for more immediate solutions, UNHCR had started relocating about 13,000 refugees to Kakuma camp in northwest Kenya. The International Office of Migration was moving the refugees in convoys of buses for the arduous three-day journey across the north of the country.

Earlier in August the UN Commissioner for Refugees, António Guterres, had visited Dadaab and described it as "the most difficult camp situation in the world." He pleaded with donors to supplement the funds that UNHCR planned to pour into Dadaab. He called the situation in the Dadaab camps "a first global priority," a priority estimated to require $92 million U.S. in upgrades, new infrastructures and support for the local community that had grown more strident over the year about the growing number of people using the scarce resources of their semi-arid land.

· There were no signs that the flow of asylum seekers would stop any time soon. The Islamist insurgents still controlled most of Somalia despite American efforts to help government forces. In late June, a U.S. State Department official told reporters that over the spring the United States had shipped "in the neighbourhood of 40 tonnes worth of arms and munitions" to Somalia's government to fight the insurgents and the al-Qaeda threat. But it didn't take long for reports to surface of soldiers losing control of arms or selling them on the open market, or for rumours to circulate that new American guns were turning up in Kenya.

Somali civilians who weren't caught in the constant fighting were facing another threat: acute malnutrition. Severe drought and instability in the delivery of food aid to Somalia led the UN's World Food Programme to report that by August 2009, the country was "facing its worst humanitarian crisis since the famine of 1991/1992, with half the population—3.64 million people"—in need of assistance.

With no end in sight to the number of refugees sneaking into its country and with reports that al-Shabab was recruiting in both the North Eastern Province and the Nairobi neighbourhood of Eastleigh, the Kenyan government had beefed up security along the border and added new restrictions to the already restricted lives of the refugees in Dadaab. One year after the eleven students had travelled on the Zafanana bus to Nairobi, the eighteen students sponsored by WUSC in 2009 were refused travel documents to move freely beyond the camps. There was no commercial bus ride for them, no days on their own in Nairobi to meet old friends or do some final shopping. They travelled on a bus arranged by the IOM and stayed in an IOM centre in Nairobi until they were transported directly to the Jomo Kenyatta Airport for their flights to Canada.

With new worries about the situation in Dadaab, Muno, in her darkest moments, thought it would be better for her to drop out of school to take any job so she could get her family out as quickly as possible. But whenever she phoned home, her parents told her not to worry, to just stay in school. "It's impossible," she said, talking about the pressure she felt, "when you have something to eat and you are safe and they are not."

Mohamed wasn't at Pearson Airport. His last exam of his summer school was scheduled for that day. After that he'd have to pack for his move the day after to an apartment a ten-minute walk from the U of T Scarborough campus. A year after he'd arrived, Mohamed had a tough second year ahead of him, but he'd managed to put to rest one of his greatest fears from a year earlier. He had lived a year in Canada—where the weather was different, where the foods tasted different, where he'd had to learn to interact with new people without the guidance of his family—and he had stayed "basically the same." He was at heart the same Mohamed who had walked with his mother to the bus stop in Dagahaley. "So far I haven't seen any changes. I'm myself."

Mohamed's friend from Dagahaley, Ibrahim, was at Pearson that day. Ibrahim, who'd arrived with the wusc students from Dadaab two years earlier, had come back the year before to see Mohamed and the others on their first day and had returned again that day. "I feel like I am also a new arrival," he said. "It helps me remember." He was there to reassure those who were coming that there was someone who would understand what they were going through. Before his classes began again, he would visit the new students in cities in southern Ontario. He would just be returning the favour done by students like Omar, who had come before him. In his talks with new students, he would advise them to try to get to know Canadians: "I think

Canada will be a very hard country if you don't socialize, but it's a great place if you are willing to trust."

In Regina, Nabiho, who'd come to Canada the same year as Ibrahim, was waiting for news of the students' arrival. Her younger sister would be among them, heading to McGill University. Montreal was too far from Saskatchewan for Nabiho to visit her sister any time soon, but it didn't matter. Her sister would be safe, out of Dadaab. Reunions could come later.

The other Dadaab students could only dream of the luck Nabiho had had. That year, her widowed mother and her youngest siblings had been resettled to the United States. Nabiho could put Ifo behind her forever, forget about the part-time jobs she'd taken to help her family. She could concentrate all her energies on the courses she hoped would lead to medical school.

In Saskatoon, Dilalesa would be at the airport to welcome three new Somali students, one from Kakuma and two from Dadaab. He was disappointed that the other Oromo teachers in the camp were too old for the scholarship, but he valued his friendship with all the WUSC students, especially with his Somali friend Abdikadar, who would soon be returning to the city. Together, they'd become a community, sharing the experiences of being students in a new country, cooking for each other when one was too busy with exams. And he had other reasons to be happy. About twenty Oromos, some from Dadaab and some from Kakuma, had arrived in Saskatoon through a resettlement program and he now had another community, one that shared his culture and celebrations.

One year after arriving in Canada, Dilalesa was starting to feel the permanence of his permanent resident status, but he would never forget he had been a refugee. It would always be part of his identity. "I believe that every great person in our whole world must have passed through the misery of life at least once," he said. "It's circumstance that forced you to become a refugee, and there is nothing wrong with being called a refugee."

In Vancouver, Siyad was waiting to greet a female Somali student from Dadaab, and in Victoria, Marwo would help her committee with the orientation of the new WUSC students. She looked forward to the socializing but bitterly regretted that none of the students coming were Somali. The unsolved problem of where she was going to live made her miss friends from Dadaab more than ever.

In Edmonton, in the midst of moving from residence to an apartment with former WUSC students, in the midst of transferring from Grant MacEwan College to the University of Alberta, Hussein would not go to the airport to greet the sponsored students. But later he would take the time to show the two new Somali students around the city of Edmonton, with its mosques, halal meat stores and Somali restaurants. Like Dilalesa, Hussein didn't mind being called a refugee "because nobody is born to be a refugee. It's just a status. I was in Kenya for seventeen years. I was born in Somalia. I am studying in Canada. I may become a citizen here. I don't mind being called any of those because I went through them all."

In Brandon, Aden posted on Facebook his excitement over the arrival of another Somali: "Brandon University—World University Service of Canada welcomes Abdirizack Sheikh from Kenya tonight!" Aden had the bicycles and camera ready for the student's first tour of Brandon. He would have a buddy on campus. They would ride the roads together. In the year since he'd arrived, Aden hadn't lost any of his enthusiasm for life. His thinking was as expansive as the prairies around him. He would marry in Canada and become a doctor, and maybe he would learn to fly an airplane—someday. "In two more years, I will be applying for my citizenship, and then I can travel internationally anywhere, even go back to Kenya to see my friends. In five years, I think I will be in medical school, be a good citizen and settled, driving my own car."

In the communal kitchen of Birch 5, Halima prepared a Somali meat dish called *odka,* with a Canadian variation, for Farhiyo's arrival to Mount Saint Vincent. For Halima the day brought back memories of her own arrival at Birch 5 one year earlier. She would never forget how lonely she'd felt in her room that first night and how she didn't eat any of the strange snacks the students had left on her desk, even though she was hungry after her flights. Farhiyo would have a Somali meal and the company of someone who spoke her language. Two days after Farhiyo's arrival in Halifax, the holy month of Ramadan would begin, and Halima would spare Farhiyo the confusion of her own first Ramadan in Canada: "No one was there to tell me where to go, where the mosque was. I can take her around." There would be some things Halima could not save another person from experiencing. Farhiyo would have to go through the loss of her family alone and make her own assessment of the transformed world around her.

At Pearson, the students were slowing emerging and connecting with their welcoming committees. When Muno saw a covered woman in the crowd, she ran over to her, speaking rapidly in Somali to find out where she was from—Kakuma—and where she was going—the University of Waterloo—as a blond woman in a red T-shirt tried to get her sponsored student's attention. Ibrahim zigzagged through the hall to greet each student from Dadaab. Asni Mekonnen of WUSC seemed able to spot all the young people she had met during the selection process in the camps. She hugged them warmly, and they clung to her for a reassuring moment. To Asni, each student arriving was a future success story in the making: "They have lived in more difficult environments than this. They are survivors."

A tall Sudanese man in a bright yellow hoodie with the letters *USA* across his chest came through the doors. He was hard to miss, and Abdirizak and the committee from University College soon found him. Now that his protégé was here, some of Abdirizak's shyness returned. He posed stiffly for a picture with Asni, the unfamiliar giant between them. But by the time enough of the students had arrived for a WUSC group photo, he had relaxed. He had earned the right to pose among the group. He had survived his first year. He crouched in the very centre of the photo, smiling broadly, while behind him the new students stared at all the cameras snapping pictures, eyes filled with bewilderment.

By five o'clock, most of the new students had been collected and were already on their way to rooms that would contain the dynamics of their internal adjustments. Only one student had not yet emerged. It was Ahmed Abdi Hassan, the student destined for the University of Toronto in Mississauga. Muno waited with her group at the end of the ramp where those arriving walked into their new lives. She grew tired and sat on the hard floor of the airport, resting her head against the welcome sign. When word came that he had finally found all his bags and was coming, Muno and the other students stood up staring at the doors. Finally, he exited and was surrounded by Asni, by old friends like Ibrahim, who would help him find his way, and by the committee from Mississauga.

Muno hung back for a moment as the others hugged the new Abdi. Then she approached. The new Abdi stuck out his hand to greet her. He was in a world where the rules could be different. There was a moment of awkwardness as the others watched to see what Muno would do. Then she reached out her own hand and shook his in welcome.

As I stood removed from the group, I thought of the expression the students used to describe their luck in being chosen: a needle in the sea. They were the few who had made it, who had escaped the hopelessness of refugee life, who had a chance and all the responsibility that came with that chance. The new Abdi was the latest needle, a shining example of success among so many others who were left behind. Dadaab might be the biggest refugee camp. It might be the worst. But it was certainly among the most ignored, and I wondered how foolhardy that public disregard was. At a time when North Americans feared young Islamic extremists, they showed not a care for the thousands of young people warehoused in camps. There just had to be more needles.

I would probably not get to know the Abdi who stood in front of me, but I understood how real and sharp his pain would be. I looked at the others I had come to know so well: Ibrahim, who had inspired me to write this story. And Muno, who, through her friendship with my daughter, would always be on my radar of concern. As I watched them both talking excitedly to the new student, I realized how familiar they had become to me. I would never be able to fully grasp the impact that their experiences, their culture and their religion had on them. There would always be a world of difference between us. But they were familiar enough to me to make it impossible not to care, not to worry about their worries. And I wondered what would happen if other Canadians took more time to get to know them, to go beyond Ibrahim's accent or see past Muno's hijab. And I wondered if I would take the time to be aware of each newcomer I met from now on and show some kindness when I could.

As the group stood there frozen in the moment between arrival and future, a professor drove another sponsored student along Highway 401 toward Huron University College, past the same green fields and under the same bridges that had been Abdi's first view of his new world a year earlier. Abdi waited in London with food to welcome his new colleague from Dadaab. Even though cooking was new to him, he would prepare all his new friend's meals until the cafeteria opened the following month. "That is how we Somalis are," he said.

Back in Ifo, Abdi had always felt anxious, fearful he would never escape "the sealed, dark room" of the refugee camp. "Now, I have a lot of opportunities ahead. I wasn't that hopeful when I was there, but right now I'm hopeful. I have ambitions. I'm into my program, thinking of completing my program in some years and doing some job or going for a master's degree. I'm a different person. There was a lot of rubbish in my mind before. But now I'm almost clean emotionally."

As another summer night ended in Canada, a year of firsts began for another round of students. Darkness finally fell in the northern hemisphere and, when dawn broke, the new students would wake up after the loneliest night of their lives, wondering what they had done. They had already gone through so much: violence, family deaths, time in a kind of prison without having committed any crime. But instead of waking up knowing that all their problems were solved, they would find their heads filled with new questions. How would they stop missing their families? How would they ever get by? Who would they become now that they were here? After a year of asking themselves these questions, the Dadaab eleven were just starting to come up with their answers.

Acknowledgements

I owe much to the people at World University Service of Canada who helped me with my research for this book, particularly to Asni Mekonnen, who meticulously and patiently answered my endless questions, and to Paul Davidson, who talked to me openly about the organization.

In Africa, I relied on WUSC's partner Windle Trust Kenya to be my sponsor for my visit to Dadaab. Marangu Njogu and Jully Odanga persisted in gaining the government's permission for my entry. On the ground, three Windle Trust teachers became valuable and lively guides in each of the camps: Jeremiah Orina, Karanja Kiiru and Catherine Kagendo. Without hesitation, Jeremiah lent me his camera after mine disappeared from my room in the main CARE compound.

Thank you to the many local WUSC committees in Canada who either offered information on how they function or made arrangements for me in their cities. I'm particularly indebted to Paula Barry and the committee at Mount Saint Vincent University in Halifax for accepting my presence throughout their orientation.

Many former WUSC students kindly shared their stories with me at length so I could deepen my understanding of the process of adjustment: Omar Ahmed Abdi, Dahabo-Noor Abdi, Abdella Abdou, Sultan Ghaznawi, Kakule Floribert Kamabu, Ambaye Kidane, Irene Kyompaire, Ruth Mathiang, Pascaline Nsekera and Ajmal Pashtoonyar.

I'd like to thank James Milner for explaining the desperate situation for protracted refugees around the world to me, and Debra Pressé for the background she provided on Canada's refugee sponsorship program.

I am fortunate to have friends and family who are there for me when I need them: I'd like to especially thank my brother, Brian Awde, for generously taking on the task of drawing maps, Anne Mason-Browne and John Kavanagh for opening their home to me in Halifax, and David and Anna Rozenshtein for offering me theirs as a retreat.

I appreciate the opportunities I had at the CBC to travel to

Mogadishu, Somalia, in 2004 and Dadaab in 2007, and to work with talented people on television pieces that inspired me to delve more deeply into the heartache of those worlds. I am constantly grateful for the ears and the kindness of my friends and former CBC colleagues, especially Donata Chruscicki, Olenka Demianchuk and Ina Kudaba.

Thank you to Scott Sellers at Random House for shepherding this project to Martha Kanya-Forstner at Doubleday. Martha's enthusiasm and grasp of the story's potential energized me and sent me off on the right course. When Martha took a maternity leave, Nita Pronovost stepped in with aplomb. Nita's editorial wisdom shines through on the final pages. And thank you to the team at Random House and Doubleday who got this book out there.

I could never have finished this book without two people who are dearest in the world to me: my daughter, Jane Goodwin, and my husband, Peter Kavanagh. Both have the souls and the minds of great writers and great human beings. I trusted their perceptions implicitly and thrived on their confidence in me.

Finally, I will always be grateful to the students of Dadaab. I am honoured to have shared their first year in Canada and remain awed by their courage.

How You Can Help

There are many humanitarian organizations that try to do what they can to ease suffering in war-torn Somalia and the refugee camps of Dadaab, or to get news out about human rights abuses. I have included just a few of the major players here as starting points so you can learn more about the current situation or donate to their efforts, if you wish.

Amnesty International www.amnesty.org
As part of its mandate to campaign internationally for human rights, Amnesty International has documented human rights abuses in Somalia and Kenya.

CARE Canada www.care.ca

CARE Canada has been part of the humanitarian effort in the Dadaab camps since 1991. CARE International provides, education, sanitation and water, and programs addressing health and social issues.

Human Rights Watch www.hrw.org

An independent organization, Human Rights Watch focuses on violations of human rights in the world, including Somalia and Kenya.

Médicins Sans Frontières/Doctors Without Borders
www.msf.ca

This medical humanitarian agency has operated in the dangerous environment of Somalia since 1991. In 2009, the agency studied the health conditions of refugees in Dadaab.

60 Million Girls / 60 Millions de Filles
www.60millionsdefilles.org/english/home.html

60 Million Girls is a public foundation based in Montreal that supports girls' education worldwide by funding two initiatives a year. In 2008, the organization funded programs to encourage girls to stay in school in the refugee camps of Dadaab and Kakuma.

Windle Trust Kenya www.windle.org

WTK is WUSC's partner in Kenya, but it does much more to advance education among refugees in the country. It is a registered non-governmental organization established by the late Hugh Pilkington.

World University Service of Canada www.wusc.ca

If you are a university student, you can check to see if there is a WUSC committee on your campus and get involved. If there isn't a committee at your university, you could contact the main office in Ottawa and learn how to start one. WUSC accepts donations for its many projects, including the Student Refugee Program.

Notes and Sources

Most of this book is based on more than one hundred interviews and hours of observation. Many of the facts here came from those interviews and observations or from multiple sources that described particular situations: newspaper and magazine stories, government reports and books. When a fact came from one specific source, I have included that source, which can often be found in some form online. I have also included the titles of a few books or reports that might be of interest to those who wish to do further reading on topics touched on in various chapters.

Introduction

Statistics Canada. *Ethnic Origin and Visible Minorities.* Release No. 7, 2006 Census. April 2, 2008.

UNHCR. *2008 Global Trends: Refugees, Asylum-Seekers, Returnees, Internally Displaced and Stateless Persons.* June 16, 2009. (Statistics used in the introduction and in Chapter 3 came from this report. It is available online at www.unhcr.org. Each year, on its well-managed website, UNHCR publishes an annual report on the numbers and locations of the world's refugees as well as information on resettlement.)

Chapter 1

Buck, Patricia, and Rachel Silver. *Report on Girls' Schooling in Dadaab.* Prepared for CARE Kenya. July 2007.

Milner, James. "Kenya." Chapter 5 in *Refugees, the State and the Politics of Asylum in Africa.* St. Antony's. New York: Palgrave Macmillan, 2009.

Chapter 2

Amnesty International. *Amnesty International Report 1998: Somalia.* January 1, 1998. (Available online at www.unhcr.org. Documents human rights abuses in Somalia between January and December 1997.)

Armstrong, Karen. *Islam: A Short History.* New York: Modern Library, 2002.

Goedhart, Gerrit Jan van Heuven. "Refugee Problems and Their Solutions." Address given by the United Nations High Commissioner for Refugees, Oslo, December 12, 1955.

Horst, Cindy. *Transnational Nomads: How Somalis Cope with Refugee Life in the Dadaab Camps of Kenya.* Oxford: Berghahn Books, 2006. (Horst spent years doing fieldwork in the camps of Dadaab.)

Immigration and Naturalization Resource Center. *Somalia: Things Fall Apart.* Alert series. Washington, DC: Immigration and Naturalization Resource Center, January 1993. [AL/SOM/93.001]

IRIN. "Kenya: UNHCR head accepts Nairobi corruption report." January 28, 2002.

Johns, Michael. *Preserving American Security Ties to Somalia.* Washington, DC: The Heritage Foundation, December 26, 1989.

Korn, Faduma, with Sabine Eichhorst. *Born in the Big Rains: A Memoir of Somalia and Survival.* Translated by Tobe Levin. New York: Feminist Press at the City University of New York, 2006. (This book is an account of the author's circumcision as a child in Somalia and her coming to terms with it in the West. Korn is an active campaigner against FGM.)

Laurence, Margaret. *The Prophet's Camel Bell.* Toronto: New Canadian Library, 1988. (First published in Toronto by McClelland & Stewart in 1963. Laurence chronicled her time in Somaliland in the early 1950s. It is an interesting portrayal of colonial Somalia and Western attitudes toward the country.)

———. *A Tree for Poverty.* Hamilton, ON: McMaster University Press, 1993. (A reprint of the original 1954 work by Laurence, in which she put to paper translations of Somali poems and folktales that had been told to her orally.)

Loescher, Gil, James Milner, Edward Newman and Gary Troeller, eds. *Protracted Refugee Situations: Political, Human Rights and Security Implications.* Tokyo: United Nations University Press, 2008.

Milner, James. "Kenya." Chapter 5 in *Refugees, the State and the Politics of Asylum in Africa.* St. Antony's. New York: Palgrave Macmillan, 2009.

Nelan, Bruce W., J. F. O. McAllister and Clive Mustio. *Somalia: A Very Private War. Time* (January 14, 1991): 17. (Available online at www.time.com.)

Smith, Merrill. "Warehousing Refugees: A Denial of Rights, a Waste of Humanity." *World Refugee Survey, 2004.* Arlington, VA: U.S. Committee for Refugees and Immigration.

UNHCR. Convention and Protocol Relating to the Status of Refugees. 1951 (Available online at www.unhcr.org.)

World Health Organization, Department of Reproductive Health and Research. *Eliminating Female Genital Mutilation: An Interagency Statement.* 2008. (Available online at www.unfpa.org.)

Chapter 3

Citizenship and Immigration Canada. *Facts and Figures 2008: Immigration Overview: Permanent and Temporary Residents.* (Available online at www.cic.gc.ca.)

Chapter 4

Amnesty International USA. "Somalia: Girl stoned was a child of 13." Press release, October 31, 2008.

Human Rights Watch. "Kenya: Protect Somali refugees." Press release, November 13, 2008.

IRIN. "Kenya: UN Warns of humanitarian crisis in Dadaab camps." November 17, 2008.

The Economist. "Somalia: The world's most utterly failed state." (October 4, 2008): 49.

Chapter 5

Catholic Information Services for Africa. "Kenya: State and UNHCR to expand crowded refugee camp." AllAfrica Global Media. February 11, 2009.

The Somali Documentary Project. *The Somali Diaspora: A Journey Away.* Photographs by Abdi Roble. Essays by Doug Rutledge. Minneapolis: University of Minnesota Press, 2008.

Chapter 6

Karim, H. Karim. *Changing Perceptions of Islamic Authority among Muslims in Canada, the United States and the United Kingdom.* Montreal: The Institute for Research on Public Policy. *Choices* 15, no. 2 (February 2009).

Chapter 7

Human Rights Watch. "From Horror to Hopelessness: Kenya's Forgotten Somali Refugee Crisis." March 30, 2009.

World University Service of Canada. *Fostering Tomorrow's Global Leaders: An Evaluation of the WUSC Student Refugee Program.* Ottawa, WUSC: 2007. (Executive summary and full report provided by WUSC.)

Chapter 8

Gettleman, Jeffrey. "The most dangerous place in the world." *Foreign Policy* (March/April 2009).

Human Rights Watch. "Kenya: Relieve Somali Refugee Crisis." June 5, 2009.

Kennedy, Elizabeth A. "Somali violence explodes as stabilization fails." The Associated Press, May 15, 2009.

Kilner, Derek. "Aid group deplores conditions at Kenya camp for Somali refugees." Voice of America News, May 15, 2009.

Médicins Sans Frontières. *Dadaab: The Unacceptable Price of Asylum.* Briefing Paper. May 18, 2009.

UNHCR. "Number of Mogadishu civilians displaced by fighting since early May tops 200,000." News Stories, July 7, 2009.

Chapter 9

Hughes, Dana, and Kirit Radia. "Somalia 'uncontrollable' because of Al Qaeda influx, PM says." ABC News, July 9, 2009.

Kilner, Derek. "UN says war crimes committed daily in Somalia fighting." Voice of America News, June 9, 2009.

Menkhaus, Ken. "Somalia: too big a problem to fail?" *Foreign Policy* (August 6, 2009).

Nebehaly, Stephanie. "Pillay accuses Somali rebels of possible war crimes." Reuters, July 10, 2009.

Petrou, Michael. "A state of terror." *Maclean's* (July 20, 2009): 26.

United Nations. *Kenya Humanitarian Update.* Vol. 51. Office of the United Nations Humanitarian Coordinator in Kenya, July 7–31, 2009.

Chapter 10

McCrummen, Stephanie. "In Somalia, a twist on 'handshake diplomacy.'" *The Washington Post*, August 6, 2009.

Shepard-Johnson, Denise. "Somali communities say 'No' to female genital cutting." UNICEF news story. December 14, 2009.

Chapter 12

Agence France Presse. "Somali refugees move from overcrowded Kenyan camp." August 16, 2009.

Aly, Heba. "How Kenya's 'Little Mogadishu' became a hub for Somali militants." *The Christian Science Monitor*, August 26, 2009.

Dickinson, Elizabeth. "Arming Somali." *Foreign Policy* (September 10, 2009).

United Nations World Food Programme. *Somalia.* Country Report. August 2009.

Index

183–85, 260–61, 280–81, 285
German Technical Cooperation (GTZ), 85
Ghaznawi, Sultan, 214–15
Goodwin, Jane, 1, 137, 156–57,
    209–10, 253, *255*, 256
Grant MacEwan College, 128–30, *233*,
    284
Gure, Abdikadar Mohamud. *See*
    Abdikadar (Abdikadar Mohamud
    Gure)
Guterres, António, 304

Hagadera refugee camp, 13, 14, 39–49,
    43, 44, 255. *See also* Dadaab
    refugee camps
halal meat, 113–14, 284
Halifax, Somali community, 182–83
Halima (Halima Ahmed Abdille),
    179–89, *186*, 217–23, 307–8
    arrival in Canada, 102–8, *104, 111*,
        111–15
    career choices, 243
    changes course of study, 141, 182, 219
    concern for family, 181–82
    dislike of winter, 168–69
    experience with Kenyan police, 37
    fear of crime in Ifo, 65–66
    financial support beyond first year, 206
    friendships, 182, 217–20, 293–95
    in Ifo refugee camp, 27–31, *29, 31*, 36
    illness, 181–83
    memories of flight to Kenya, 59–60
    money management, 220–21
    at Peggy's Cove, *223*
    personality change, 152–53, 184–85
    reliance on Loyan, 180
    search for familiar foods, 124–25
    secondary education, *79*, 79–80
    at WUSC annual assembly, *143, 145*
Hassan, Ahmed Abdi, 309–10
"head tax," 3
health care, 84–86
henna, 27, 45, 254
hijab, 44–45, 154, 166, 281
    and employment prospects, 204
homelessness, 164, 167, 262
homesickness, 4, 101–3, 108–9, 118–20,
    129, 131, 137, 173, 182, 248–50,
    279, 307
Horst, Cindy, 69–70
hospitals, 84–86
"hotels," in refugee camps, 25–26, 193
human rights
    abuses in Somalia, 56–57

in Canada, 29–30
Human Rights Watch, 139
humour, 32, 44, 153, 170, 273, 292
Huron University College, 207–9
Hussein (Mohamed Hussein Ismail), 27,
    232–36, *233*
    arrival in Canada, 101, 109–10
    experience with Kenyan police, 53
    in Ifo refugee camp, 32–33
    loneliness, 116–17, 127–32
    memories of Somali civil war, 58–59
    search for summer job, 232–33
    transfer to University of Alberta, 284
    views on women, 235–36, 283

Ibrahim (Ibrahim Aden Mohamed), 3–4,
    20, 98–100, *99*, 108, 136–38,
    172, 305, 308, 309–10
ice skating, 116–17
identity
    alteration of, 274–75
    cultural. *See* cultural identity
    imposition of, 86–88
    manipulation of, 170, 191, 273
    search for, 171
    split, 258–59
"Ifo Highway," 31–32
Ifo refugee camp, 26–36. *See also* Dadaab
    refugee camps
The Illustrated Journey (storytelling
    project), 213
impurities, 42
incontinence, 82–83
independence, 34–35, 162–63, 258–61,
    302–3
individualism, 166–67
inflation, 259
integration
    into campus life, 224
    vs. assimilation, 192, 251, 262, 281
    of WUSC students into Canadian
        society, 211, 213–14, 264
International Organization for Migration
    (IOM), 17, 54, 95, 303, 305
Internet access
    on campus, 135
    in Kenya, 24–26
Islam
    impurities, 42
    teachings on clans and tribes, 61
    teachings on dogs, 42, 157
    teachings on status of women, 28,
        183–88, 229–31, 235, 252, 283, 285
    teachings on tolerance of cultural

33, 72–73, 74–75
Union of Islamic Courts (UIC), 138,
176, 236
United Kingdom, colonization of
Somalia, 56
United Nations. *See also* World Food
Programme; World Health
Organization
Office of Internal Oversight Services,
70
Operation Restore Hope, 68
United Nations High Commission for
Refugees (UNHCR), 2, 14, 39, 140
attempt to open fourth refugee camp,
257
Convention and Protocol Relating to
the Status of Refugees, 63
extortion scheme, 70
relocation of Dadaab refugees to
Kakuma, 303
responsibility for Somali refugees,
62–65, 75–77
United States
backing of Ethiopian military in
Somalia, 138
Battle for Mogadishu, 68–69
Committee for Refugees and
Immigrants, 63
diplomatic visit to Somalia, 280–81
expectation to assimilate, 297
interest in politics, 164–65
military aid to Somalia, 304
perception of Muslims, 133
resettlement of refugees, 95
support of Siad Barre, 56–57
universities, support for sponsored
students, 204
University of British Columbia (UBC),
47, 207, 212–13
University of Toronto
Mississauga campus, 153–54
Scarborough campus, 19
St. George campus, 224
university scholarships, 72–74

Van Heuven Goedhart, Gerrit Jan, 64
Vector Marketing, 209–10

Victoria, British Columbia, housing
market, 278

walking, 18, 32
"Wavin' Flag," 298
West Edmonton Mall, 116–17
Windle Trust Kenya, 5, 71–75, 96, 149
winter weather, 167–69, 172, 177, 189
women
adoption of Western dress, 154, 166
education of, 27–28, 79–82, 145,
183–84, 229–30
erosion of rights in Somalia, 183–84
health care, 85–86
Muslim teachings about status of, 28,
183–88, 229–31, 235, 252, 283,
285
privacy from men, 42
status in Afghanistan, 183
status in Somali culture, 28, 177,
229, 235, 250
violence against, 35, 66–67
wearing of hijab, 44–45
Woolf, Virginia, 175
World Food Programme, 20–21, 71, 304
World Health Organization, 82
World Refugee Day, 63
World University Service of Canada
(WUSC), 73, 93–98
annual assembly, 142–52
bankruptcy, 211–12
disparity of support for students,
204–10
graduation and integration of
students into society, 211–15
selection of student candidates,
96–97, 232, 294
student attrition, 141, 210
students' feeling of abandonment
after first year, 259
support for students beyond first
year, 138, 203–4, 206–8, 212,
220, 234, 295

Zafanana bus company, 17–18
Zapf, Serina, 231–32, 280
Zhao Meng, 124–25